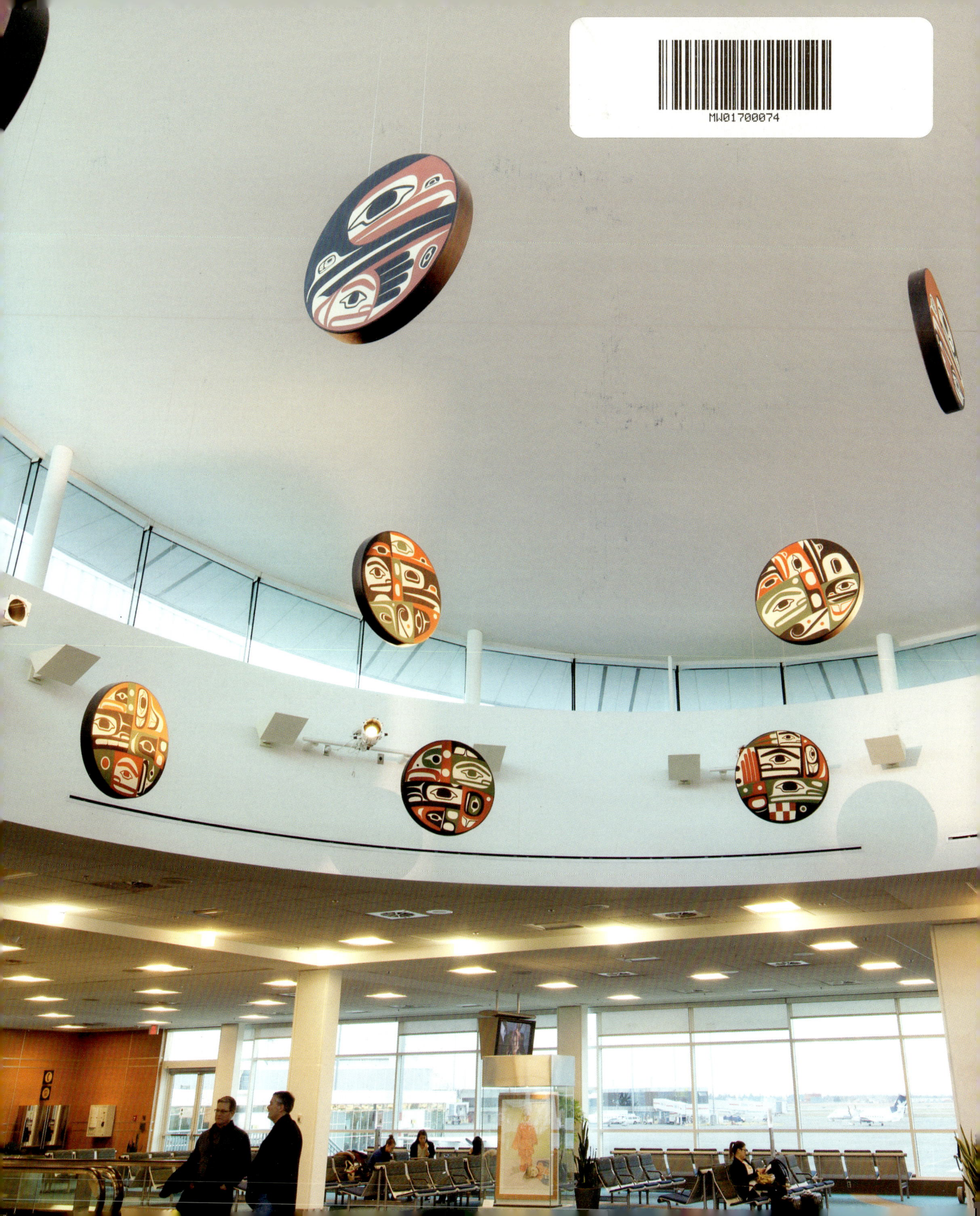

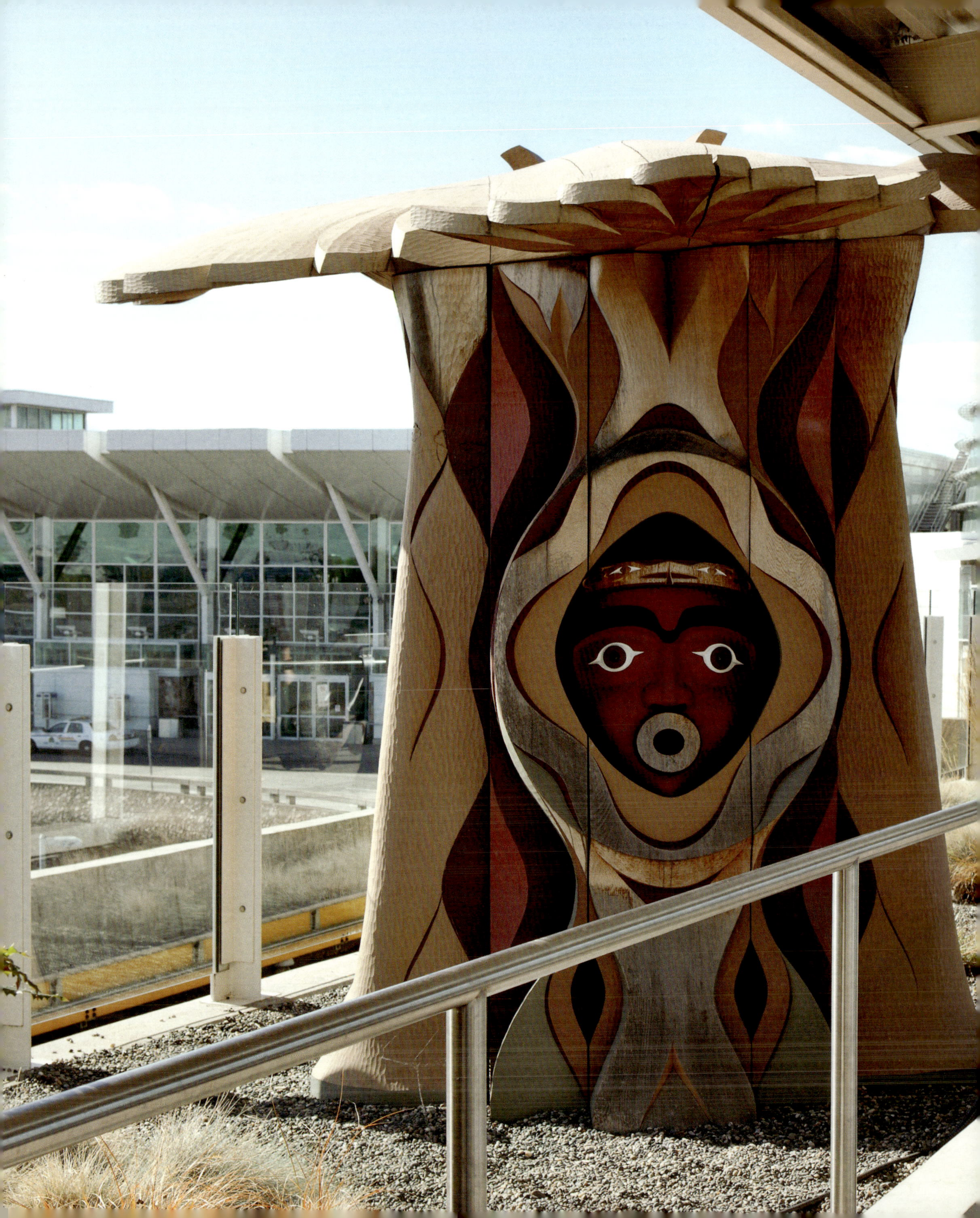

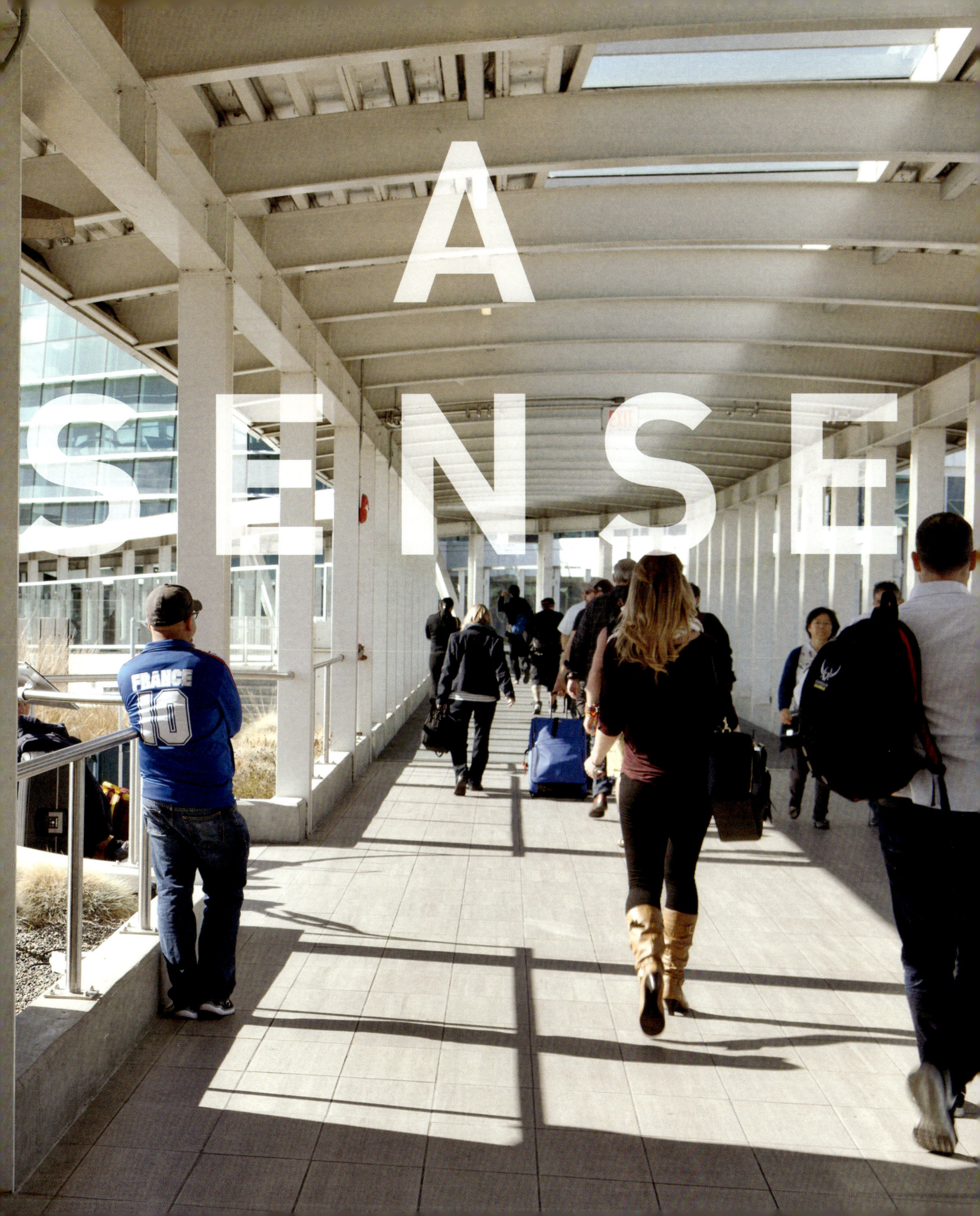
A
SENSE
FRANCE
10

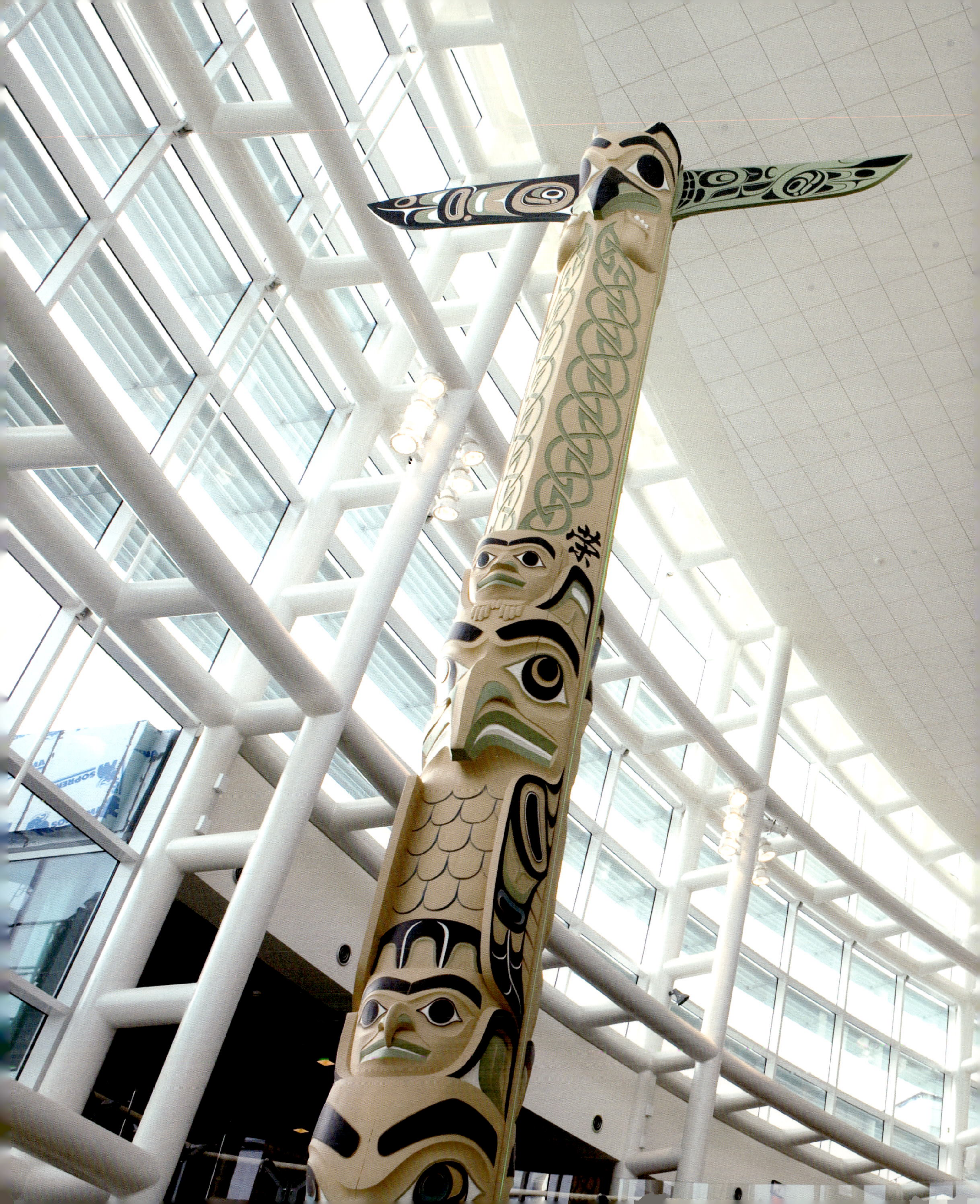

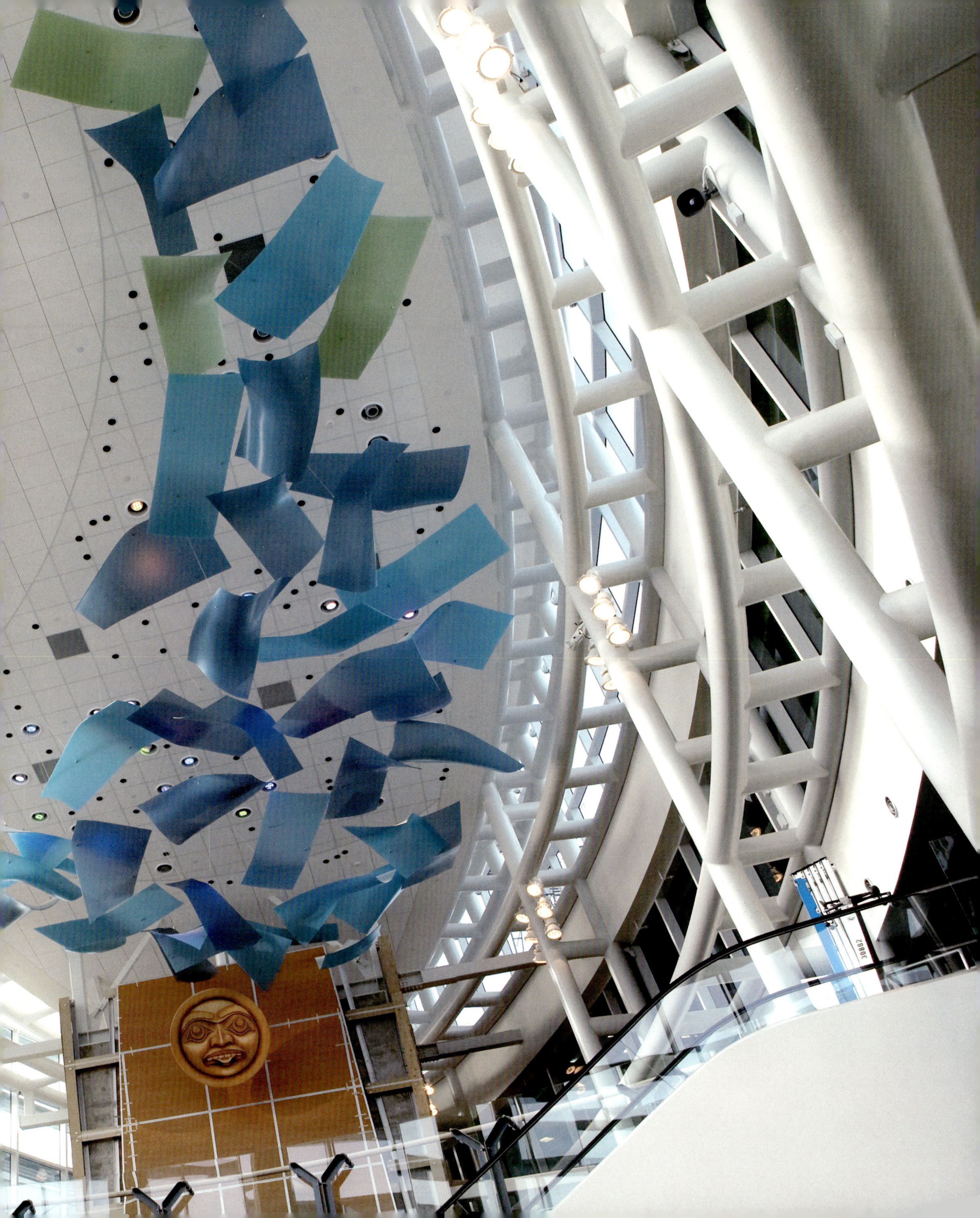

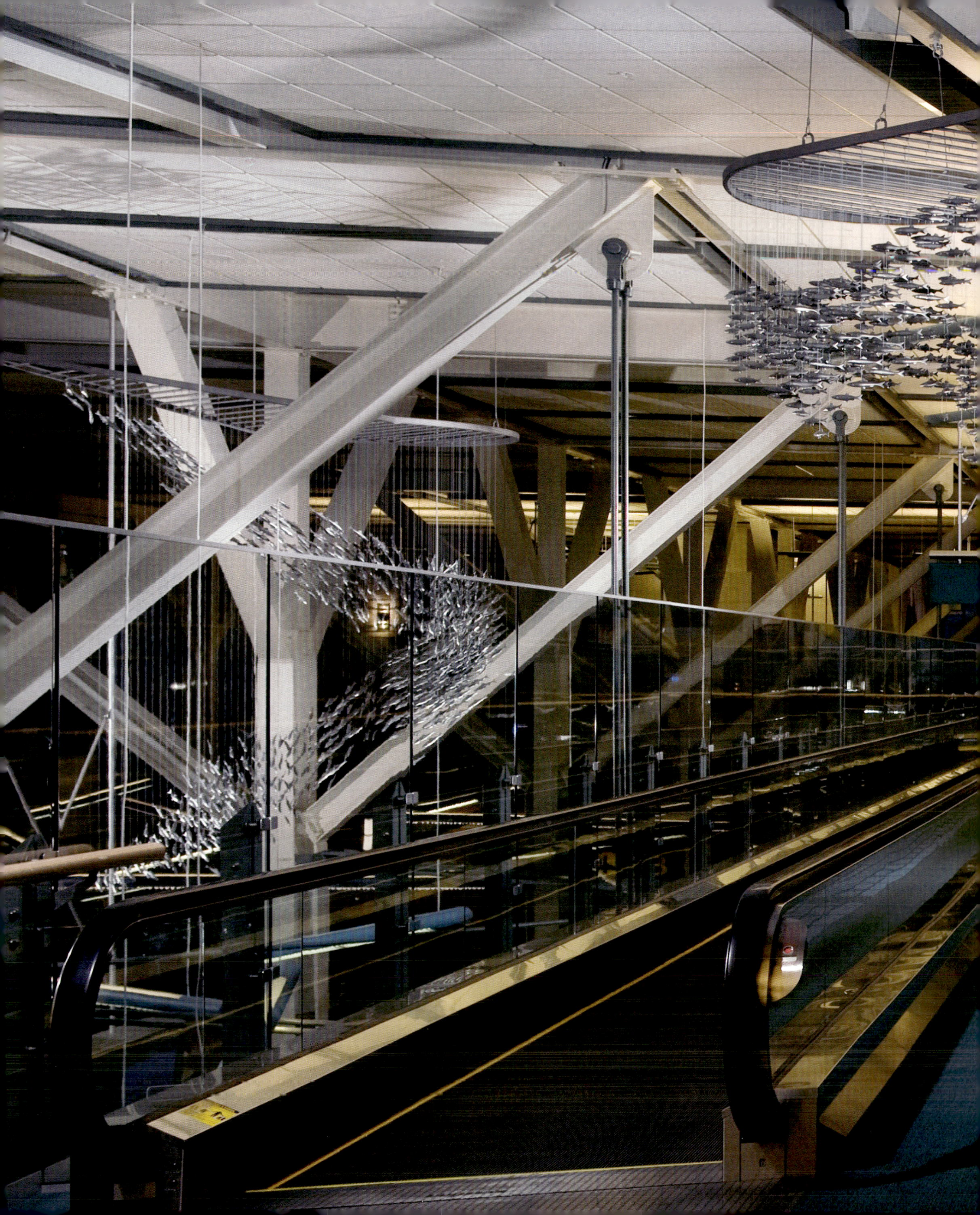

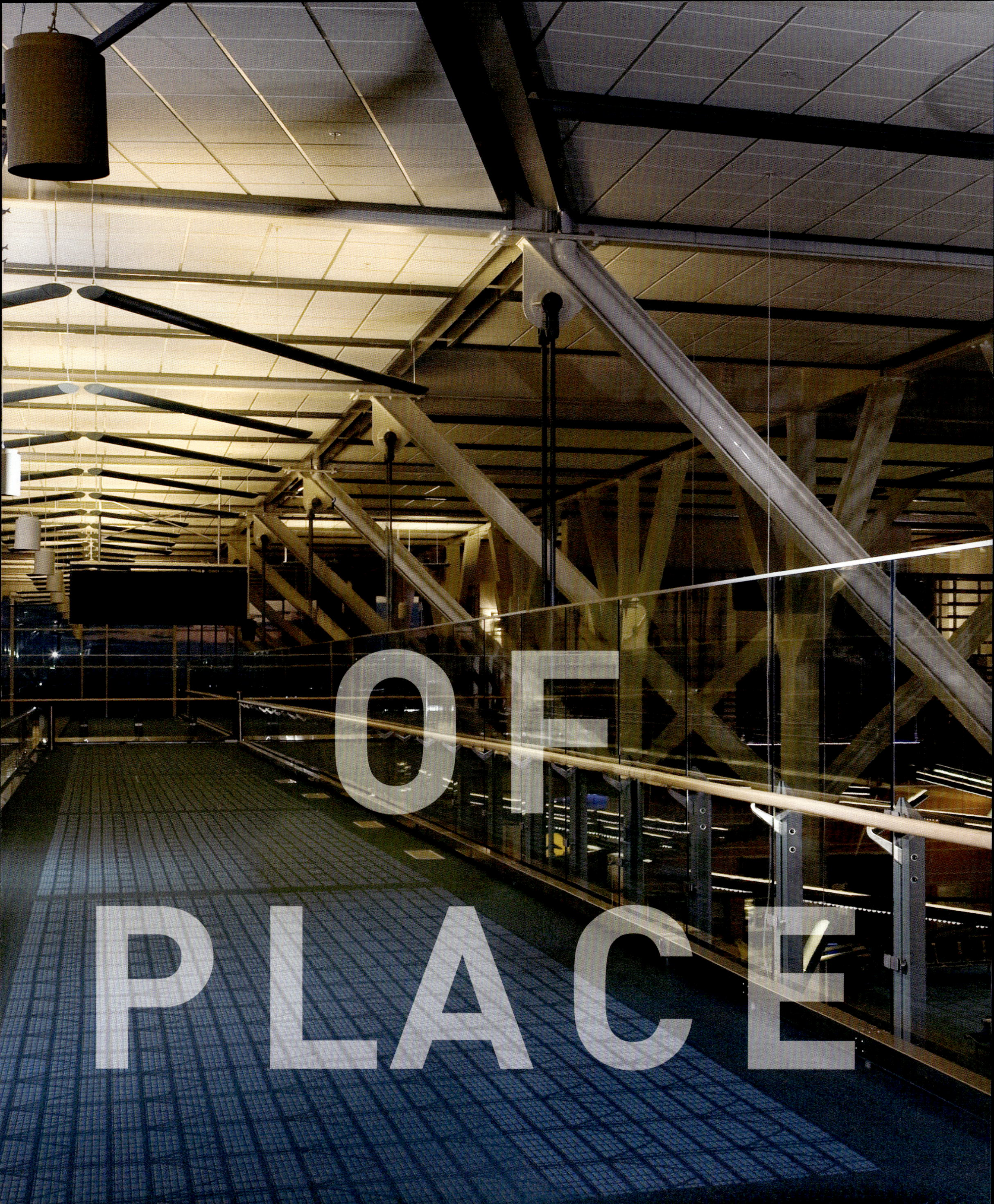
OF
PLACE

A SENSE OF PLACE

ART AT VANCOUVER INTERNATIONAL AIRPORT

ROBIN LAURENCE

Figure.1
Vancouver / Berkeley

CONTENTS

INTRODUCTION

As travellers from abroad arrive at Vancouver International Airport (YVR) and enter the International Terminal, they experience a powerful and unique welcome. Having passed long walls of glass framing views of ocean, mountains and deep green forest, they encounter a high view of Canada Customs Hall from a large and beautiful landing. The landing serves as a kind of stage, where distinctive cultural and natural elements enact a drama of place. Here, water cascades down a vertical rock face behind an enormous wooden sculpture. Carved in red cedar by leading Musqueam artist Susan Point, the sculpture is based on the shape of a traditional Coast Salish spindle whorl. It depicts stylized eagles, salmon and human figures, all caught up in a current of swirling movement and gesture and representing the intertwined themes of flight, welcome and cultural identity. Orbs realized in both positive and negative space symbolize the sun, the moon and the planet Earth, and the circular shape of the spindle whorl itself suggests the great encompassing cosmos.

Beyond this work, four richly hued weavings hang like celebratory banners in space, incorporating the patterns and designs of traditional Coast Salish blankets. Created by Debra Sparrow, Robyn Sparrow, Krista Point, Gina Grant and Helen Callbreath, they represent an honoured and ancient craft practiced by the First Nations women of the region. Past the spindle whorl and the weavings, down a set of stairs and escalators separated by rushing streams of water, two large wooden welcome figures, male and female, also carved by Point, extend their greetings to all who pass by. Even on overcast days, light floods the high-ceilinged hall, contributing to the sense of wonder and delight.

The Musqueam Welcome Area at the entrance to Canada Customs Hall is a dramatic example of YVR's thematically linked art, architecture and interior design, and their integration into an overarching theme of land, sea and sky. It also and more importantly conveys a powerful sense of place, communicating elements of the natural environment and aboriginal cultures of British Columbia and making the airport distinctive, enjoyable and memorable within the global network of aviation hubs. The sculptures and weavings on view are representative of YVR's groundbreaking art program, which, in concert with its architectural design, has captivated millions of travellers who pass through the airport each year, garnered numerous awards, inspired wide media coverage and served as a model to other airports around the world.

In the late 1980s, while YVR was still being managed by Transport Canada, modest efforts were made to enliven the facility through the display of contemporary aboriginal art from British Columbia. However, the commissioning and display of such art had yet to become a priority at what was considered "a very functional and in some ways undersized airport."[1] Things changed dramatically in 1992 when Vancouver Airport Authority took over the management of YVR and plans were made for an ambitious and visually arresting expansion and renovation of the passenger terminals. At that time, a commitment was made to direct up to one percent of building capital expenditures to the commissioning of art for placement throughout YVR, and to fully consolidating these works with the overall architectural plan.

The mission statement for art and architecture in the newly expanded airport called for the celebration of the natural beauty and cultural heritage of British Columbia. Both could be used to tell the story of this place—to convey to visitors the unique character of the province the airport serves. Essential to YVR's vision was and is the presentation of outstanding works—from figurative sculptures, silkscreen prints and copper panels to transformation masks, ceremonial paddles and totem poles—by contemporary First Nations artists from British Columbia. The YVR Art Foundation was established in 1993. This charitable organization fosters the development of B.C. First Nations art and artists through scholarships and other programs. As a further commitment to YVR's art program, a curator was hired to oversee the growing collection, which now numbers over two hundred works and is one of the most significant of its kind in the world.

In the mid-1990s, the creation of the Musqueam Welcome Area and the purchase and installation of Bill Reid's acclaimed bronze sculpture *The Spirit of Haida Gwaii: The Jade Canoe* dramatically launched YVR's comprehensive art program. The additions powerfully identified the airport with the most distinctive visual art created in British Columbia. But who are the people whose cultural presence has contributed so much to the story of this place?

Isolated by mountains, forests and long, wet winters on the narrow, broken margin of the sea, the first peoples of the North Pacific Coast of North America evolved, over many thousands of years, sophisticated fishing, hunting and gathering technologies and complex systems of religious belief, social structure and economic exchange. They also developed a distinctive material culture, with a monumental scale and wealth of expression that were unmatched in Native America anywhere north of pre-Columbian Mexico. The abundance of food sources on the Northwest Coast (most pivotally, the annual salmon runs) allowed for a seasonal division of the year. Summers were spent accumulating and processing food. In the winter, they planned and performed social and religious rituals, using the art that they produced for the ceremony. Towering and abundant evergreens, such as red cedar, provided the basic material for much of the art and all of the architecture.

The nature-based mythology at the heart of Northwest Coast First Nations culture explains the making of the world and its inhabitants, and recounts ways in which distant ancestors garnered special privileges through encounters with supernatural animals and beings. These privileges, including dances, songs, masks, stories and the right to display crest images, were and are regarded as private property. Fiercely guarded, they have been passed from generation to generation through properly observed public rituals such as the feasting and gift-giving events known as potlatches. The art of the Northwest Coast makes visible complex social orders, records important family histories and describes the individual's place within the cosmos. The best known of the area's art forms are carved and painted totem poles, internationally esteemed for their impressive scale, technical accomplishment and visual impact. (The term "totem pole" is a misnomer, since the figures represented are more heraldic than totemic; however, it is so widely used that it has become established and accepted.)[2] Carved in cedar, they vary in form, content and function, and include memorial poles, house frontal poles, interior house posts and mortuary poles.

Because of their shared, homogeneous environment, Northwest Coast peoples developed similar technologies and mega-cultural traits but remain divided by language and distinctive art styles and traditions. Running mostly from north to south, the Northwest Coast First Nations of British Columbia are identified as Tlingit, Tahltan, Haida, Nisga'a, Gitxsan, Tsimshian, Haisla, Heiltsuk, Nuxalk, Oweekeno, Kwakwaka'wakw, Nuu-chah-nulth and Coast Salish. Within these nations, smaller subgroups exist, distinguished by their own dialects and cultural traditions.[3] For example, the Musqueam, on whose traditional lands YVR stands, are a Coast Salish people who spoke a dialect of the Salishan language Halkomelem. Their lengthy history, rich culture and traditional claim to this place are integral to the Musqueam Welcome Area at YVR. A wide range of art from different First Nations traditions, representing other areas of the province, has also been installed throughout the International and Domestic Terminals.

Although European contact and trade with Northwest Coast First Nations stimulated art production in the eighteenth and early nineteenth centuries, the increasing colonial presence eventually proved disastrous. By the early twentieth century, disease, depopulation, missionizing and government policies (such as anti-potlatch laws and the imposition of the residential school system) had badly eroded traditional indigenous cultures. For a few decades, mask-making and large-scale carving were actively preserved in only a few communities and lay dormant in many others. In some cases, remnants of classical Northwest Coast design survived in the form of miniature poles, figures and canoes produced for the tourist market. The art was never completely extinguished, however, and from the 1950s onward it has seen an extraordinary resurgence, attracting national and international acclaim and finding an honoured place in non-Native collection and display, while also serving First Nations ceremonial needs and stimulating the recovery of other, more ephemeral cultural practices. New masks have been danced, new poles have been carved and raised, and the transfer or bestowal of family stories, names and privileges has been validated through potlatches.

The important decision to focus on aboriginal art from British Columbia in the development of YVR's art program has meant commissioning and exhibiting major works from leading First Nations artists, many of whom have been active as teachers and mentors to younger generations. YVR has also supported the production of monumental art by emerging First Nations artists. For some, such commissions have resulted in the largest sculptures or installations of their careers to date. The works created specifically for the International and Domestic Terminals reveal a deep respect for cultural traditions and, at the same time, a willingness to explore new and innovative forms, styles and materials. For those travelling through YVR, such art expresses the powerful presence and creativity of the first peoples of British Columbia, alerting us to the extraordinary and particular place in which we find ourselves. ■

---

1 Frank O'Neill, in an interview with the author, August 22, 2014. 2 Hilary Stewart, *Looking at Totem Poles* (Vancouver/Toronto: Douglas & McIntyre; Seattle: University of Washington Press, 1993), p. 12. 3 Cheryl Shearar, *Understanding Northwest Coast Art* (Vancouver/Toronto: Douglas & McIntyre; Seattle: University of Washington Press, 2000), p. 9.

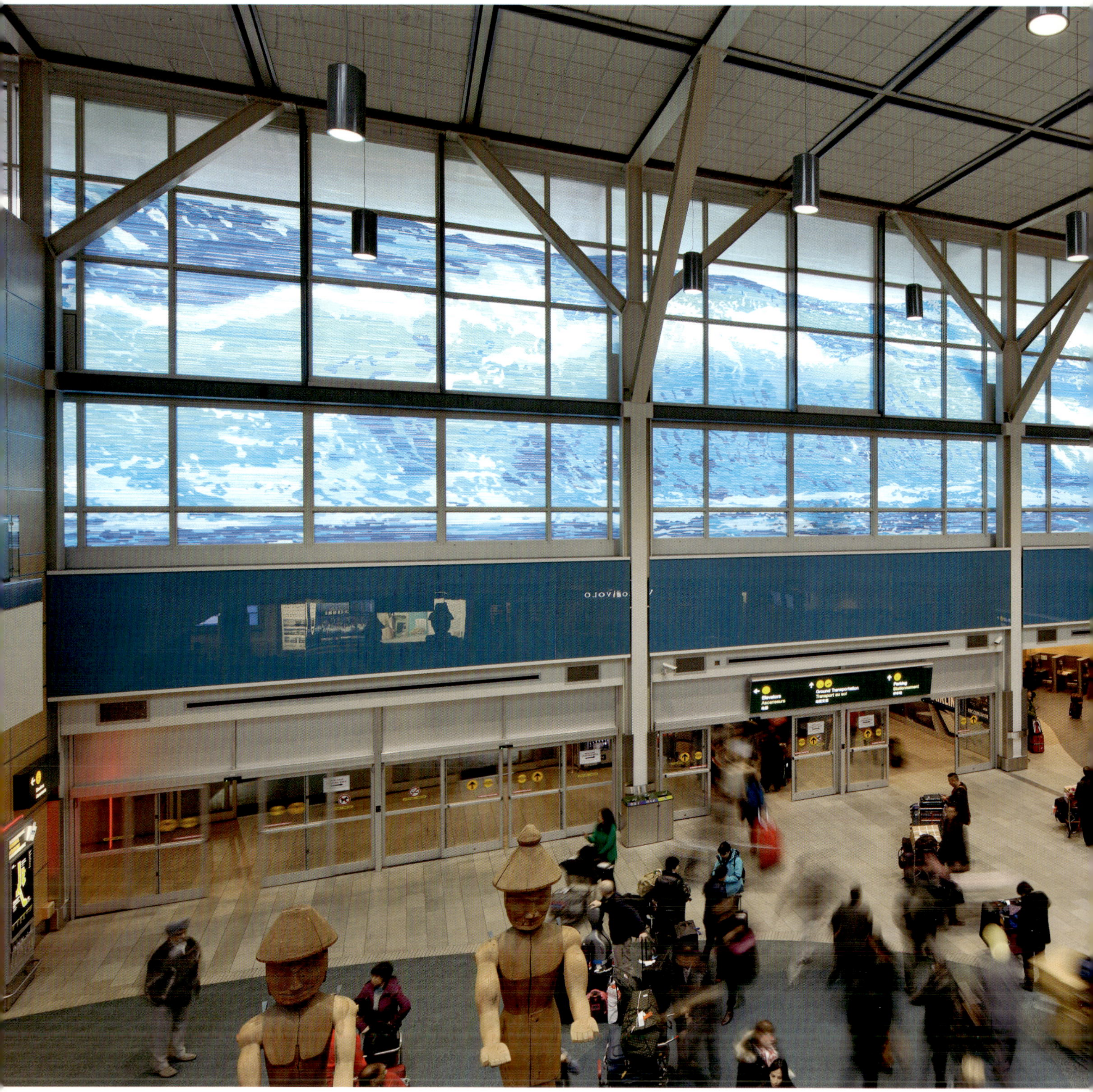
Elevators
Ascenseurs
Ground Transportation
Transport au sol
Parking
Stationnement

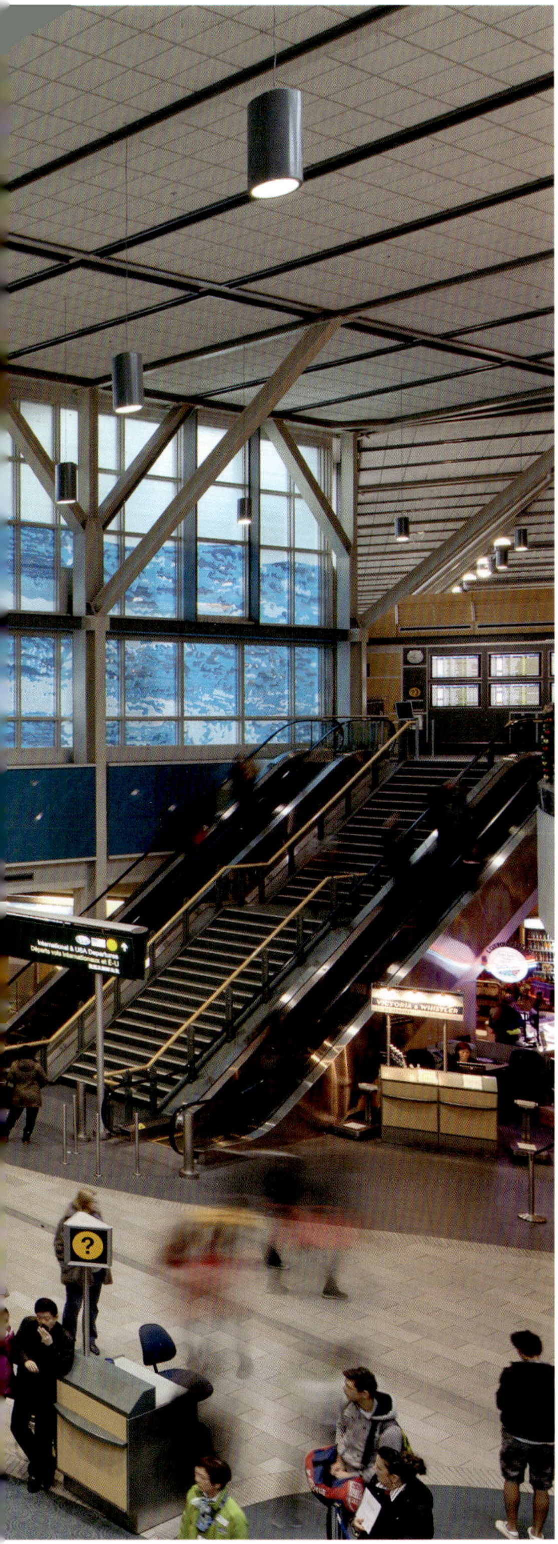

A SENSE OF PLACE

In early 1996, a team of workers, using a large construction crane, manoeuvred a six-ton sculpture into place at Vancouver International Airport (YVR). Conceived and designed by Haida artist Bill Reid, it had been modelled in clay and moulded in plaster in Reid's studio in Vancouver, cast in bronze in the Tallix Foundry in Beacon, New York, and displayed for an interim period in a pavilion on Vancouver's Granville Island. On that momentous day, as it came to rest at YVR, and with the later blessing of the Musqueam First Nation, on whose traditional territory the airport is located, the sculpture found its permanent home.

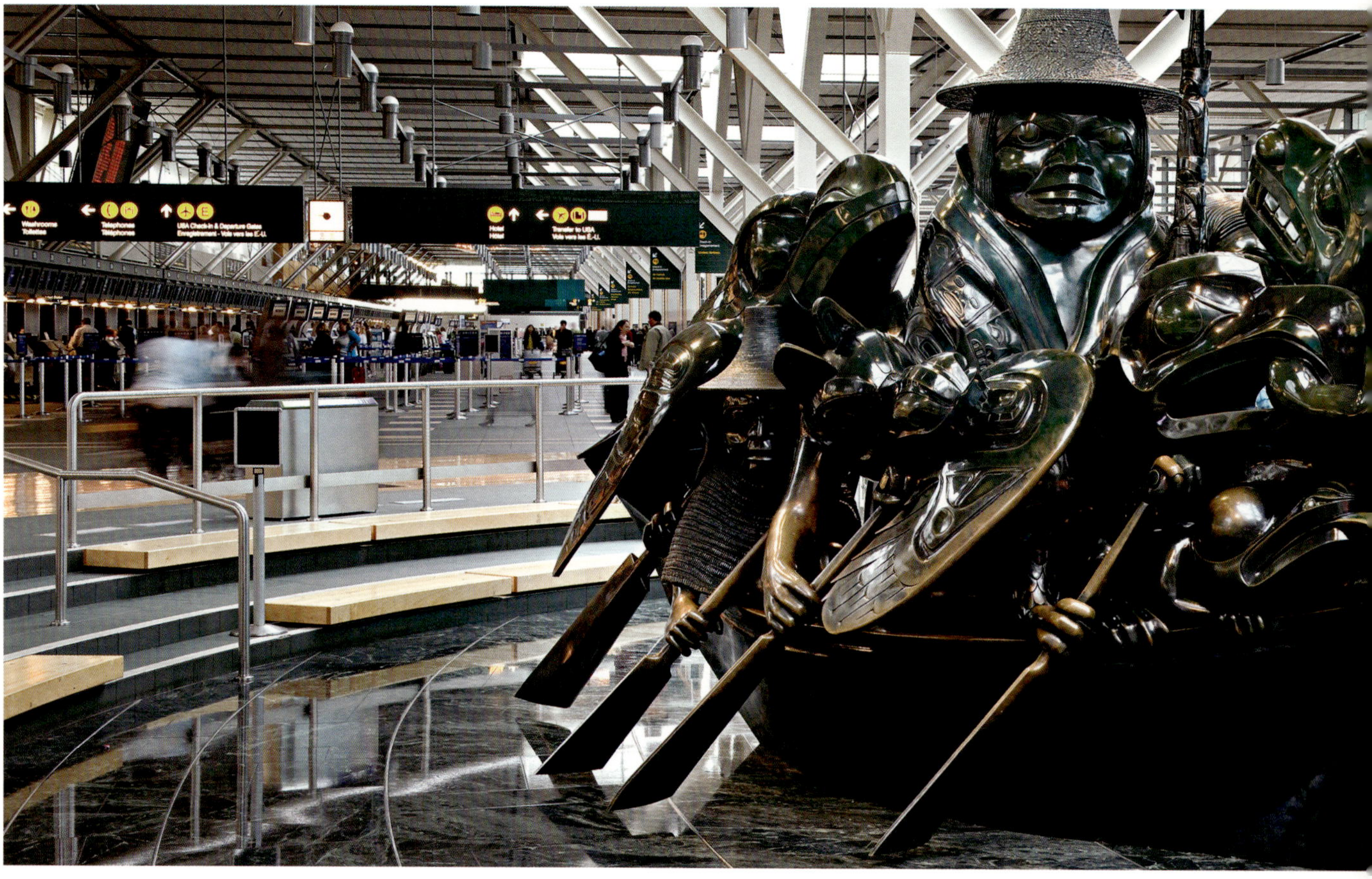

The Spirit of Haida Gwaii: The Jade Canoe has since become a touchstone for travellers from all parts of the world, and an anchor for YVR's renowned collection of British Columbian First Nations art.

The sculpture's first casting had been given a black patina and was installed in 1991 in the Chancery of the Canadian Embassy in Washington, D.C. A second and final casting, patinated in blue-green to evoke the naturally occurring jade of British Columbia,[1] was completed in 1994 and purchased by Vancouver Airport Authority for placement in its new International Terminal.[2] Among those witnessing the installation of this celebrated work, widely known by its subtitle, *The Jade Canoe*, were airport and museum officials, architects and contractors, as well as the artist and his wife. Seated in a wheelchair, ailing in body but strong in mind, Bill Reid seemed to be the living embodiment of the journey depicted in his sculpture. An ancient and enduring culture was being revalidated, old stories were being reinterpreted and new materials

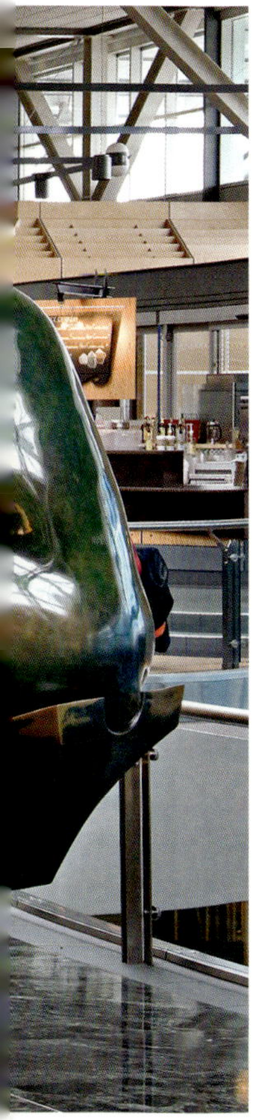

THE SPIRIT OF HAIDA GWAII: THE JADE CANOE

Bill Reid

SEE PAGE 34

and techniques were being explored. As a high-profile artist of mixed Haida and German-American descent, Reid was an important bridge between cultures when non-Native people began to take notice of the indigenous art of the Northwest Coast in the middle of the twentieth century.

The form and content of Reid's sculpture were inspired by nineteenth-century miniature canoes carved in argillite, a black sedimentary stone mined on Slatechuck Mountain, on the densely forested archipelago known as Haida Gwaii, "the Islands of the People." Created by Haida artists for trade with visitors to the Northwest Coast, argillite works (including platters, bowls, boxes, pipes and miniature poles) often drew their subjects from long-held aboriginal themes and stories. In the early years of Reid's career, when he was educating himself in classical Haida style and techniques, he had closely studied such objects in museum collections.

The work was also informed by the artist's late-life experience collaborating in the carving and launching of a suite of full-size cedar canoes. The metaphor of a vessel, crowded with crest figures and myth-time creatures and travelling to an unseen destination, resonated deeply with Reid—and continues to resonate with those passing through YVR. (In a poem titled "The Spirit of Haida Gwaii," written to accompany the sculpture, Reid explored the levels of meaning conveyed by the canoe and those aboard it.)[3] The journeying theme, imposing scale and lively passengers of *The Jade Canoe* are beautifully suited to a busy international airport. And, in fact, the airport is beautifully suited to them.

Over the past two decades, the Airport Authority has designed new and expanding passenger terminals around the large-scale artworks it has commissioned, rather than dropping the pieces into previously built spaces. This innovative strategy has led to a wondrous unity of art and architecture rarely seen at airports before. Of special note is the Musqueam Welcome Area at the entrance to the Canada Customs Hall in the International Terminal, created to convey the presence as well as the greetings of the Musqueam people. It is of the highest significance that iconic sculptures by Susan Point and beautiful weavings by Krista Point, Robyn Sparrow, Debra Sparrow, Gina Grant and Helen Callbreath are among the first artworks encountered by international travellers arriving at YVR. While expressing the cultural traditions of the Coast Salish peoples, the sculptures and weavings also speak to YVR's Sea Island site, in the estuarial mouth of the Fraser River, traditional Musqueam territory. The water cascading through the Musqueam Welcome Area signifies the salmon-bearing

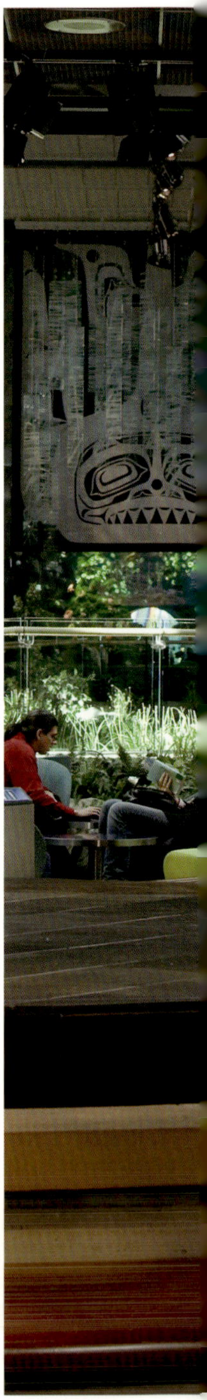

THE STORY OF FOG WOMAN AND RAVEN
Dempsey Bob
SEE PAGE 42

river that is of such great importance to the First Nations people of the region. Travellers from afar enter the city of Vancouver, the province of British Columbia and the country of Canada by passing through lands etched with millennia of aboriginal history.

The public area of the International Terminal, where Reid's sculpture stands, was also designed around the artwork. Conceived as a town square encircled by shops and restaurants, the area functions as a public space where people pause in their journeys to eat, drink, shop and contemplate *The Jade Canoe* and the voyage it symbolizes. More importantly, however, Reid's sculpture communicates its power within YVR's thematic master plan, the intention of which is to evoke the natural beauty and the cultural heritage of British Columbia, creating a memorable portrait of a particular place. For many visitors, YVR provides both their first and last impressions of British Columbia.

The architecture and interior design of the International and Domestic Terminals reiterate the province's natural forms, materials and colours, while the art emerges from and directly represents its Native cultures. In tandem with the powerful works commissioned for the Musqueam Welcome Area, the arrival of *The Jade Canoe* signified an enduring commitment from YVR to collect and display First Nations art of British Columbia. Performing an additional and wholly practical function, aligned with traffic flow, orientation and way-finding, major works have been placed at gates, portals and other spots where important directional changes are made by travellers. *The Jade Canoe*, the most photographed sculpture at YVR—often described as the heart of the airport—provides a popular meeting place for both locals and visitors navigating the terminal.

Acting as a dramatic backdrop to *The Jade Canoe* is an enormous glass wall, created by Lutz Haufschild. Some forty metres in length and composed of thousands of pieces of tinted float glass, *The Great Wave* depicts a seascape of high waves and pounding surf. In its subject and its title, the work pays homage to the famous woodblock print by nineteenth-century Japanese artist Hokusai, a reference suggestive of YVR's important Pacific Rim connections. This imagery also aligns itself with YVR's mission to reflect the natural beauty of British Columbia and the overarching thematic elements of land, sea and sky. Although Haufschild is of European rather than First Nations descent, his architectural glass work speaks directly to Reid's ocean-going canoe. In a subtextual way, too, it reminds us of the importance of the Pacific Ocean as a source of food, a medium of transportation and a begetter of myths, legends and oral histories for British Columbia's peoples.

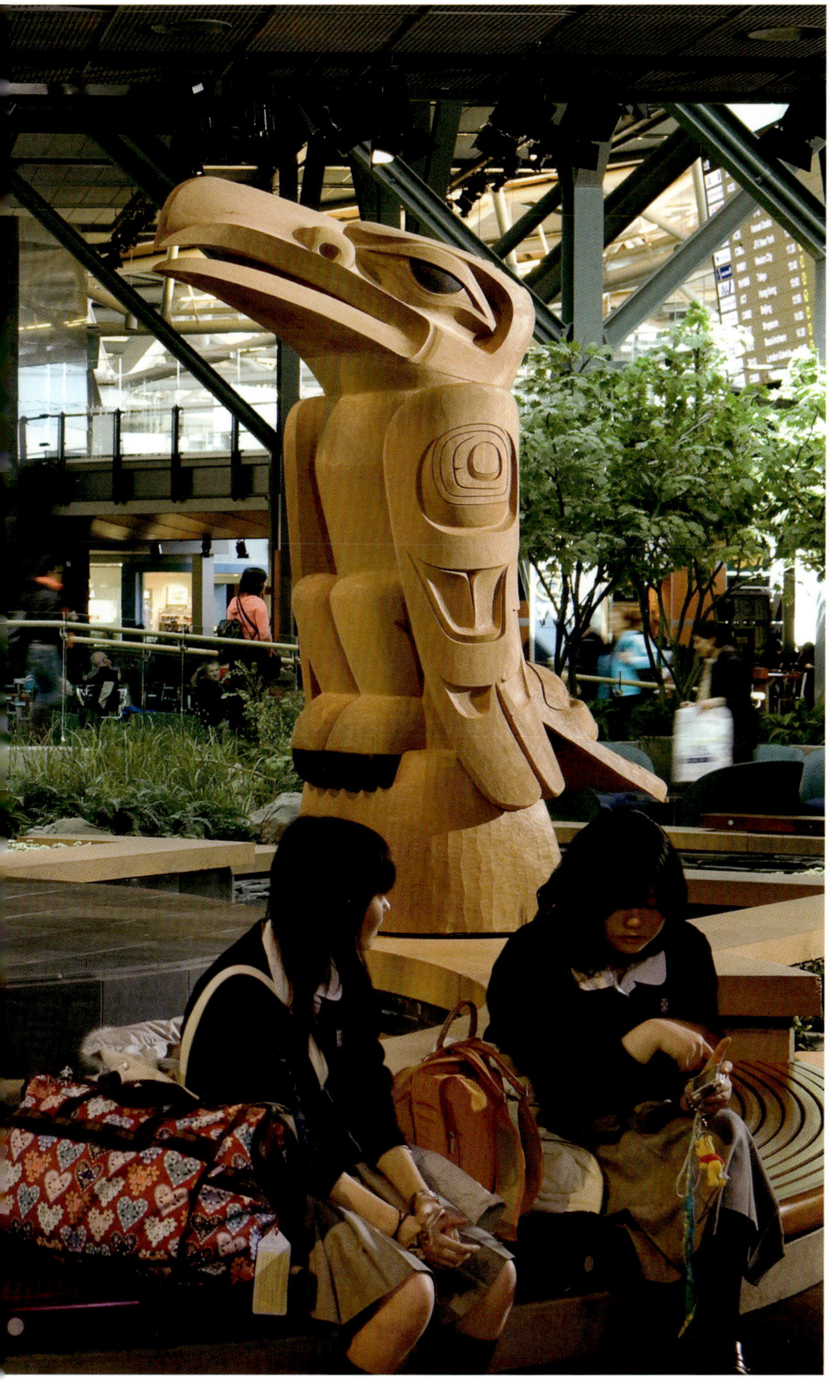

Passengers departing on flights from the International Terminal experience a powerful series of sculptures, glass art, architectural forms and water features. Having checked into their flights and passed through security, they have the time and leisure to fully explore the theme of waterways of the Pacific as they walk among artworks suggestive of streams and rivers flowing to the coast and out into the open ocean.[4] At the head of this symbolic system, posed around the edge of a dark pool, is the figurative sculpture *The Story of Fog Woman and Raven*. Carved from red and yellow cedar by the renowned Tahltan-Tlingit artist Dempsey Bob, this work tells a version of a creation myth, explaining how the annual salmon run originated to benefit the Tlingit people of the northern coast of British Columbia and the southern coast of Alaska. The beneficent Fog Woman, her hair streaming with salmon, a frog pressed against her back, kneels opposite her greedy husband Raven. She embodies the life cycle of spawning salmon that has been essential to the survival of Northwest Coast peoples. At the same time, the artwork recognizes the need to honour and respect the natural environment that sustains these splendid fish.

Downriver, at the opposite end of this setting, is a 114,000-litre aquarium filled with hundreds of sea creatures and underwater plants indigenous to North Pacific coastal

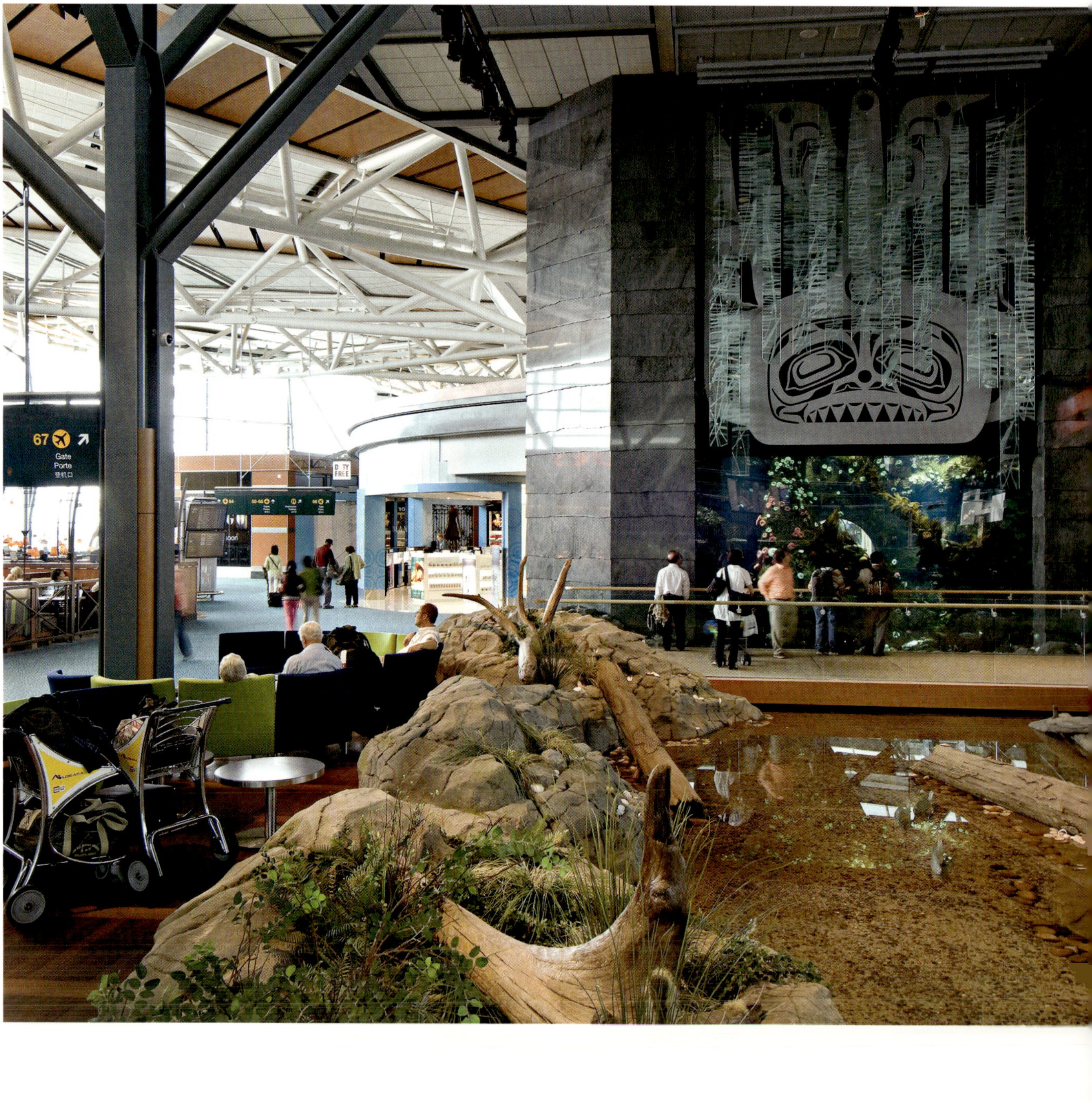
67
Gate
Porte
DUTY FREE

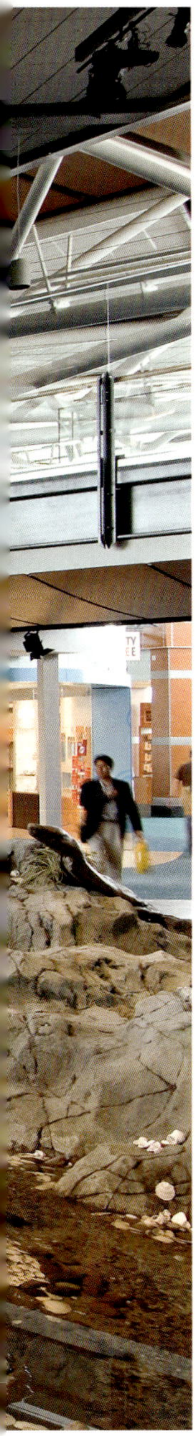

ORCA CHIEF AND THE KELP FOREST
Lyle Wilson and John Nutter
SEE PAGE 47

waters. Majestically installed above and in front of the aquarium is *Orca Chief and the Kelp Forest*, a collaborative installation by multidisciplinary Haisla artist Lyle Wilson and Anglo-Canadian glass artist John Nutter. Wilson's immense aluminum panel depicts the Orca Chief as the foremost ruler of the ocean, his subjects reiterated by the live sea creatures in the aquarium. The kelp that, in myth, surrounds the Orca Chief's copper big house is represented by Nutter's vertical panels of etched glass, which are also suggestive of the beautiful and ecologically important kelp forests that thrive in the cold waters off the Northwest Coast.

Beyond and attuned to these live examples and artful depictions of undersea life is Eric Robertson's installation *Net Work*, three cast aluminum and steel sculptures that hang like swirling silver clouds above the heads of travellers. Suspended from abstracted dip nets, hundreds of silver-coloured fish represent herring balls, the pattern of movement of herring when their school is under attack from predators, both animal and human. Robertson, of mixed Gitxsan and Euro-Canadian heritage, drew upon his fine art education in Vancouver and Montreal along with knowledge gleaned from working in fisheries to create a dynamic evocation of life energy and environmental concern.

The fierce and striking *Transformation Mask* by Kwakwaka'wakw artist Stan Wamiss is the focal point of a dramatic display in the departures area of the International Terminal that serves travellers bound for the United States. The lighting and materials used in the display evoke the winter ceremonials of Northwest Coast First Nations people, performed in longhouses around flickering fires. Large and complex, with hinged sections operated by a cord or by the movements of the dancer, a transformation mask traditionally represents one creature or being in its closed position and another in its open and spread position. The outer being on Wamiss's mask is Raven, culture hero and Trickster; the inner being is Bak'was, commonly known as Wild Man of the Woods. His attributes include deep-set eyes, prominent cheekbones and an overall skeletal appearance, identifying him as the ghost-like chief among the spirits and the keeper of drowned souls.

The positioning of *The Spirit of Haidi Gwaii: The Jade Canoe*, *The Story of Fog Woman and Raven*, *Orca Chief and the Kelp Forest* and *Net Work* as a series of Northwest Coast "farewells" to travellers bound for international destinations is contrasted by the "greetings" extended by the Musqueam Welcome Area. Other scenes of welcome include the extraordinary Pacific Passage

NET WORK
Eric Robertson
SEE PAGE 48

in the International Terminal, marking the arrival of passengers from the United States and symbolizing another kind of journey through realms both natural and supernatural. Here, diverse examples of contemporary Northwest Coast First Nations art—arising from quite different traditions and ranging in size from miniature to monumental—play off each other and their surroundings. All the art is set within a diorama intended to evoke a coastal environment of forests, cliffs and shoreline, enhanced by the sound of ocean waves and the calls of wild birds. The four artists commissioned to produce work for the Pacific Passage—Stephen Bruce, Tim Paul, Connie Watts and Lyle Wilson—were asked to communicate a time of creation, alluding to myth-age stories explaining the awakening of human consciousness. They also explored the themes of epic voyages and animal-human transformation.

Hovering above travellers as they walk through the passage is an immense, articulated Thunderbird, created by Watts out of unexpected construction materials. Watts, improvising on design components of traditional Kwakwaka'wakw art, riveted natural and painted birch panels to echoing forms of aluminum. Further elaborated by depictions of other symbolic creatures and celestial bodies, these parts are then joined together with aluminum rings. Titled *Hetux*, the work represents a contemporary variation on the giant supernatural bird known as the keeper of the sky. This creature dwells high in the mountains, creates thunder with the flap of its wings and lightning with the blink of its eyes, and hunts large prey, such as Killer Whale, by hurling Lightning Snakes like spears.[5] Watts, who is descended from three different Northwest Coast First Nations (Nuu-chah-nulth, Kwakwaka'wakw and Gitxsan), bestowed her Thunderbird with the name and personality of her determined and creative grandmother, Hetux.

Also hanging in the "sky" of the Pacific Passage area is Wilson's etched glass and polished aluminum disk *Origin of Light*. It is based on the story of Raven (Wee-git in the Haisla language) stealing light in the form of the sun, moon and stars and releasing it to the world. In Wilson's telling, Raven's release of the ball of light becomes a metaphor for the dawning of human consciousness. Culture, language and thought emerge out of what had been primordial darkness. Like Watts, Wilson employed new materials to articulate ancient beliefs, and brought new interpretations to traditional imagery.

Representing the realm of the sea is Paul's *Rainbow off the Beach*, a contemporary realization of a traditional Nuu-chah-nulth whaling canoe. Named for Paul's Hesquiat ancestors, known as the Rainbow People, this

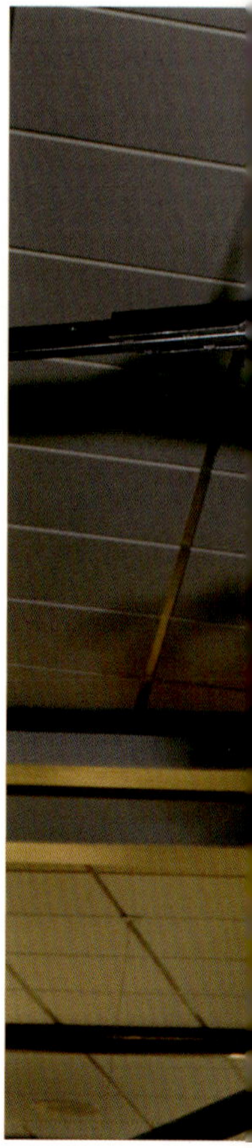

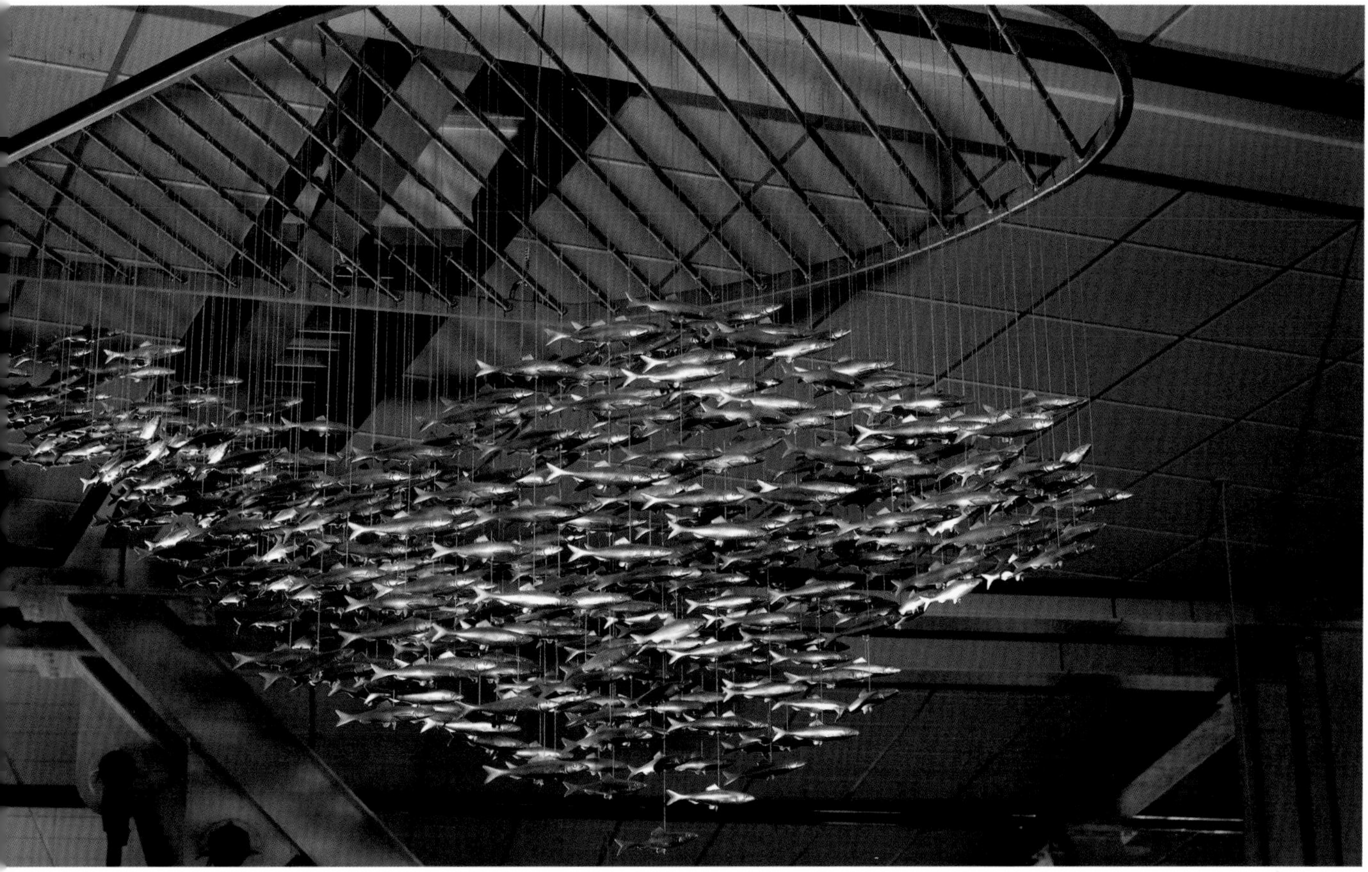

eleven-metre-long cedar vessel especially honours the artist's grandfathers, uncle and father, who carried forward the specialized knowledge of canoe-making. Historically, the Nuu-chah-nulth, who live on the west coast of Vancouver Island, were skilled and powerful whalers, taking their canoes into the open ocean, harpooning their large prey and hauling them back to shore. As a consequence, their whaling canoes had to be strong and extremely seaworthy — as did the men who paddled and steered them. Paul, acclaimed for his pole commissions in Canada and abroad, painted this, his first large canoe, with a Great Sea Serpent, a moon design and an image of "our ancestor gone before us."

Bruce, a Kwakwaka'wakw artist of the Namgis First Nation, has based his carvings of animals and birds on tales of the time when creatures took off their skins and became human. Posed among the cliffs, forests and shoreline represented within the Pacific Passage diorama, the creatures represented are part family crest, part

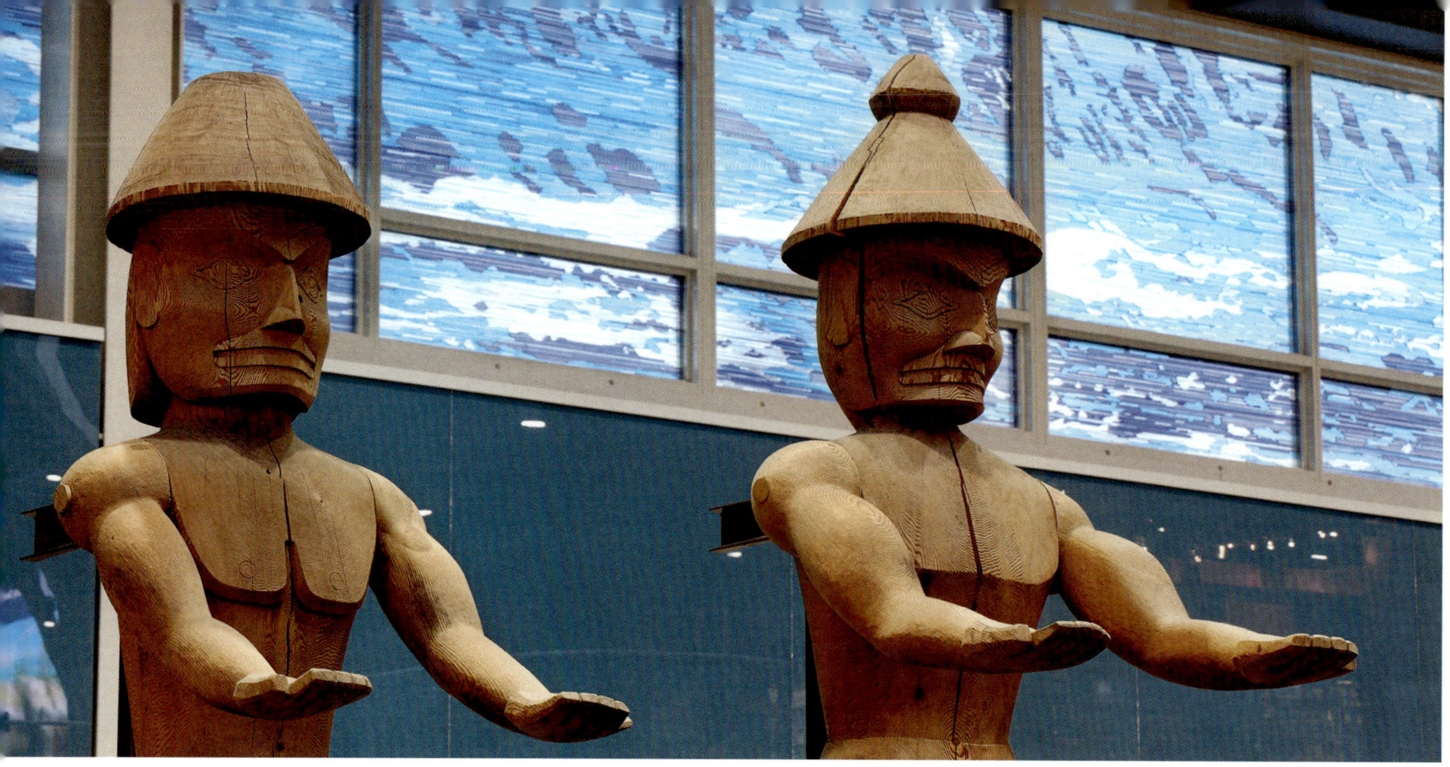

closely observed nature and part evocation of the meeting place between the past and the present. As disembarking passengers from the U.S. progress through the Pacific Passage toward the Musqueam Welcome Area, it is as if they are experiencing the dawning of this land and all those who have inhabited it.

Once travellers make their way through the Canada Customs Hall, they emerge into the thronging meeters and greeters area of YVR's International Terminal. There, they are received by friends and family and two large, imposing wooden figures, male and female. Arms extended, palms turned upward, such welcome figures are traditional to the Nuu-chah-nulth First Nation, and were often set up on beaches to welcome visitors to village feasts. The figures at YVR were originally commissioned in the mid-1980s from Nuu-chah-nulth artist Joe David to stand at the entrance of the British Columbia Pavilion at Expo 86, the world's fair held in Vancouver during the city's centennial year and thematically dedicated to transportation and communication. After the fair ended, they were installed outside the Vancouver Museum (now the Museum of Vancouver), where, unfortunately, they were damaged and then placed in storage.[6] In the 1990s, the Airport Authority borrowed them from the museum, arranged for their restoration and erected them on concrete pedestals in the International Terminal's arrivals area. In this location, they greet passengers and highlight YVR's ongoing collaboration with leading local museums to express a sense of place through the powerful representation of B.C. First Nations cultures. In addition to borrowing and siting art from the permanent collection of the Museum of Vancouver, YVR has worked closely with advisors from the UBC Museum of Anthropology, one of the world's leading institutions for the display and study of aboriginal art of the Northwest Coast.

WELCOME FIGURES

Joe David

SEE PAGE 33

Standing just outside the International Terminal, in Chester Johnson Park, are three tall and beautiful poles created more than four decades ago by the esteemed Gitxsan artists Earl Muldoe and Walter Harris. Collectively identified as the K'san Totem Poles after the historical village on the Upper Skeena River in north-central British Columbia where they were carved, they demonstrate the intricate relief style and interlinked forms of classical Gitxsan art. Specifically, they tell stories of supernatural beings and creatures associated with the family lineage and cultural heritage of each artist. Eagle, Frog, Killer Whale and Grizzly Bear of the Sea are among the figures on Harris's pole, while Muldoe's poles depict Watchman, Raven, Bear, Hawk and Owl, among others. Also on loan to YVR from the Museum of Vancouver and erected with the approval of the Musqueam people, these works stand among low benches and towering evergreen trees. While representing a point of rest and contemplation, they can also be viewed by travellers walking past them at ground level or from the glassed passageway leading to the rapid transit station above.

Celebrating Flight, a tall and dynamic pole by Don Yeomans, dominates the light-filled Graham Clarke Atrium, which joins the International and Domestic Terminals at YVR. An acclaimed artist of Haida and Metis descent, Yeomans brings his considerable skill and experience to this tribute to air travel, that is, to the knowledge and technology that enable humankind to fly. Incorporated into this innovative pole are not only figures from Haida mythology but also visual and linguistic expressions from other cultures, such as Celtic knot-work and Chinese characters. Set into either side of this multi-referenced pole, which recognizes YVR as a meeting place of many peoples and cultures, are soaring vertical lines of bright green light, drawing the eye upward. Hanging in a "sky" filled with curving blue panels, representing the aurora borealis, is a moon mask by Trace Yeomans. An artist of Haida and Ukrainian descent best known for her paintings and dance regalia, she has often worked with her husband Don on large-scale commissions. As with *The Jade Canoe*'s setting in the International Terminal, the curved seating around *Celebrating Flight* in the Graham Clarke Atrium invites travellers to rest for a moment and contemplate the artwork. It also functions as a popular meeting place for the public and for YVR employees, and as a significant point of recognition for those taking self-guided art tours of the airport.

Through both art and architecture, the celebration of British Columbia's natural

HUGGING THE WORLD
Robert Davidson
SEE PAGE 86

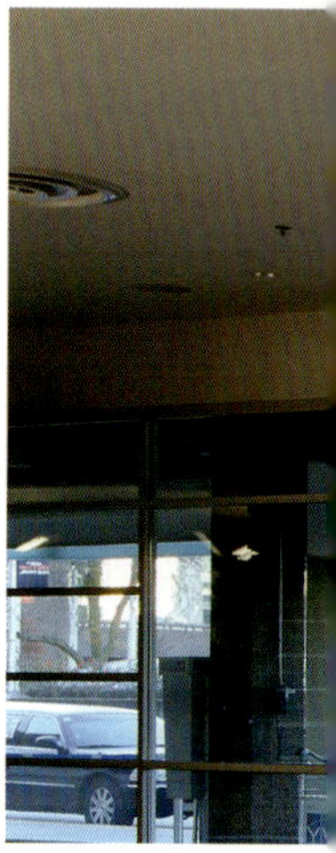

environment and First Nations cultures is beautifully continued in the Domestic Terminal. One of the most spectacular displays in this building is Supernatural World, located within the arrivals concourse, spanning levels one and two. Dempsey Bob, Robert Davidson and Richard Hunt, three renowned artists from distinct linguistic groups and style traditions, have created important works that exude individual power when viewed on their own but that also participate in a complex conversation with each other, across time, place and belief. The intention of Supernatural World is to evoke the creatures and beings, both seen and unseen, that occupy the realms of land, sea and sky. These entities may be the ancestors of the families who use them as crest figures, and they may also have the power to transform themselves at will.[7]

Supernatural World greets travellers arriving from other parts of the province and the country while marking a space of physical transition and culture dialogue. Standing on a shell and shingle beach, designed by the distinguished landscape architect Cornelia Hahn Oberlander, is Hunt's two-part sculpture *Thunderbird and Killer Whale*. In both style and subject matter, the work reflects his Kwakwaka'wakw heritage. It depicts the supernatural Thunderbird, wings spread, about to swoop down on Killer Whale, his eternal enemy and favourite prey. Hunt also takes as his inspiration ceremonial dances in which participants wear Thunderbird and Killer Whale masks and regalia.

Bob's enormous *Bear/Human* and *Human/Bear* masks, carved in red cedar and mounted on poles at either end of the Supernatural World, articulate the Tlingit belief in the profound connections between people and animals, and the ability of certain animals to assume human form. In one mask, a small human figure crouches between the ears of a bear with huge fangs and hooded eyes. In the other, this configuration is reversed: the small face of a bear (with human teeth and extended tongue) is perched on the forehead of an ancestral human. Both works suggest the attributes and understanding shared between bears, the biggest and most important land animals on the Northwest Coast, and the humans who seek safe passage among them.

Davidson's *Hugging the World* is suspended high above the ground floor of the Domestic Terminal, visible through big windows to travellers on the second-level sidewalk outside as well as to those using the encircling ramp and escalators inside. The most renowned of contemporary Haida artists, Davidson has both honoured the traditional art of his people and innovated upon it through his use of a range of two- and three-dimensional forms. Facing in opposite directions, the immense Eagle and Raven of his large, red cedar sculpture

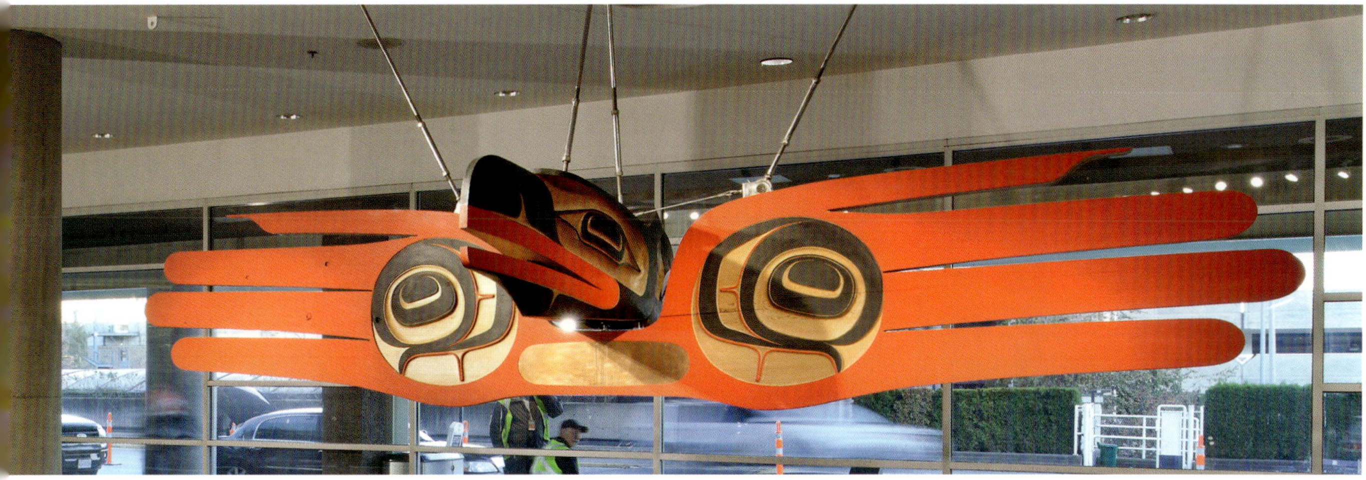

share the same pair of flat, outstretched wings, shaped and painted to resemble open human hands. Both birds are symbolically resonant, assuming multiple roles in culture, myth and social organization among the Haida people.

The A-B Connector, part of the Domestic Terminal expansion, was recently opened at YVR. The A-B Connector evokes British Columbia's vineyards, orchards and fishing lodges, and the Fraser River's canyon. The space is anchored by the contemporary art piece *The Rivers Monument*, by Marianne Nicolson (Tayagila'ogwa). Perched atop each of two glass poles, which bear pictograph-style images of humans, fish, wildlife and water, is a carved and painted red cedar eagle. Together the imagery, forms and materials symbolize the power and natural abundance of the Pacific Northwest's great river systems,[8] while also mourning the losses that have occurred in the past two hundred years. Of special concern to Nicolson, a critically acclaimed Kwakwaka'wakw artist and scholar, are declining fish runs in the Fraser River and the flooding, in 1957, of thousands of pictographs at the Celilo Falls site in Washington State, as a result of the construction of the Dalles Dam on the Columbia River. Nicolson's new work reasserts the "submerged histories" told by those pictographs, bringing them back to life symbolically.[9]

Powerful works have also been installed in the departures area on level three of the Domestic Terminal, where the architectural design is intended to suggest the Sea to Sky Highway that runs north from the city of Vancouver to the mountain resort of Whistler. *Snuw'uy'ulth*, by John Marston (Qap'u'luq), a Coast Salish artist from the Chemainus First Nation, is composed of an array of extraordinary canoe paddles. Carved and painted to tell the stories of Marston's people and to suggest "different animals, their spirits, and the forms of life and culture associated with them,"[10] they are suspended in the air above architectural features representing

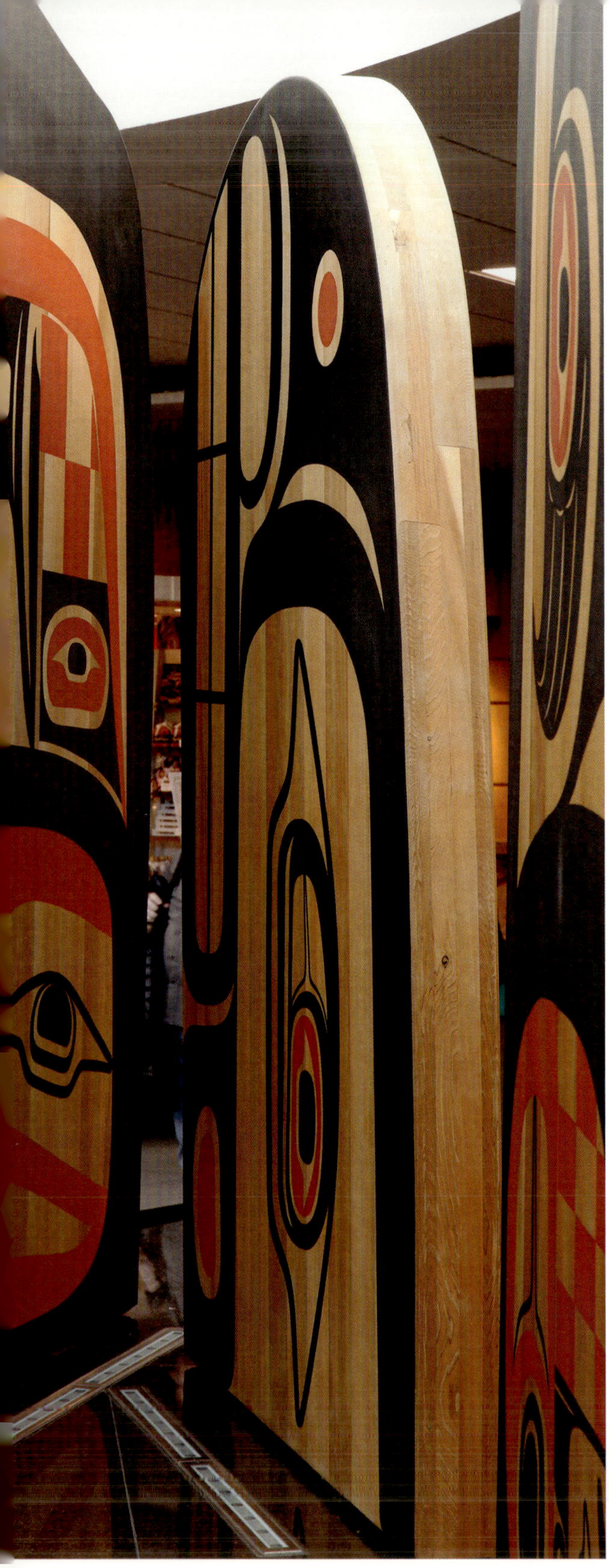

FREEDOM TO MOVE

Steve Smith

SEE PAGE 75

falling and flowing water. The impact is immensely lively and complex. The colours of and relief carvings on the paddles express not only their Coast Salish origins but also reveal style influences from Japan and Papua New Guinea, where Marston has participated in cultural exchanges. Despite this sense of innovation and vitality, the mood conveyed is also somewhat ghostly. It is as if an unseen canoe, with highly visible paddles and invisible paddlers, were gliding along an imaginary shoreline, calling up the spirits that dwell in the forest beyond.

Kwakwaka'wakw-Oweekeno artist Steve Smith has created two major installations for YVR's Domestic Terminal, *Freedom to Move* and *Sea to Sky*. The latter alludes to the significance of drumming within First Nations ceremonial culture, employing painted maple wood and elk hide to create very large, contemporary interpretations of the traditional instruments. Just as guests are welcomed to a ceremonial event with the sound of drums and then drummed out again as the event ends, Smith's *Sea to Sky* silently sounds the arrival and departure of travellers as they pass through YVR daily.[11] In reference to the overarching theme of land, sea and sky, the Vancouver-based artist painted his drums with abstracted images of creatures from all three realms: Killer Whale, Salmon and Octopus; Bear and Man; and finally, Eagle and Raven.

Freedom to Move alludes to the canoe travel that characterized the movements of Northwest Coast peoples in times past while also presiding over a place of rest and contemplation for today's airline travellers. The six large, laminated red cedar panels, their highly abstracted designs executed in acrylic paint, stand upright on a black granite platform set in a pool of water. Stylistically innovative and physically commanding, they represent a host of creatures and crest figures in a state of transformation.

In 1990, Roy Henry Vickers was commissioned to create cedar house posts and painted panels for a duty-free shop in the old Vancouver International Airport. Of Tsimshian, Haida, Heiltsuk and British ancestry, Vickers is best known for his silkscreen prints of Northwest Coast scenes. He is also a skilled carver, as revealed by his *Raven House Posts*, which now frame a doorway in the arrivals area of the Domestic Terminal. Here, Raven can be seen to embody all his contradictions: culture hero and Trickster, transformer and teacher, organizer and troublemaker, "intelligent, curious, innovative and resourceful, yet selfish, greedy, deceitful and mischievous."[12] Raven, in fact, is very much like humans, those complicated creatures he released from a clam shell in the Haida creation myth. As depicted in Vickers's house posts, the wily creature seems to recognize this kinship—a bond with both people and place—and to watch us as we pass through Vancouver International Airport on our many and various journeys. ■

---

1 Jade is British Columbia's official gemstone, prized by jewellers and sculptors locally and abroad. According to the Ministry of Energy and Mines, all the known jade deposits in B.C. are of the nephrite variety and the province supplies three-quarters of the world jade market. See www.empr.gov.bc.ca/Mining/Geoscience/MINFILE/Jade for more information. 2 Robin Laurence, "Introduction," in Ulli Steltzer's *The Spirit of Haida Gwaii: Bill Reid's Masterpiece* (Vancouver/Toronto: Douglas & McIntyre; Seattle: University of Washington Press, 1997), p. 16. 3 Bill Reid, "The Spirit of Haida Gwaii," accessed at www.billreidfoundation.ca/banknote/spirit.htm. 4 Architecttura, *YVR Thematic Master Plan*, January 2002, p. 4. 5 Cheryl Shearar, *Understanding Northwest Coast Art: A Guide to Crests, Beings and Symbols* (Vancouver/Toronto: Douglas & McIntyre; Seattle: University of Washington Press, 2000), p. 104. 6 YVR Art Foundation, *Land Sea Sky: Art at YVR* (Vancouver: YVR Art Foundation, 2003), p. 4. 7 Ibid., p. 20. 8 Marianne Nicolson, artist's statement, 2014. 9 Ibid. 10 John Marston, artist's statement, 2009. 11 Steve Smith, artist's statement, 2011. 12 Shearar, *Understanding Northwest Coast Art*, p. 88.

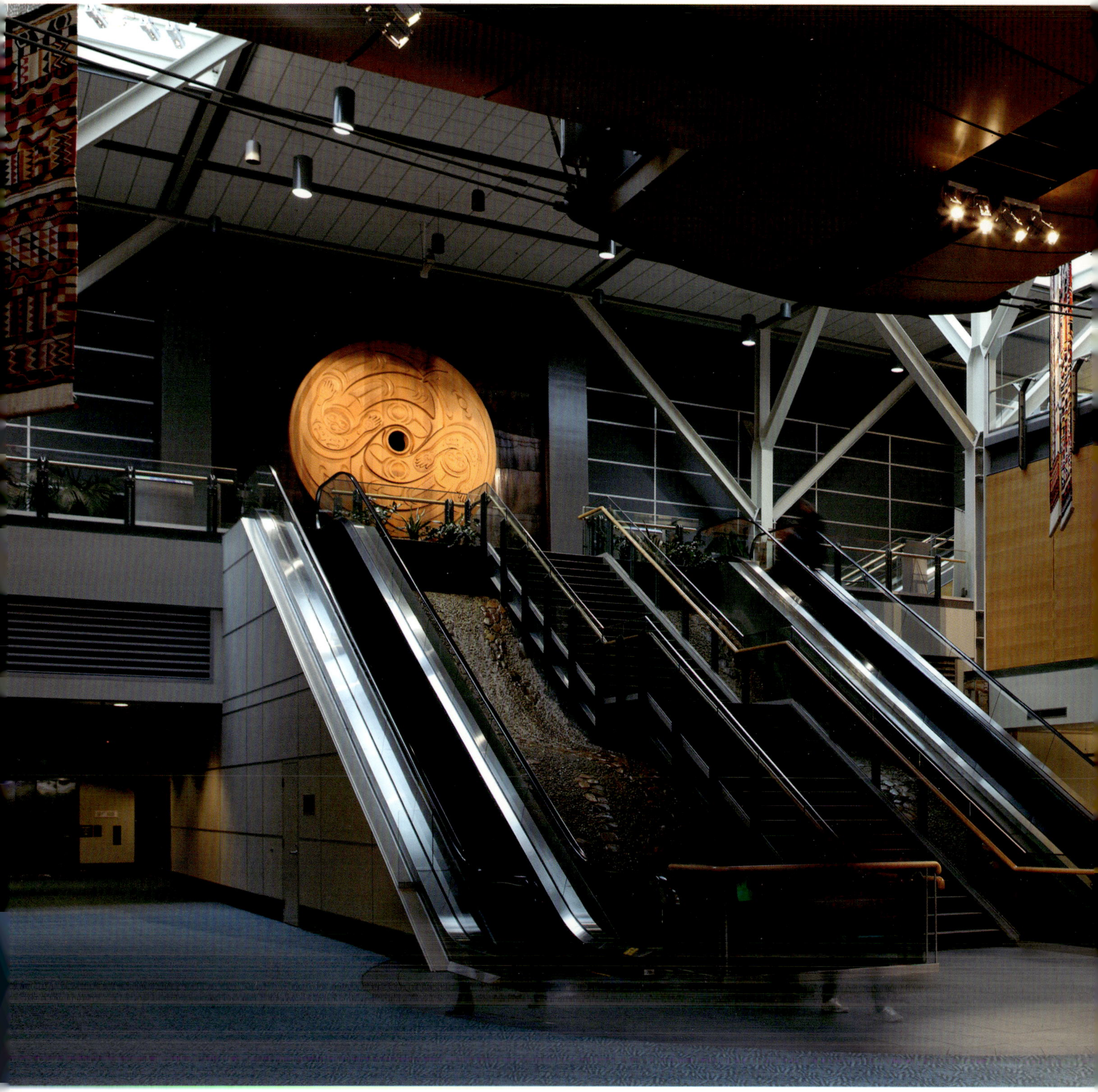

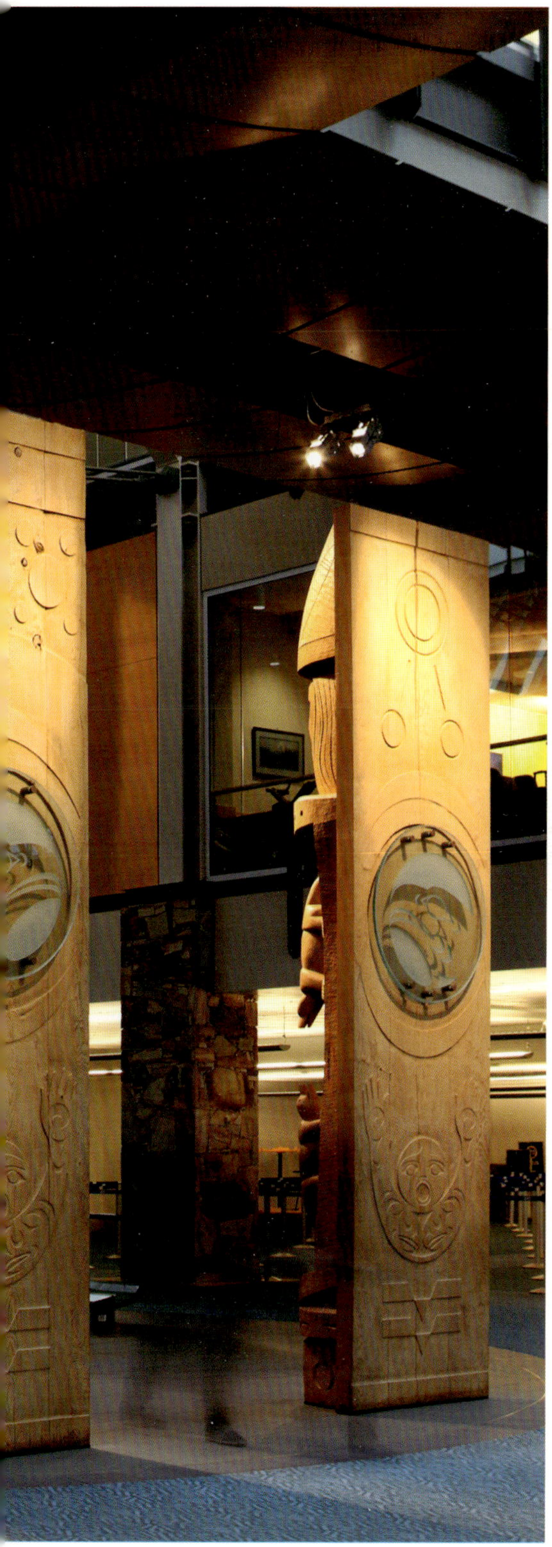

1

MUSQUEAM WELCOME AREA

CANADA CUSTOMS HALL

(POST-SECURITY)

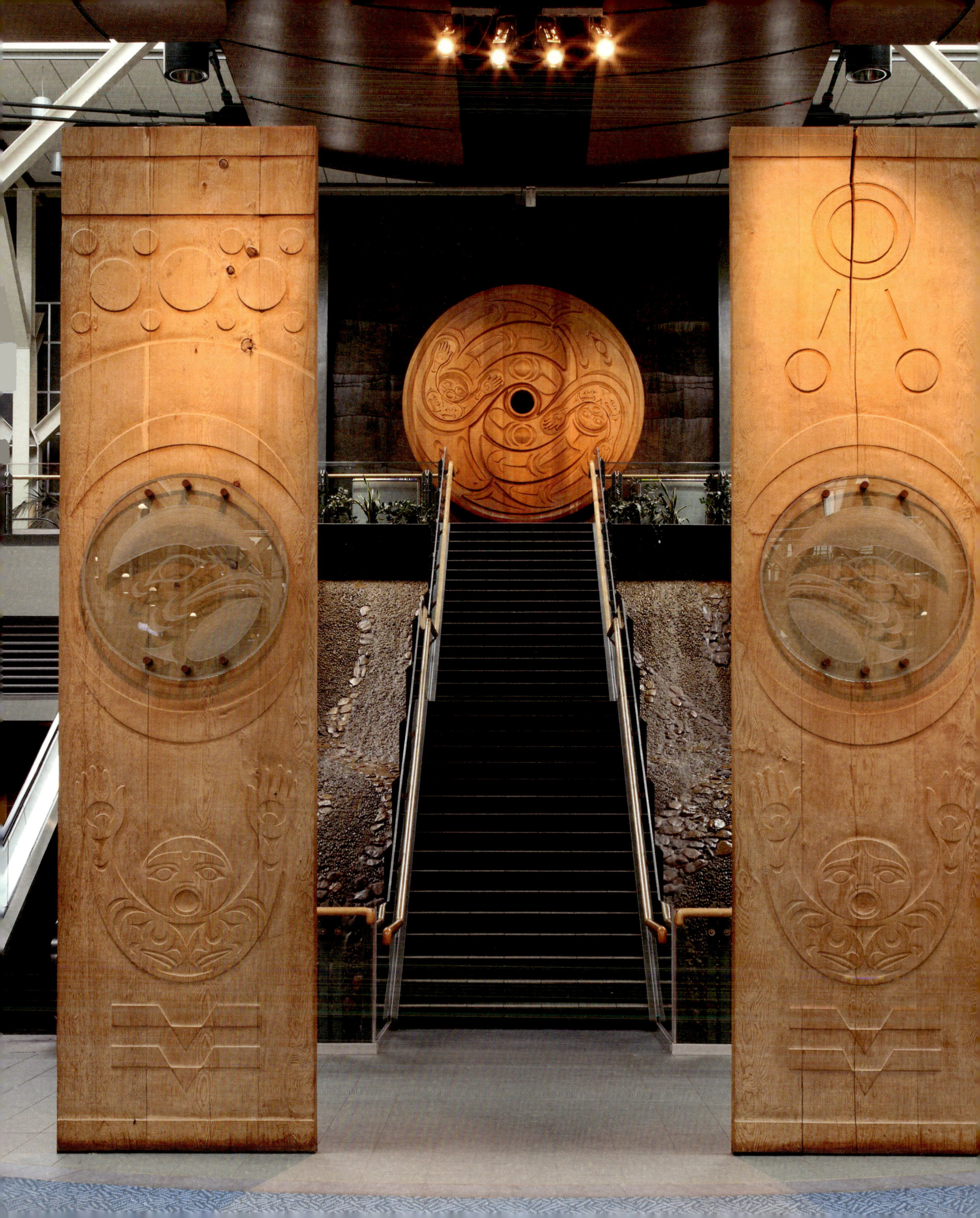

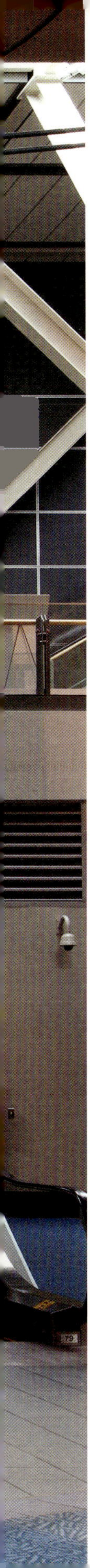

MUSQUEAM WELCOME FIGURES

Susan Point

1996 red cedar, glass | 5.2 × 1.3 × 0.2 m each

Susan Point's striking pair of welcome figures, standing near the bottom of the escalators, stairs and streams in Canada Customs Hall, extend a First Nations greeting to international and cross-border travellers. The deeply carved frontal aspects of both figures are inspired by historical Coast Salish house posts, while the back panels reveal the artist's innovations on traditional images and motifs. The female figure is depicted wearing a basketry hat with feathers, signifying her gender and high social status. She also wears a ceremonial blanket, adorned with buttons and fishers. Fishers, which are members of the weasel family, figure importantly in Coast Salish sculpture and are associated with cleansing rites.[1] The male welcome figure is more shallowly carved and bears depictions of sea serpents and of eagles, the latter reiterating the eagles on Point's monumental *Flight (Spindle Whorl)* located on the nearby landing.

The back panels of both figures have been sand-etched and inscribed with additional images and forms. The depictions of human figures with arms raised, seen in *Flight (Spindle Whorl)*, are repeated here, and the salmon images on their chests symbolize the Coast Salish people who have lived and fished along the banks of the Fraser River for thousands of years. On one panel, circular motifs symbolize the stars, the moon and the sun. On the other, the sun carries two valises filled with valuables, an image found on historic Coast Salish house posts. The back panels of both figures have been inset with round glass depictions of eagles, conveying again the theme of flight, and the bottoms of the panels have been carved with the "flying geese" pattern seen in the Salish weavings hanging nearby.

1 Susan Point, artist's statement, 1996.

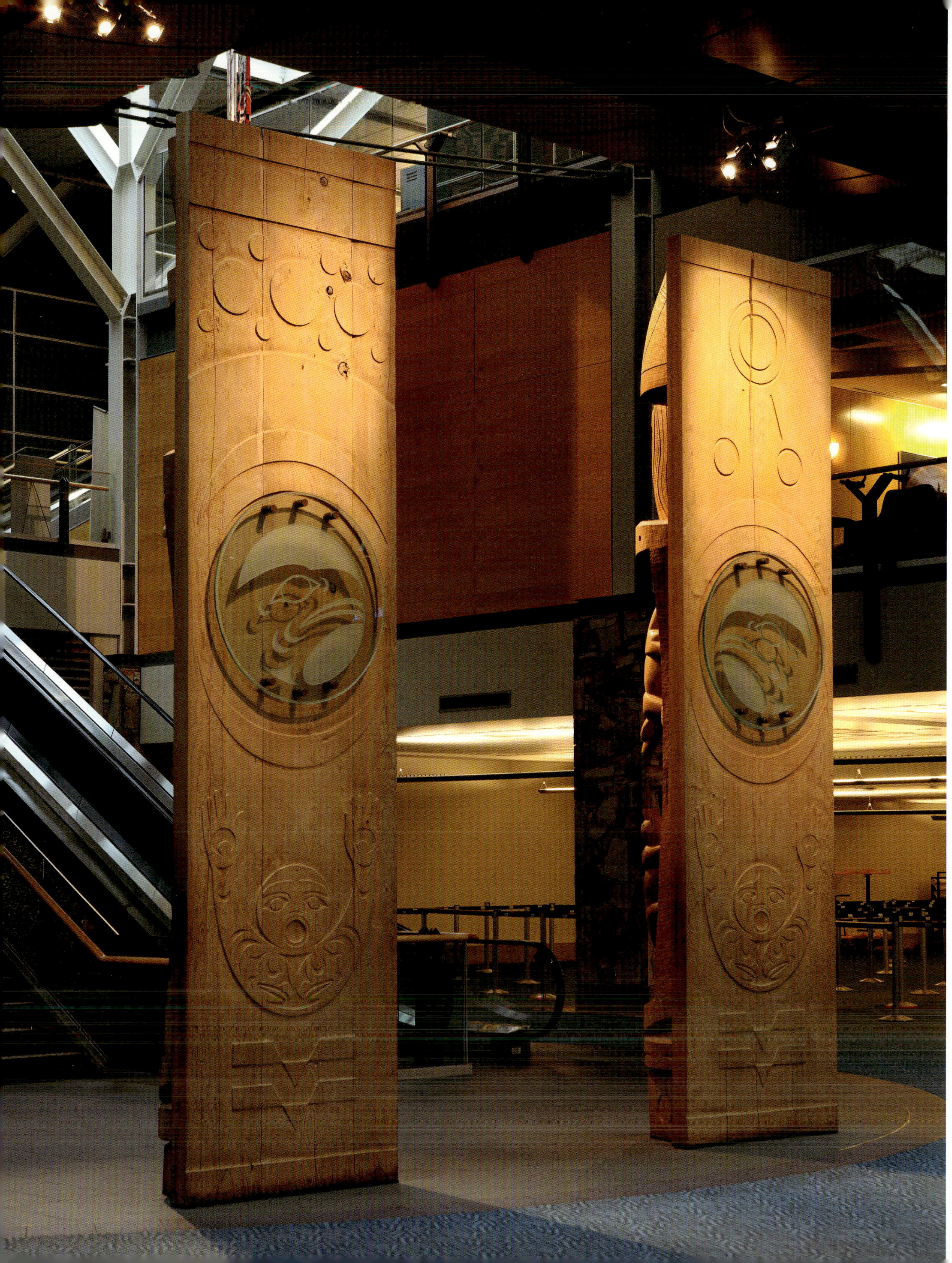

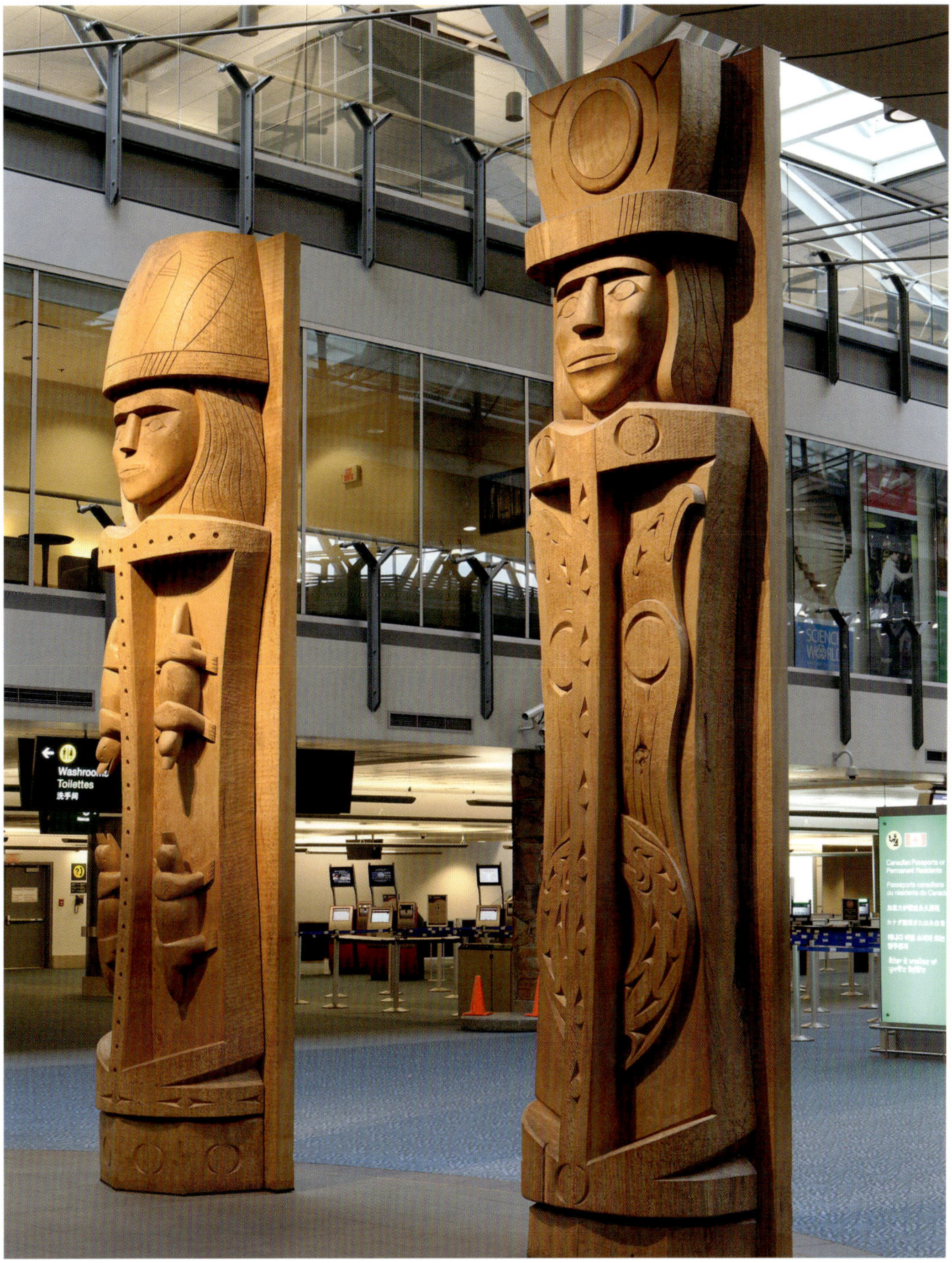
Toilettes
洗手间

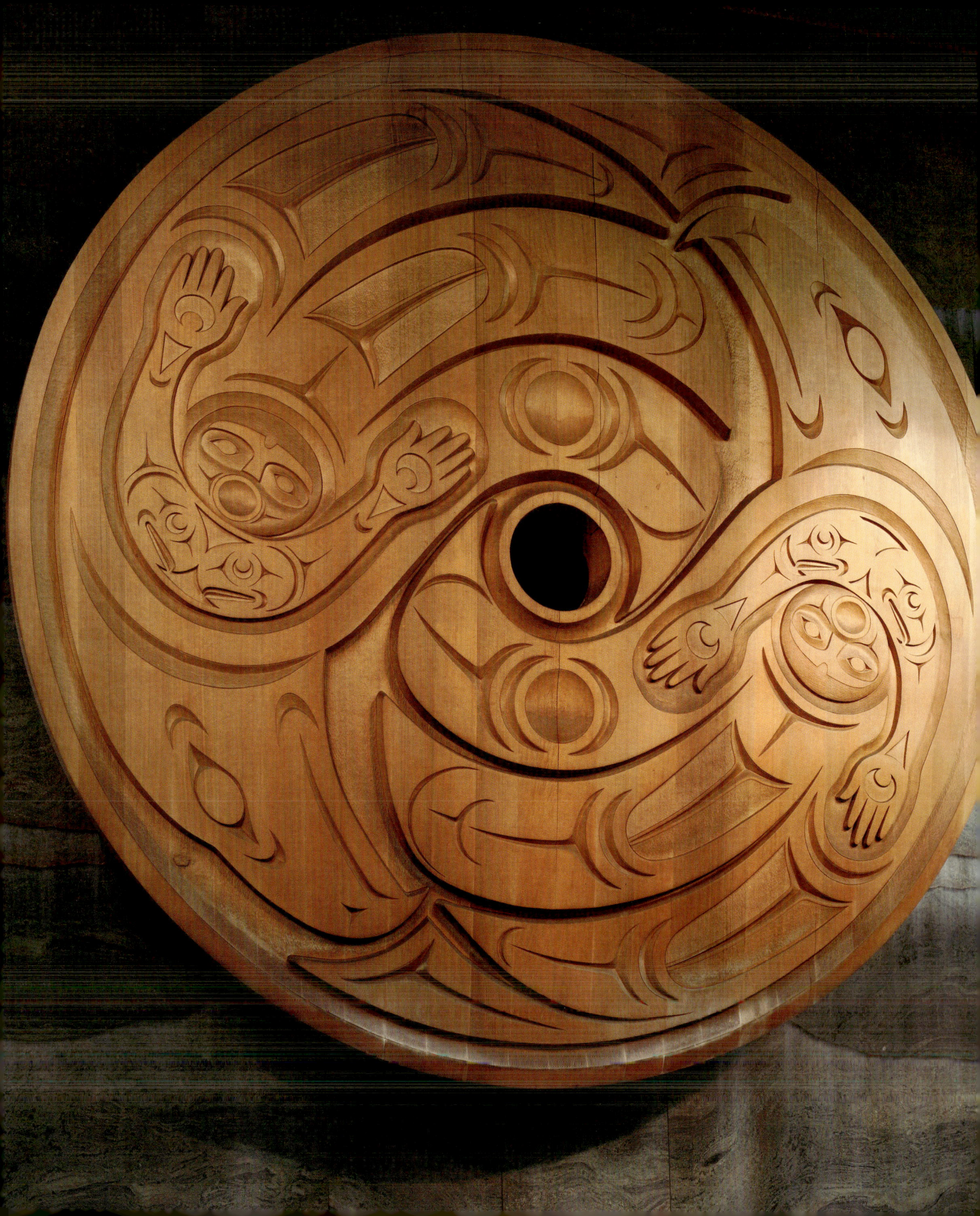

FLIGHT (SPINDLE WHORL)

Susan Point

1995 red cedar | 4.8 m in diameter

Susan Point's immense spindle whorl, carved in red cedar, twines together a number of themes and traditions. The images incised into the overall circular form include eagles, salmon and human figures, their arms raised in a gesture of welcome and also as a suggestion of flight. The eagles symbolize power while the salmon, whose sleek bodies are incorporated into the human arms, represent the Coast Salish First Nations who have lived and fished along the Fraser River for millennia. Musqueam Village, where Point lives, is located near the mouth of the river and is surrounded by the city of Vancouver; YVR, built on Sea Island in the municipality of Richmond, stands on traditional Musqueam territory. In spite of the intense urbanization that has taken place around them, the Musqueam people retain an active cultural and political presence in the Metro Vancouver area.[1] These facts inform all aspects of the Musqueam Welcome Area in the International Terminal where *Flight (Spindle Whorl)* is installed.

Point has drawn inspiration for the overall shape and design of her sculpture from historic spindle whorls, flat disks approximately twenty to twenty-five centimetres in diameter, made from wood or stone.[2] Carved with figurative or abstract designs and having a hole in the centre where the spindle was inserted for spinning wool from mountain goat hair, such objects were essential in the creation of Coast Salish blankets.

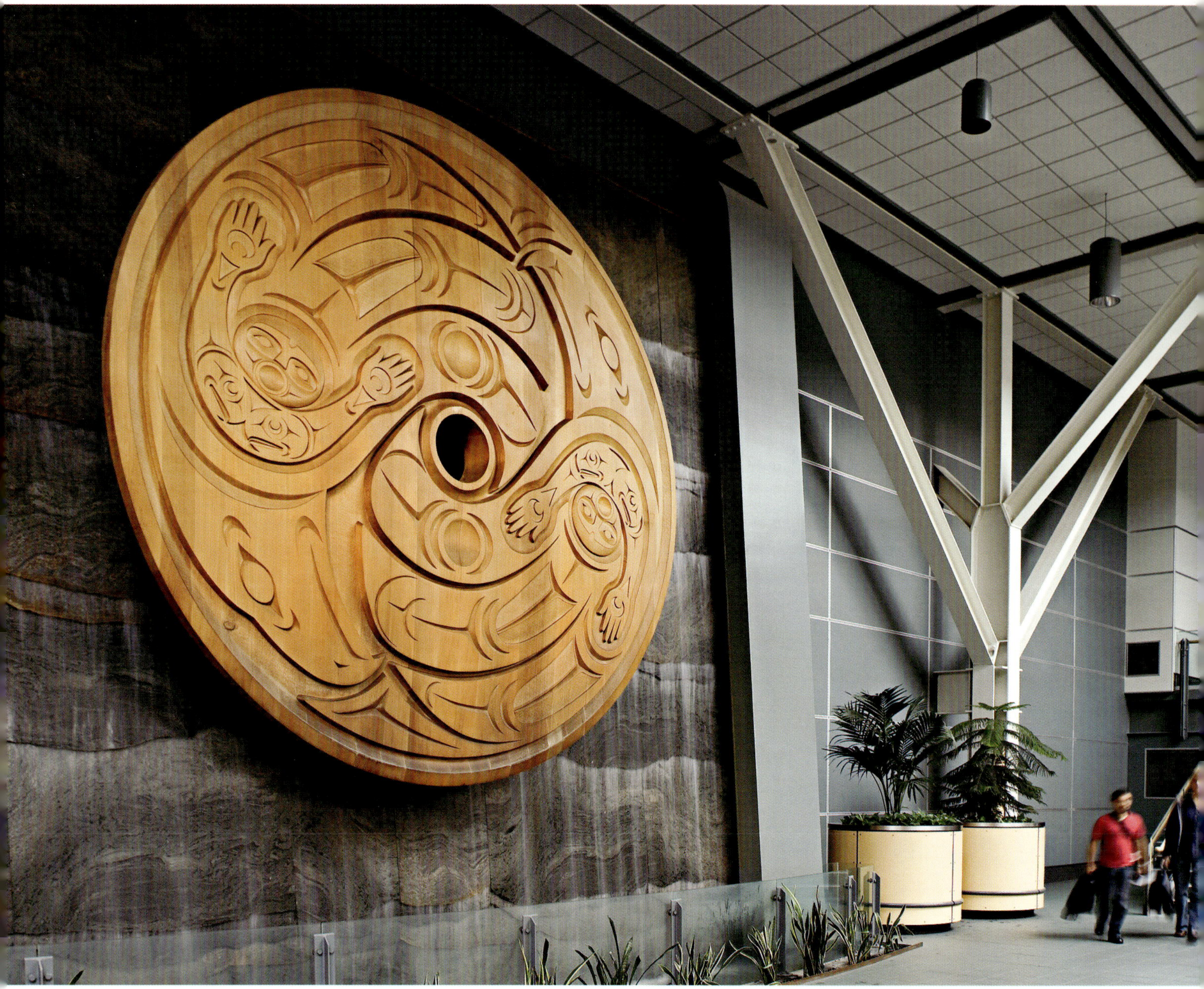

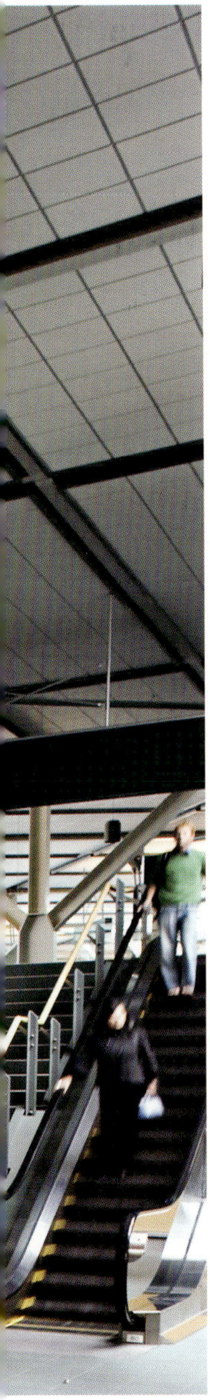

These blankets were symbols of wealth, and could be used as a sort of currency,[3] and spindle whorls were also accorded great respect. The form of Point's monumental relief sculpture—the largest spindle whorl in the world—also honours countless generations of Salish women who produced both the wool and the blankets that served their people's social, religious and economic systems.

Susan Point is one of the leading artists of her generation and has won numerous public art commissions. Self-taught and immensely prolific, she has worked across multiple disciplines, including painting, printmaking and sculpture, in a range of contemporary and traditional materials.

1 YVR Art Foundation, *Land Sea Sky: Art at YVR* (Vancouver: YVR Art Foundation, 2003), p. 1. 2 Gary Wyatt, "Introduction," *Susan Point: Works on Paper* (Vancouver: Figure 1 Publishing, 2014), p. 5. 3 Dale R. Croes, "Showing the Wealth on Paper, Echoing the Archaeological Past," *Susan Point: Works on Paper*, p. 10.

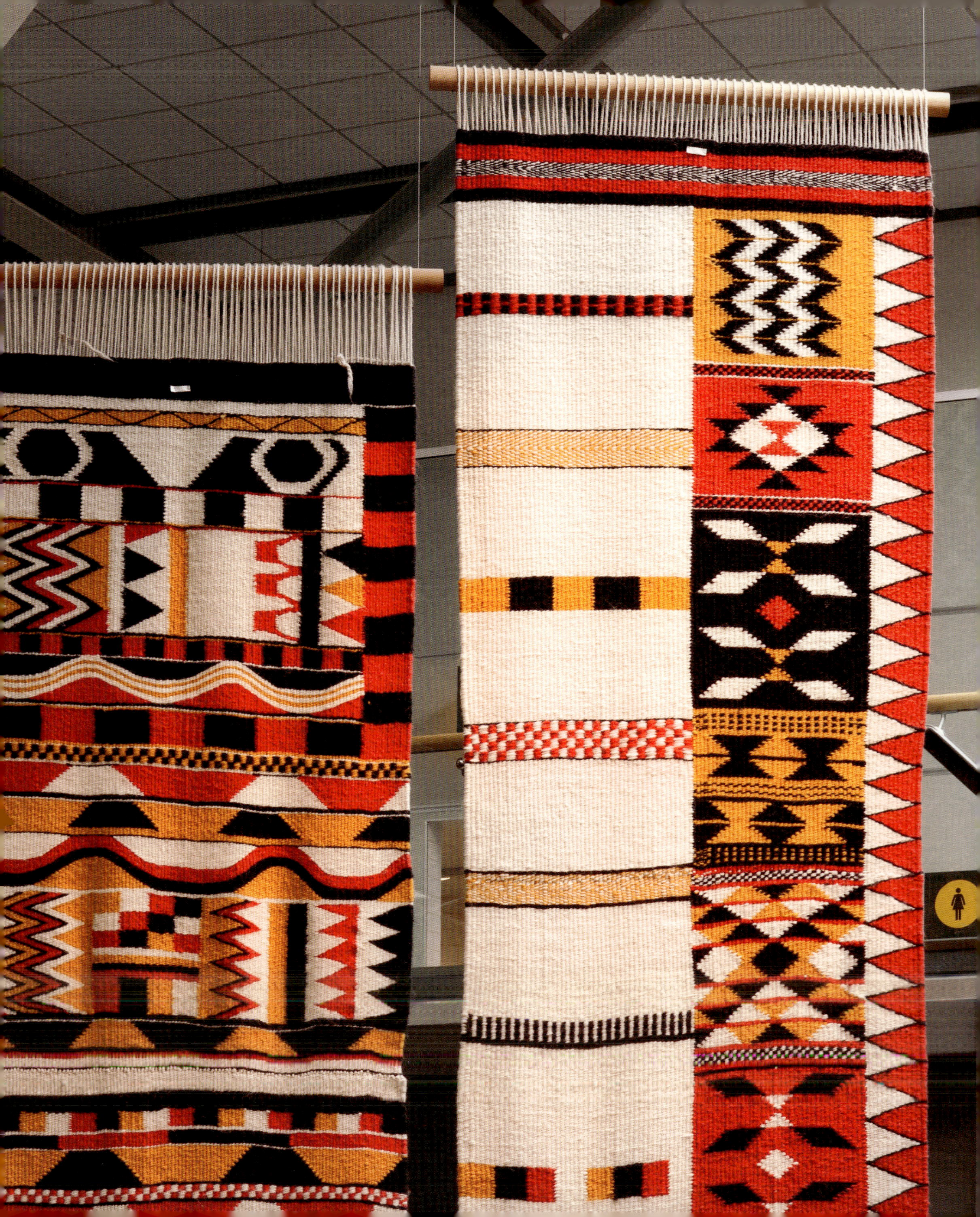

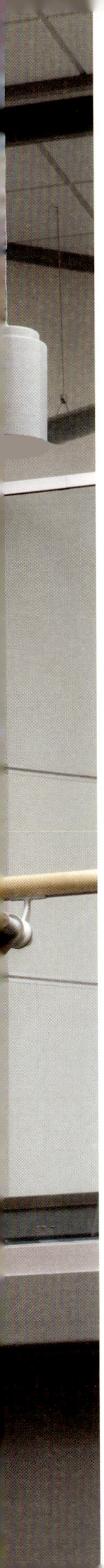

OUT OF THE SILENCE

Krista Point, Robyn Sparrow, Debra Sparrow, Gina Grant and Helen Callbreath

1996 hand-dyed, hand-spun sheep's wool | each 4.9 × 1.5 m

The four large weavings hanging in the Musqueam Welcome Area represent an esteemed and enduring art form among the Coast Salish people. For many centuries before European contact, intricately woven Coast Salish blankets, made from mountain goat hair and other natural fibres, were worn or distributed during social and religious ceremonies. They might identify individuals of high standing or be part of the regalia of participants in spirit dances. Plain or complexly patterned and made by women who handed down weaving techniques to younger generations (usually grandmother to granddaughter), such blankets were very highly valued, and came to function as a form of currency. When given away at potlatches, they signified the wealth and raised the prestige of the potlatch host. As well, spiritual value accrued to the mountain goat hair itself, to the labour-intensive process of carding, spinning, dyeing and weaving, and to the different patterns and motifs incorporated into the overall design.

As with many First Nations traditions, Salish weaving declined drastically as a result of European colonization and the abundance of cheap trade blankets manufactured elsewhere. Since the 1960s, however, weaving has enjoyed a dynamic recovery. The group of women who created *Out of the Silence* chose to use a number of traditional patterns, made up of diamonds, squares and zigzags, to honour the endurance of their craft and to signify their identities as weavers. The vivid colours of the weavings add warmth and vibrancy to the setting.

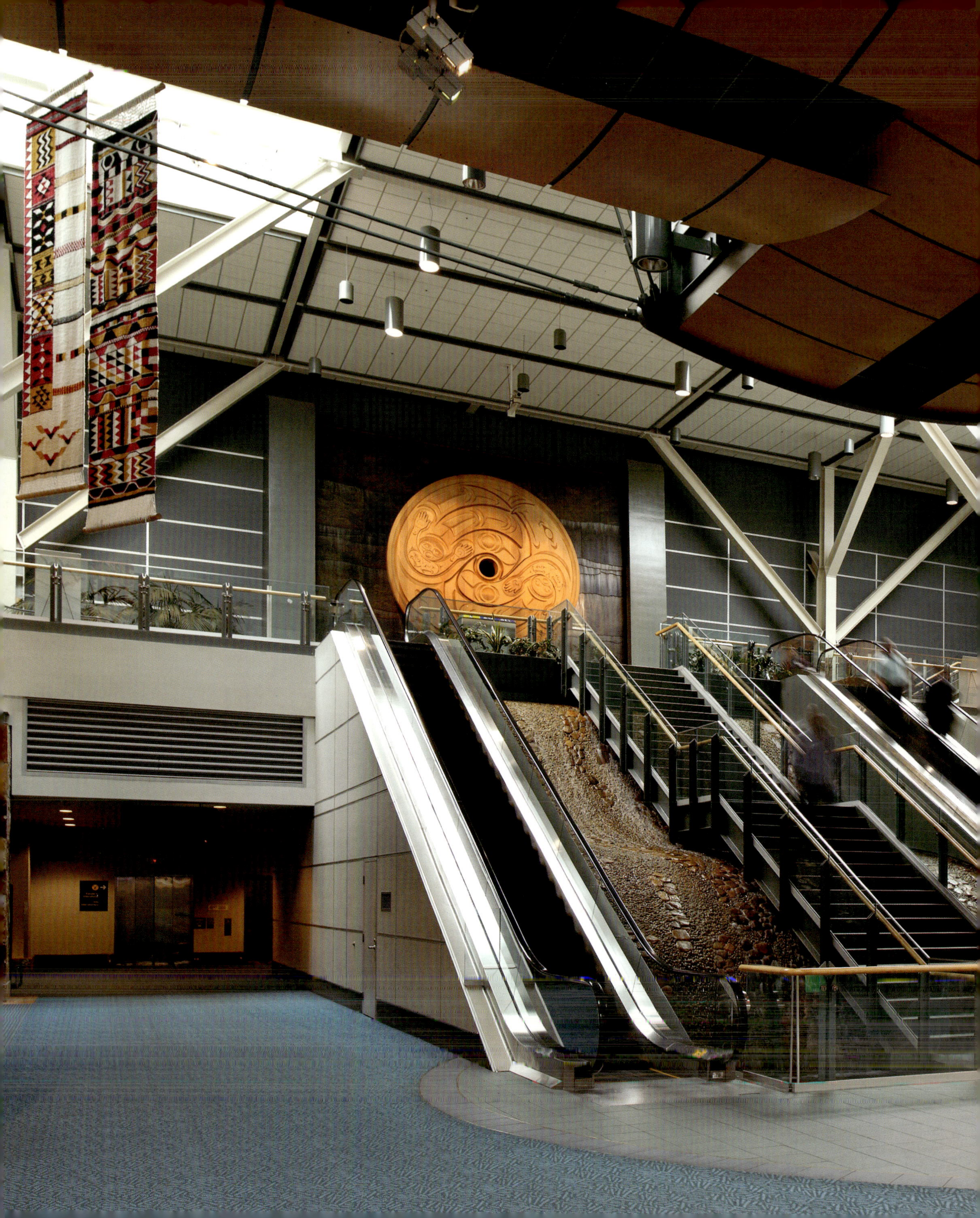

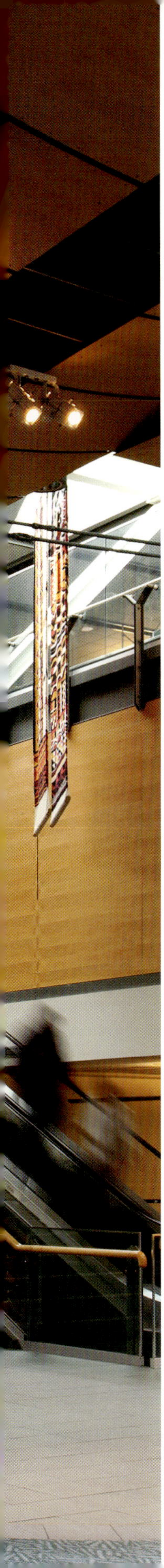

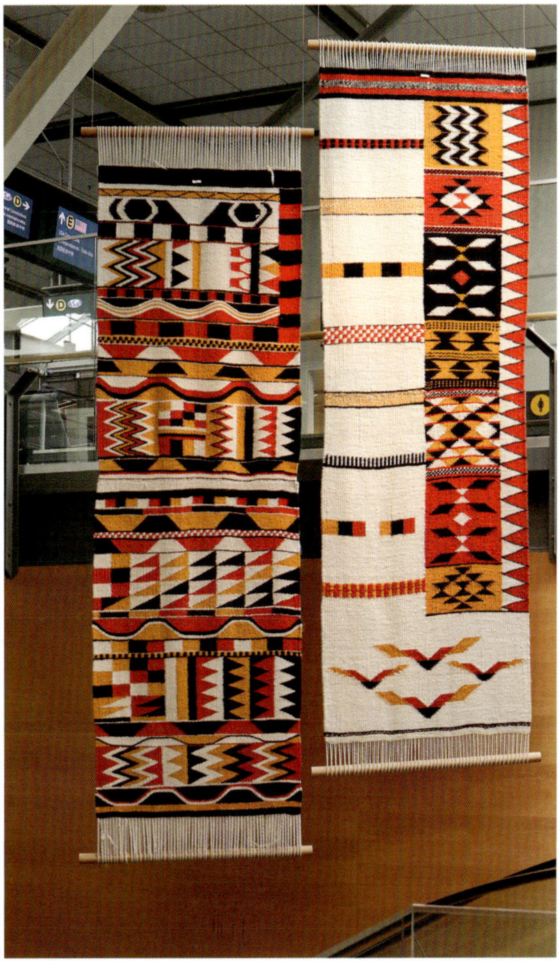

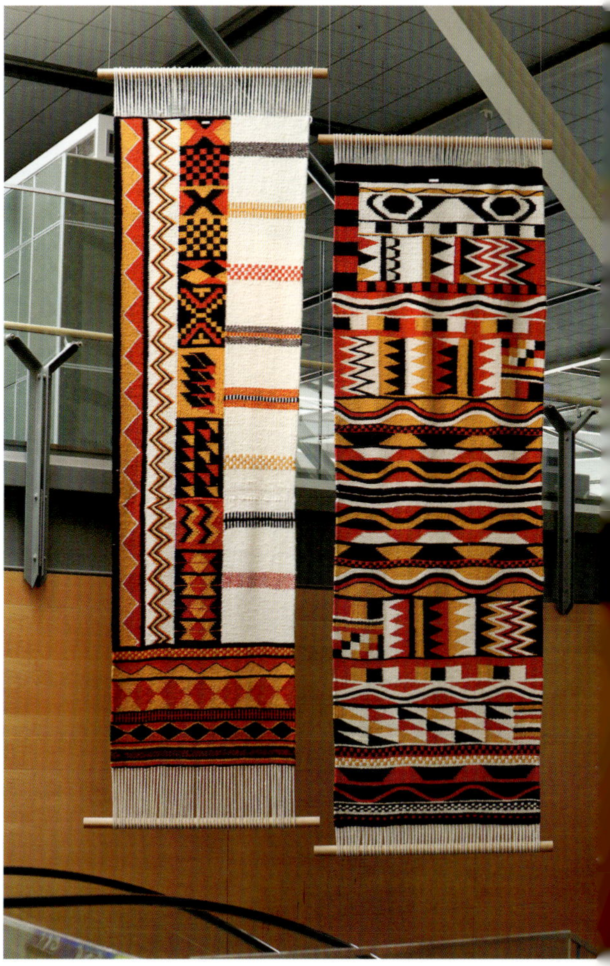

(FROM LEFT TO RIGHT) Weavings by *Krista Point* | *Debra Sparrow* | *Robyn Sparrow* | *Helen Callbreath and Gina Grant*

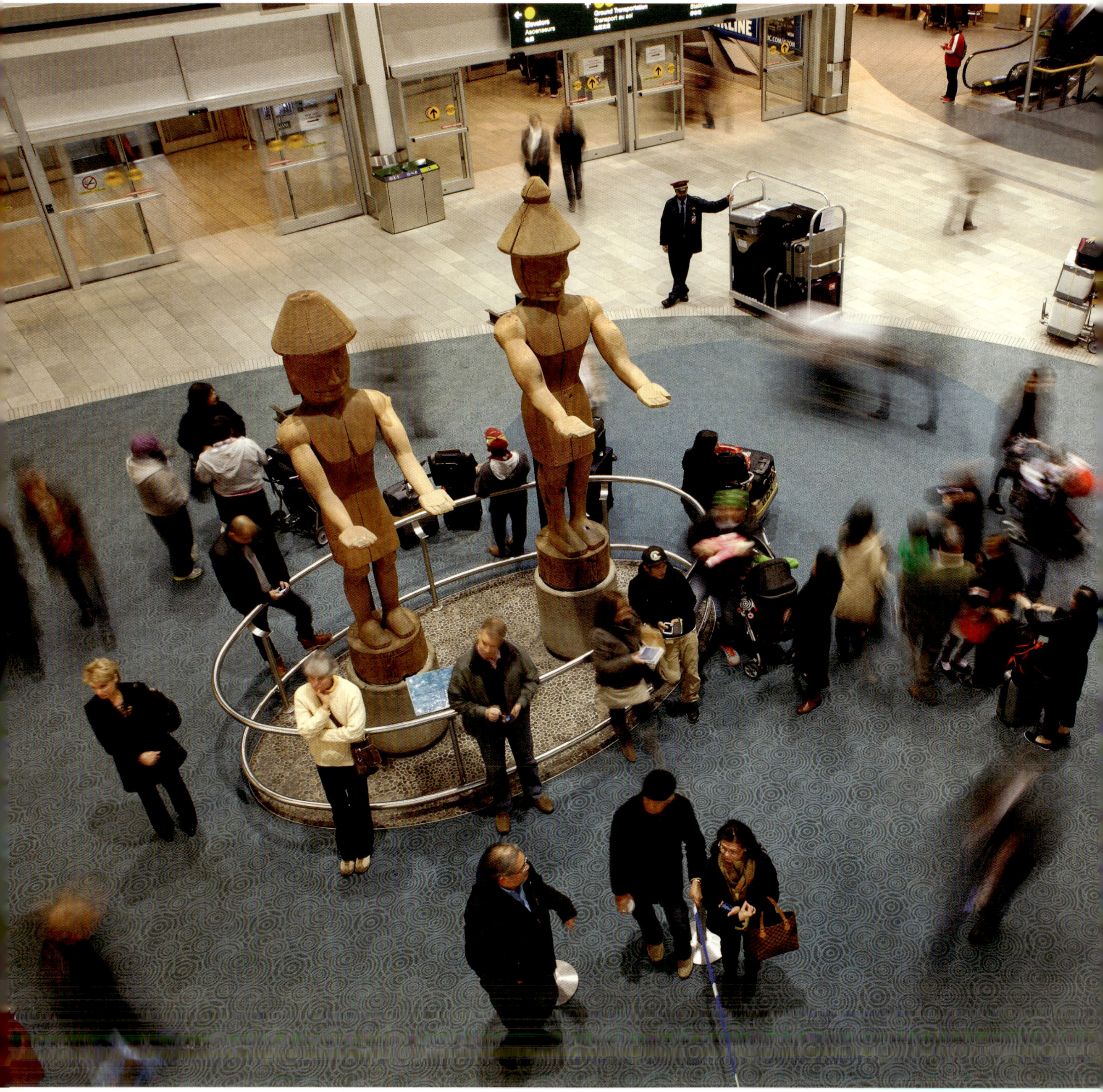
Elevators
Ascenseurs
Ground Transportation
Transport au sol

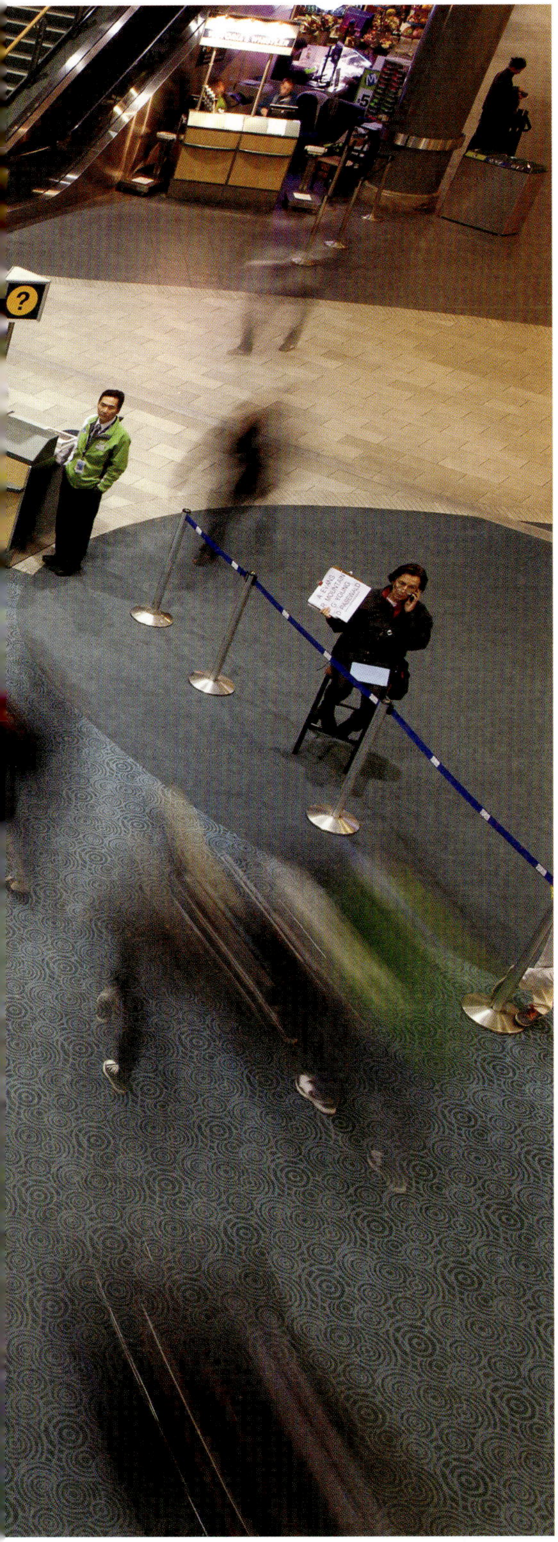

2

THE HEART OF THE AIRPORT

INTERNATIONAL TERMINAL BUILDING

(PRE-SECURITY)

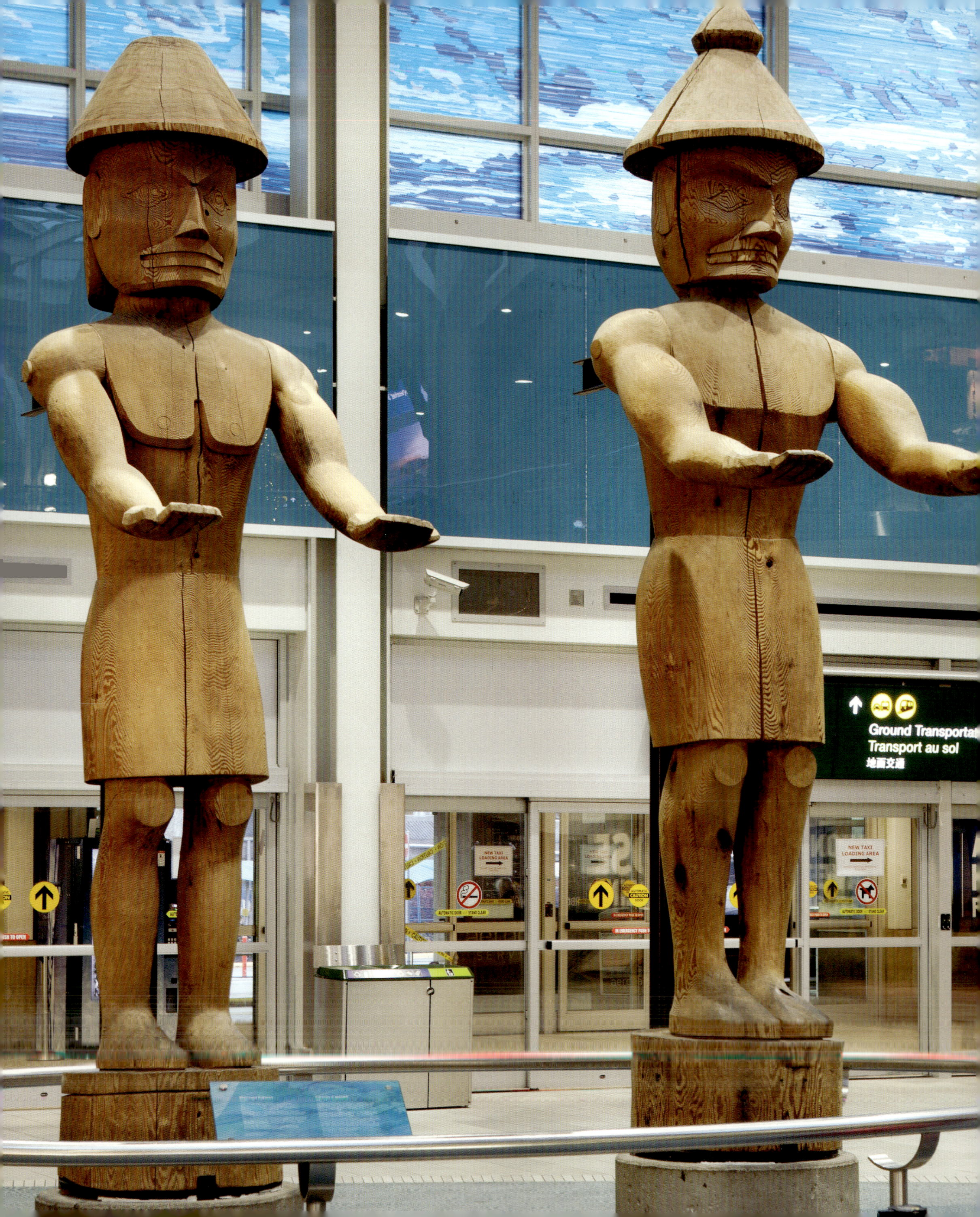

Transport au sol
地面交通
NEW TAXI LOADING AREA

WELCOME FIGURES

Joe David

c. 1986 red cedar | MALE 3.3 × 1.2 × 1.1 m | FEMALE 3.0 × 1.1 × 1.1 m

Carved by Joe David in the Clayoquot tradition of the Nuu-chah-nulth people, these welcome figures are based on those that would be placed on the beach in front of a village or a big house, to greet guests invited to special events such as potlatches. Because visitors would arrive from other villages by canoe, each figure is designed to look out to sea, arms raised, palms facing upward. The arms are constructed so that they can swivel at the shoulder, to be raised in welcome when needed and lowered to facilitate storage.[1]

The male figure wears the traditional knobbed hat of a high-ranking person such as a whaling chief; the female figure has a more common domed hat. Both wear skirts that would have been woven from the softly shredded inner bark of the cedar tree.[2] David originally created these figures on commission, to stand at the entrance to the B.C. Pavilion during Expo 86. After that world's fair ended, they were accessioned by the Vancouver Museum (now the Museum of Vancouver), which subsequently loaned them to YVR, to place in the post-customs arrivals area of the International Terminal. David reports that he carved the welcome figures from cedar logs he salvaged from West Coast beaches,[3] adding an environmental footnote about wasteful logging practices to the journey that brought them to this place.

Nuu-chah-nulth artist Joe David was born at Opitsaht, a Clayoquot village on Meares Island, off the west coast of Vancouver Island. During the 1960s and 1970s, he intensively studied the art and culture of his people, and he is one of the most respected master carvers and graphic artists on the Northwest Coast. His wood, silver, bronze and glass works have been collected internationally, as have his prints and drawings.

---

1 Hilary Stewart, *Looking at Totem Poles* (Vancouver/Toronto: Douglas & McIntyre; Seattle: University of Washington Press, 1993), p. 70. 2 Ibid., p. 70. 3 Ibid., p. 70.

THE SPIRIT OF HAIDA GWAII: THE JADE CANOE

Bill Reid

1994 bronze cast, 2/2, jade green patina | 6.05 × 3.89 × 3.48 m

Often identified as the heart of YVR, this acclaimed sculpture by Bill Reid was inspired by nineteenth-century miniature canoes carved in argillite, a soft, sedimentary rock that is found near Skidegate on Haida Gwaii. The blue-green patina that covers this second and final casting of *The Spirit of Haida Gwaii*, however, is a reference to British Columbia's naturally occurring jade, the province's official gemstone. As with many historic examples of miniature canoes, Reid's monumental vessel is crowded with creatures and beings, their identities drawn from the legends and oral histories of the Haida, and their forms energetically and sometimes fiercely interacting with each other in the manner of rivalrous siblings.

Standing at the canoe's centre is the unnamed chief, resplendent in his ceremonial regalia and indifferent to the squabbling and wrangling around him. His tall hat, Chilkat robe, speaker's staff and dignified bearing symbolize his importance and that of his journey.[1] Crowded together in the prow are Bear and Bear Mother and their two cubs, along with Wolf, Eagle and Frog, all realized in Reid's distinctive, three-dimensional style and yet also recognizable from their features and attributes in classical Haida art. For instance, Frog's tongue is extended, which is a frequent motif in northern Northwest Coast culture, thought to symbolize the creature's role as an agent of transformation or shamanic power.

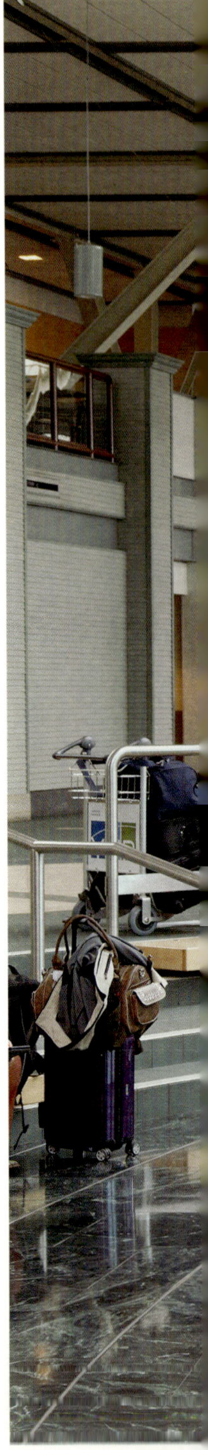

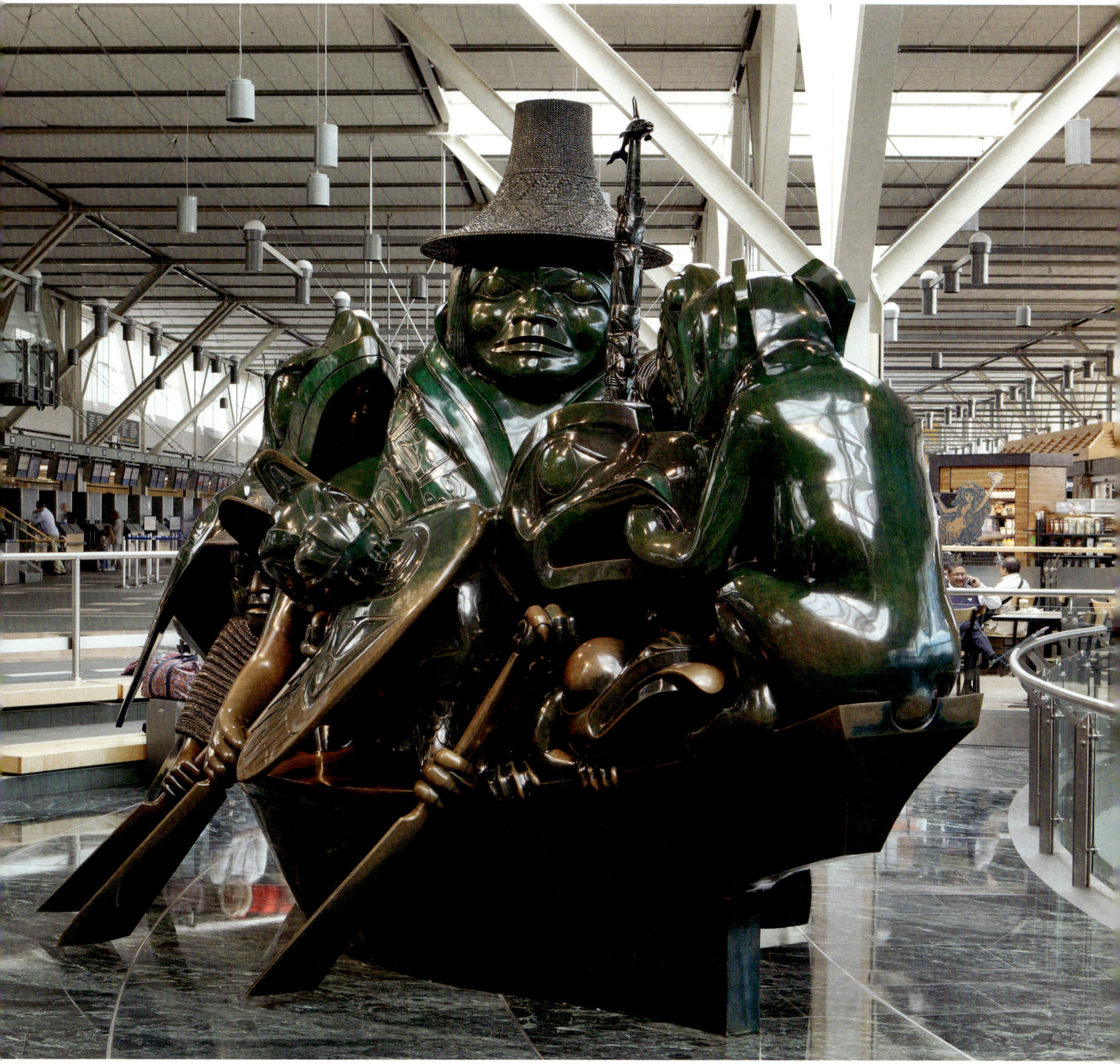

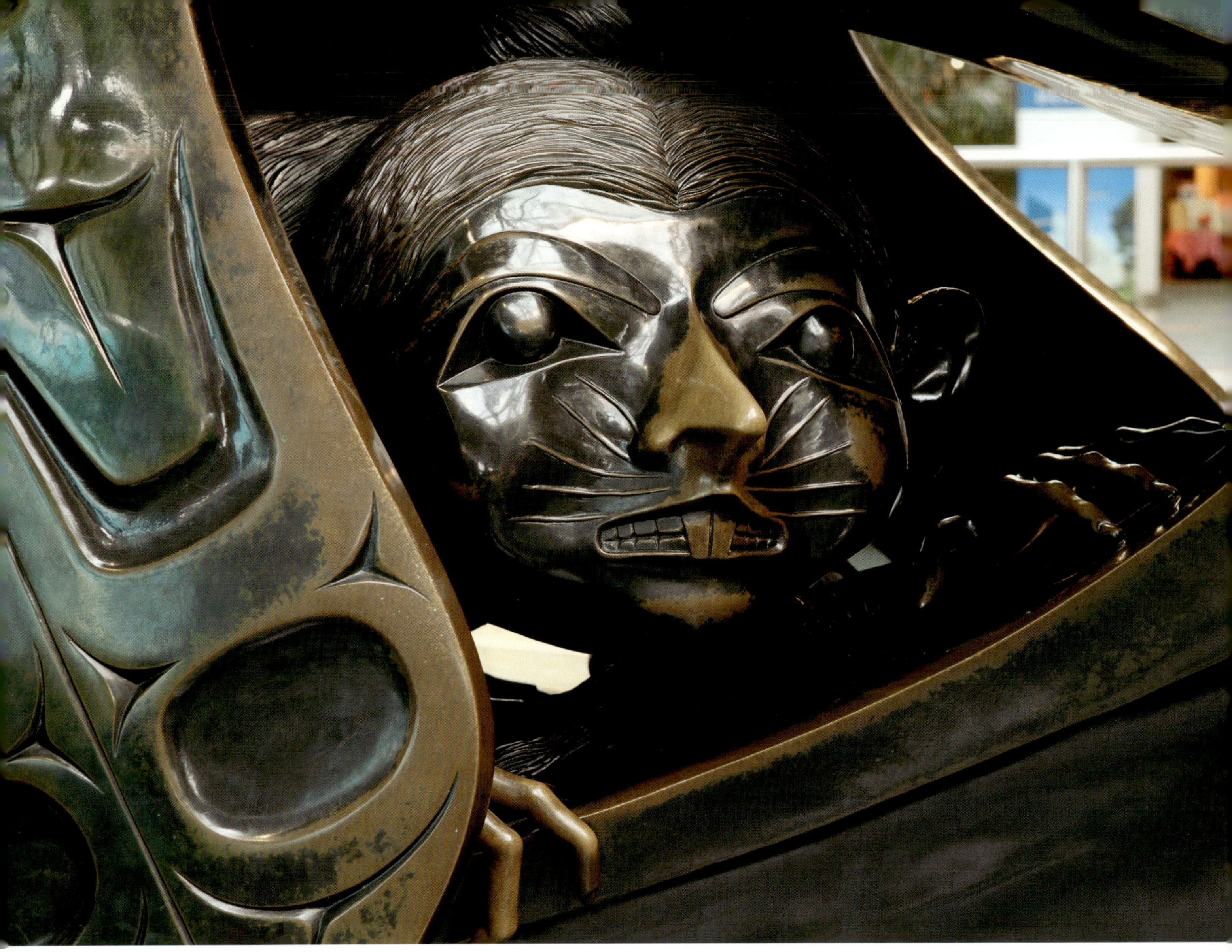

In the middle of the canoe, on either side of the chief (who may also be a shaman) are Beaver and Dogfish Woman, and crouched beneath Raven's wing is the wise grandmother, Mouse Woman. Raven himself is perched at the stern of the canoe, using his tail and wings to steer the craft. Trickster and culture hero of the Northwest Coast, Raven features prominently in Haida origin myths.

The small human paddler tucked under Raven's wing on the starboard side of the canoe is a self-portrait of the artist as "The Ancient Reluctant Conscript." As with Reid's mixed German-American and Haida heritage, this figure consolidates two different cultural traditions. His name is borrowed from the Carl Sandburg poem "Old Timers," but he also seems to allude to a Haida myth of a "supernaturally gifted slave" who voyages to the bottom of the sea.[2]

(FROM LEFT TO RIGHT) Mouse Woman | The Ancient Reluctant Conscript | Bad Cub

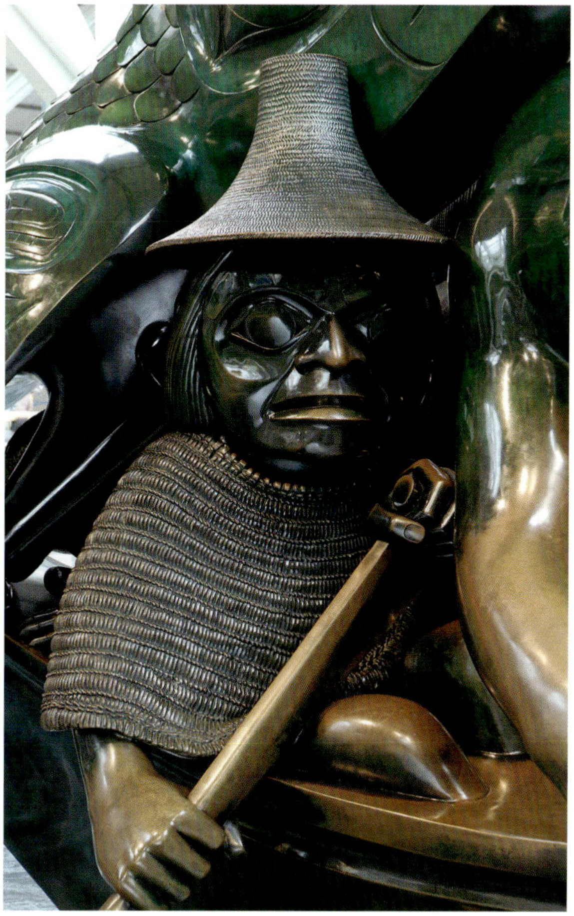

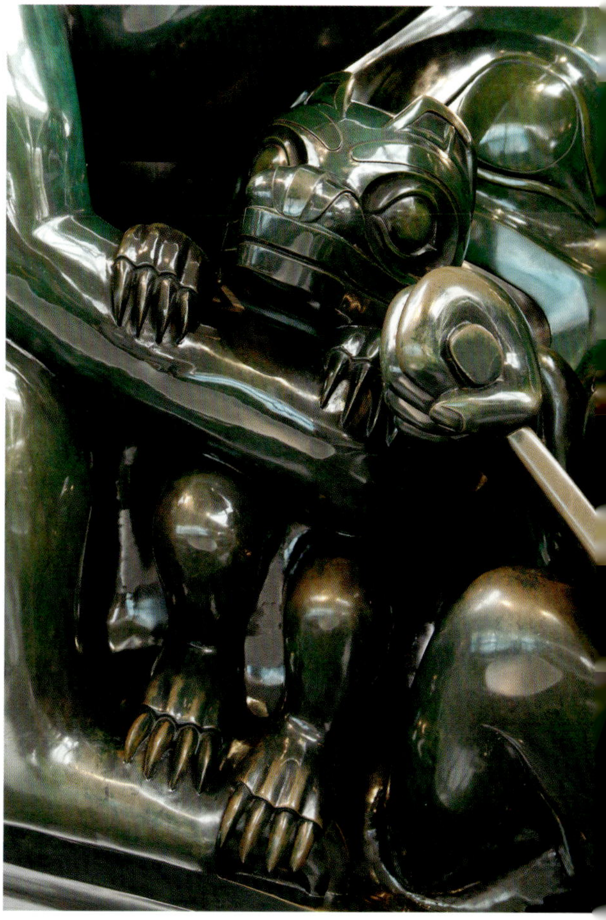

In its entirety, the sculpture suggests that life is a journey, filled with struggle and uncertainty but also with beauty and endurance. Despite their apparent jostling for position and power, all the beings depicted here co-operate in the paddling of the canoe. Their entwined and interacting forms suggest not only human-animal transformation but also the interconnectedness of all living creatures, whether they inhabit the land, the sea or the sky. ■

---

1 Robin Laurence, "Introduction," in Ulli Steltzer's *The Spirit of Haida Gwaii: Bill Reid's Masterpiece* (Vancouver/Toronto: Douglas & McIntyre; Seattle: University of Washington Press, 1997), p. 11. 2 Robert Bringhurst and Ulli Steltzer, *The Black Canoe: Bill Reid and the Spirit of Haida Gwaii* (Vancouver/Toronto: Douglas & McIntyre, 1992), p. 58.

THE GREAT WAVE

Lutz Haufschild

1996 glass | 10 × 40 m

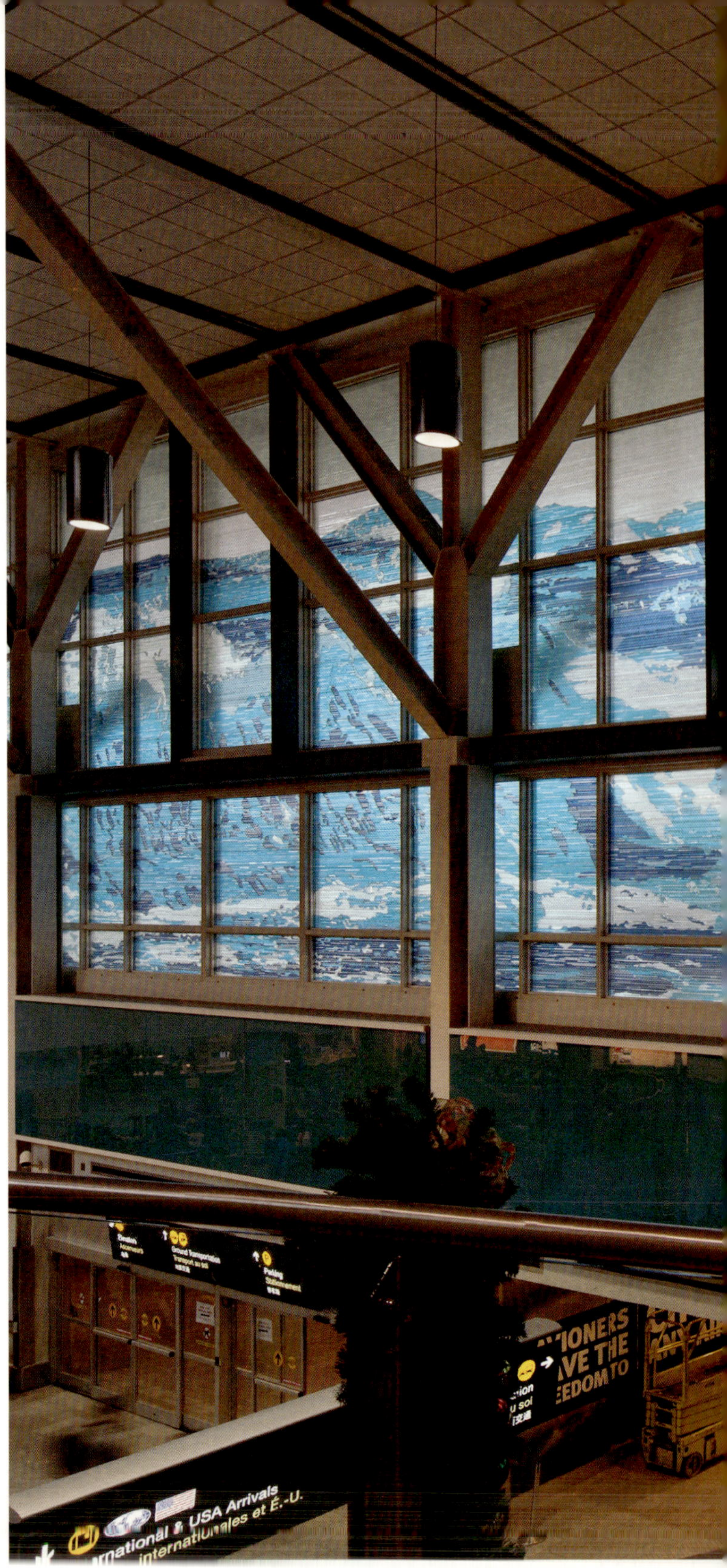

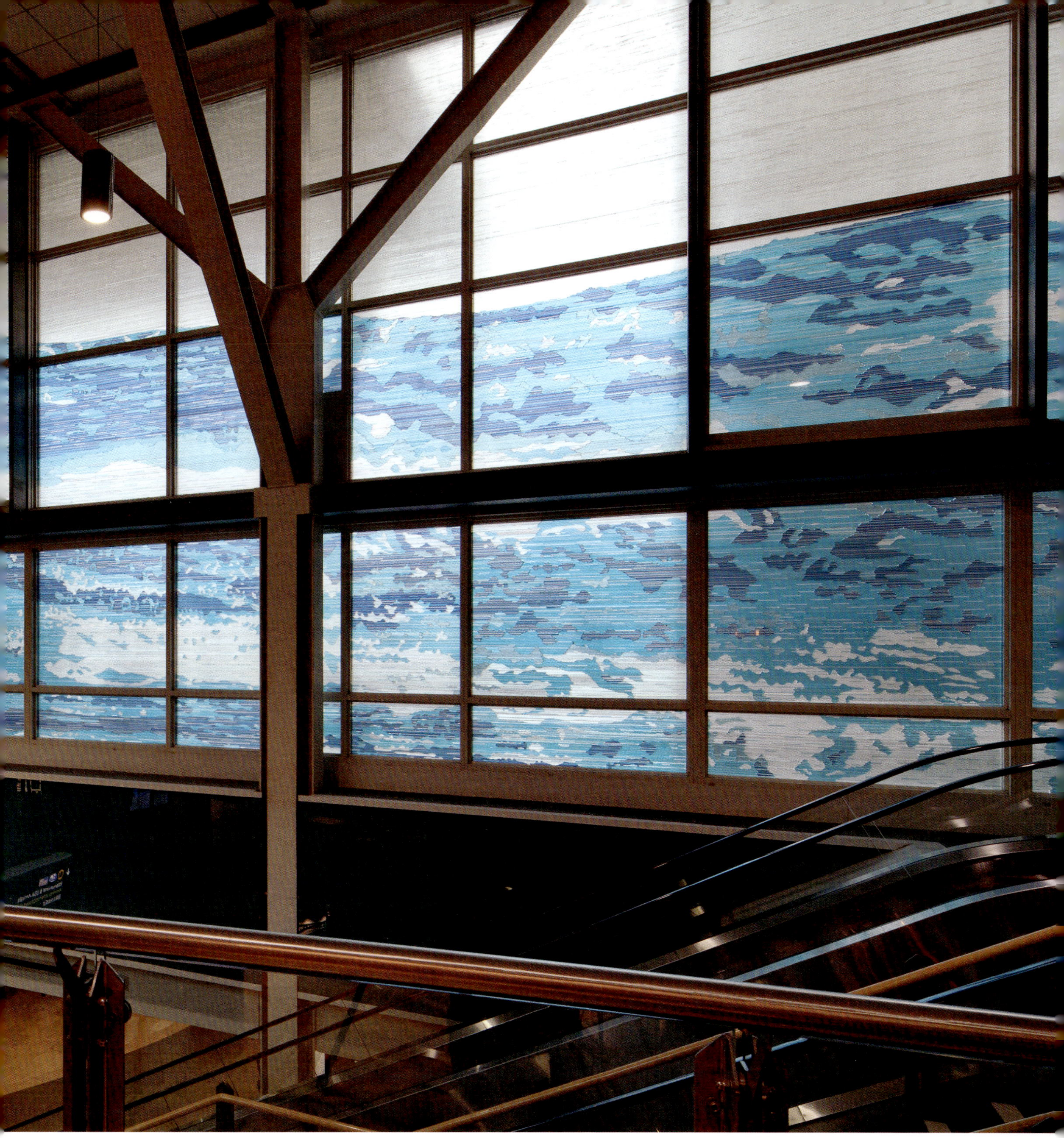

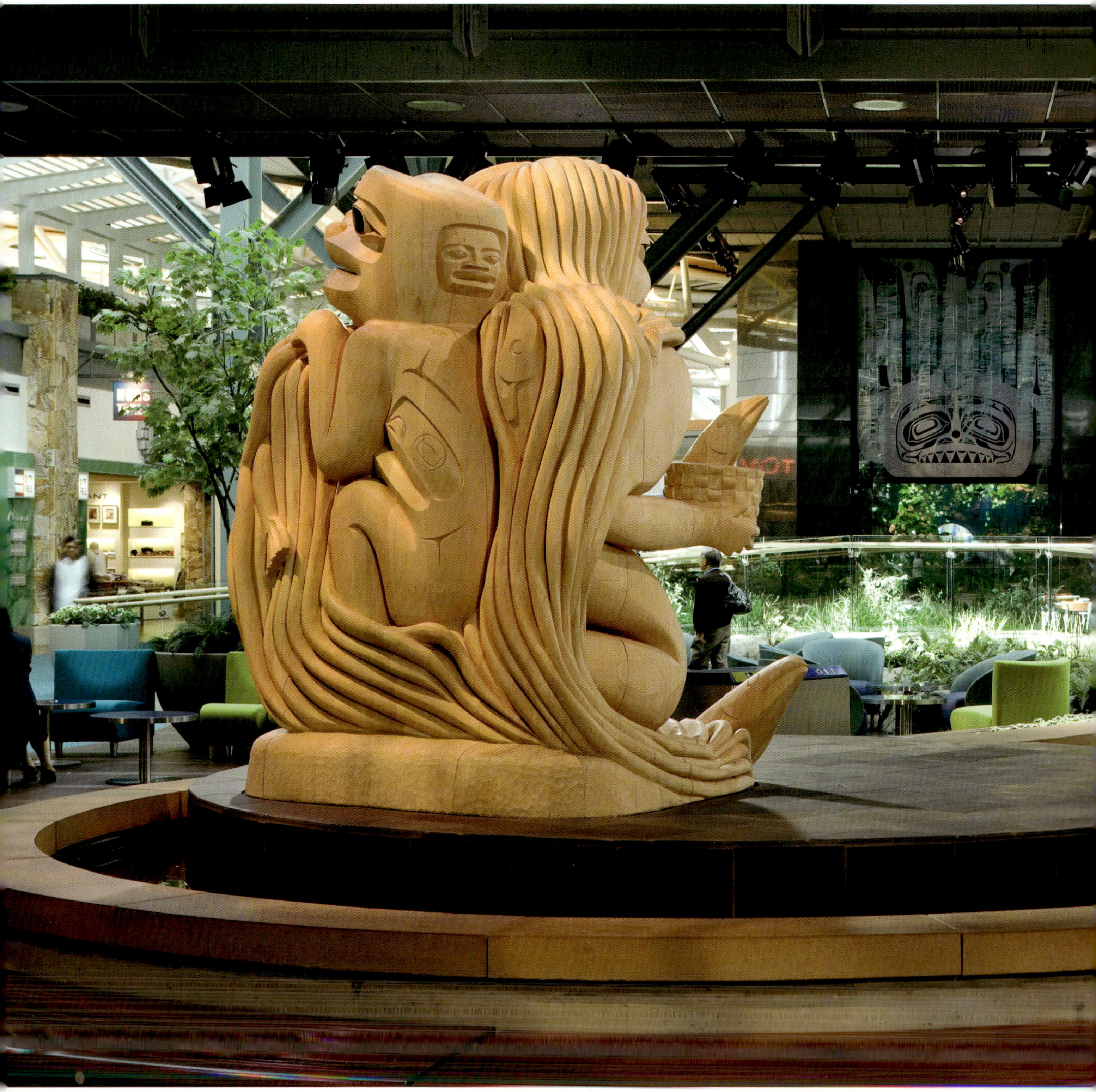

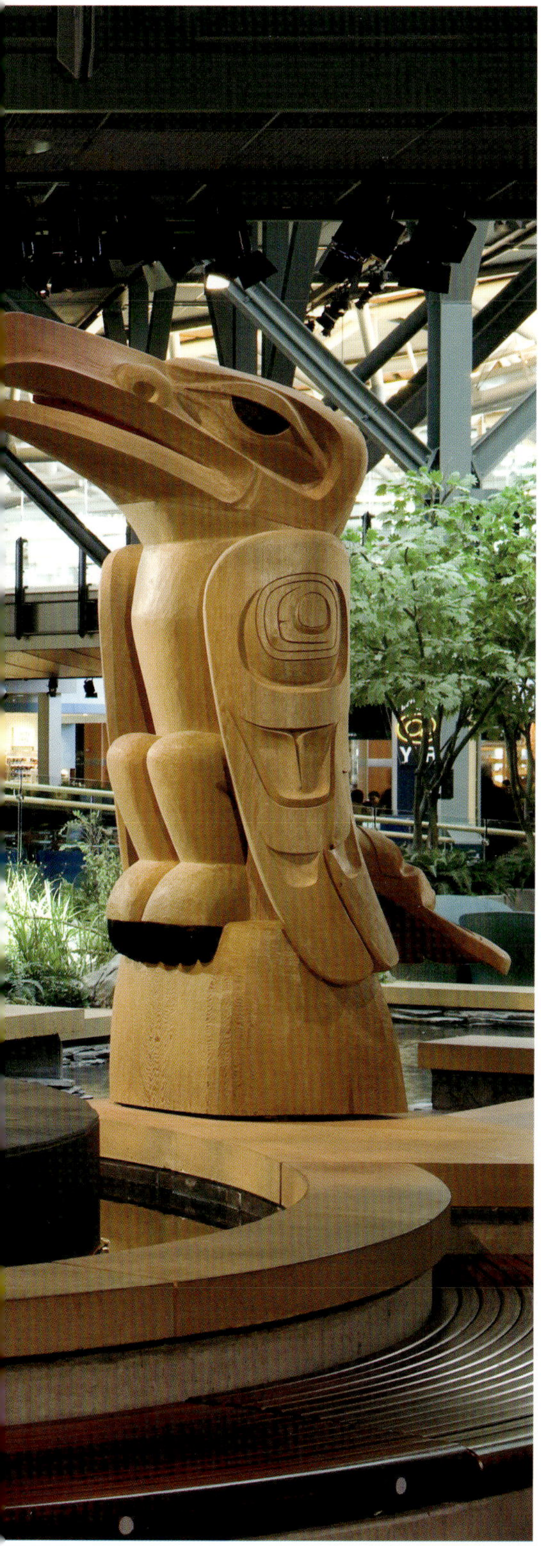

3

SPIRIT OF THE SEA

INTERNATIONAL TERMINAL BUILDING

(POST-SECURITY)

THE STORY OF FOG WOMAN AND RAVEN

Dempsey Bob

2007 laminated yellow cedar, red cedar, acrylic paint, stone |
FOG WOMAN 198 × 142 × 134 cm | RAVEN 213 × 81 × 178 cm

This complex work by Dempsey Bob, an acclaimed artist of Tahltan and Tlingit descent, tells the story of how the annual salmon run originated to benefit the people of the northern coast of British Columbia and the southern coast of Alaska. There are a few recorded versions of the myth of Fog Woman and Raven; all relate to a distant myth-time, before the salmon existed as a food source for the Tlingit people. In Bob's telling, Fog Woman created and controlled the salmon, that most delicious and nourishing fish. Raven, the notoriously greedy, selfish and cunning Trickster of First Nations legend, married Fog Woman in order to have access to her salmon, and became wealthy and, for a while, content. Eventually, however, Raven grew bored and ungrateful and mistreated Fog Woman, who then left him and called back all the salmon, including those hanging in his smokehouse. When Raven realized what was happening, he ran after his wife, trying to catch her. However, she wrapped herself in fog and slipped out of his grasp. Still, Fog Woman was not vindictive and allowed the salmon to return each year to spawn, for the benefit of the people.

Carved from a red cedar log in Bob's distinctive style, Raven perches on the side of the pool, beak uplifted, smiling and well fed. Fog Woman, carved from a block of laminated yellow cedar, kneels at the head of a stream, which flows metaphorically toward river and ocean. Her attributes include her stone labret, indicating her gender and her high social status, and her woven spruce root basket, from which salmon emerge. Salmon also stream through her long, flowing hair, emphasizing her alignment with the bodies of water where salmon spawn.

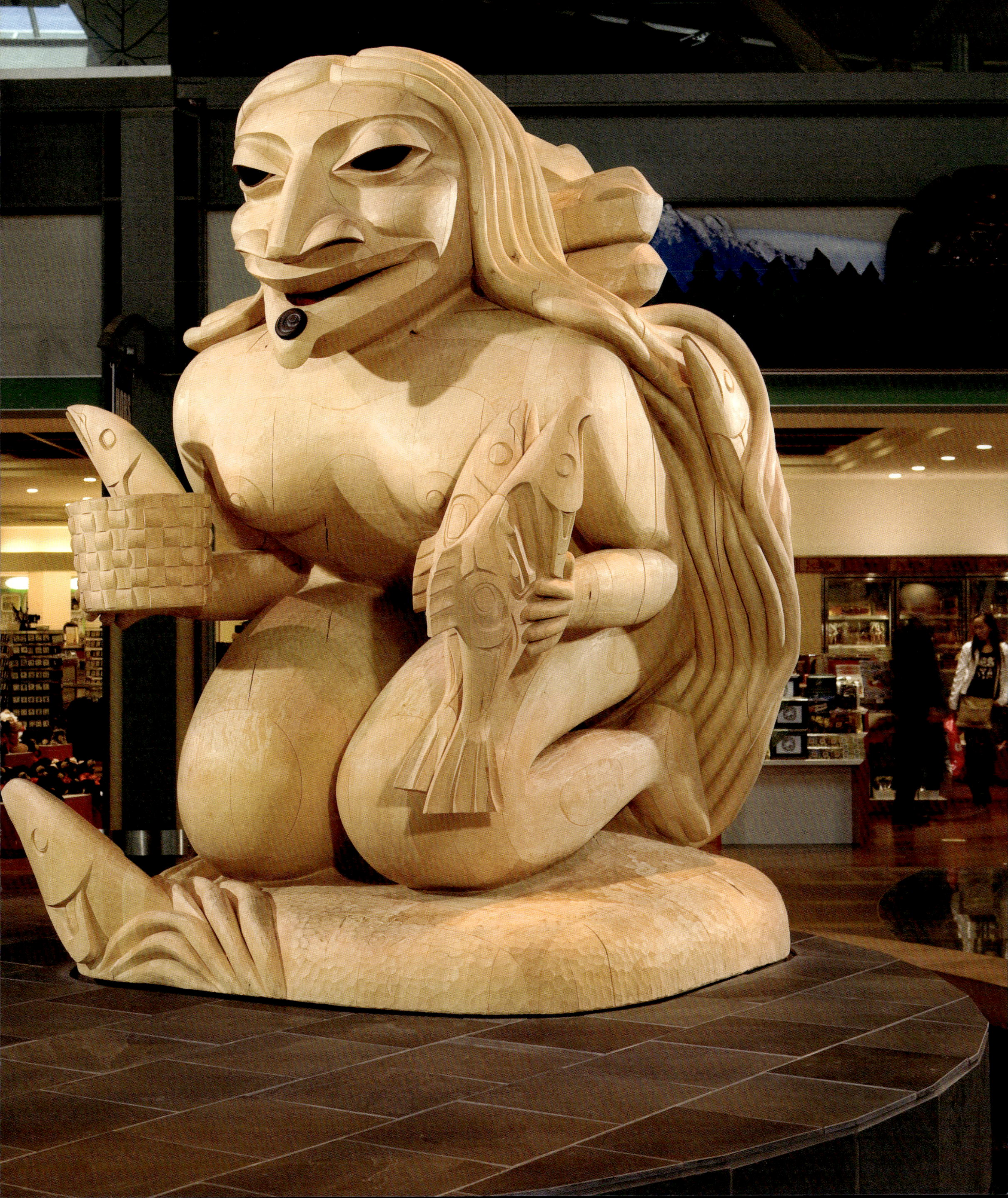

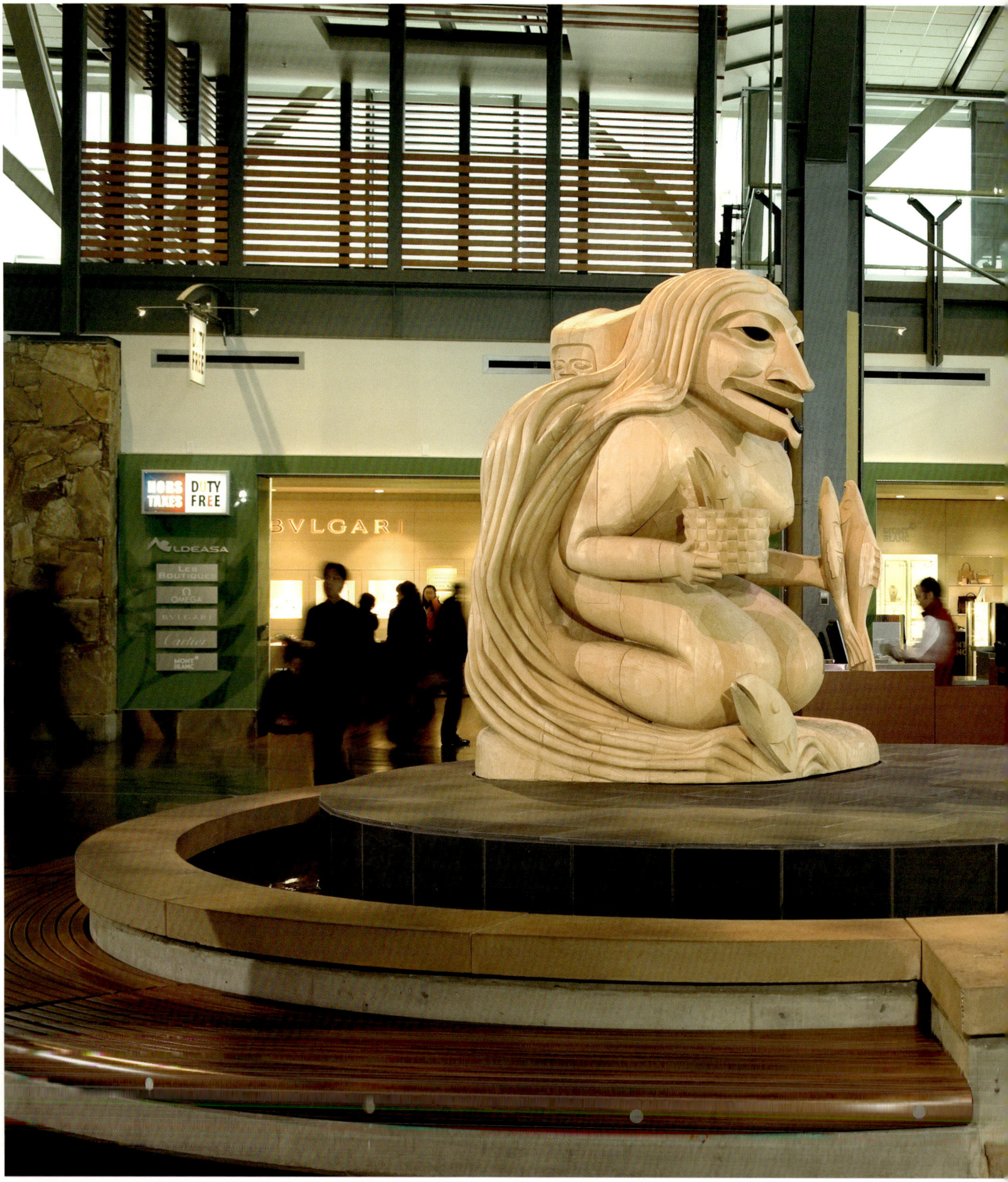
DUTY FREE
HORS TAXES
DUTY FREE
BVLGARI
Les Boutiques
OMEGA
BVLGARI
Cartier
MONT BLANC

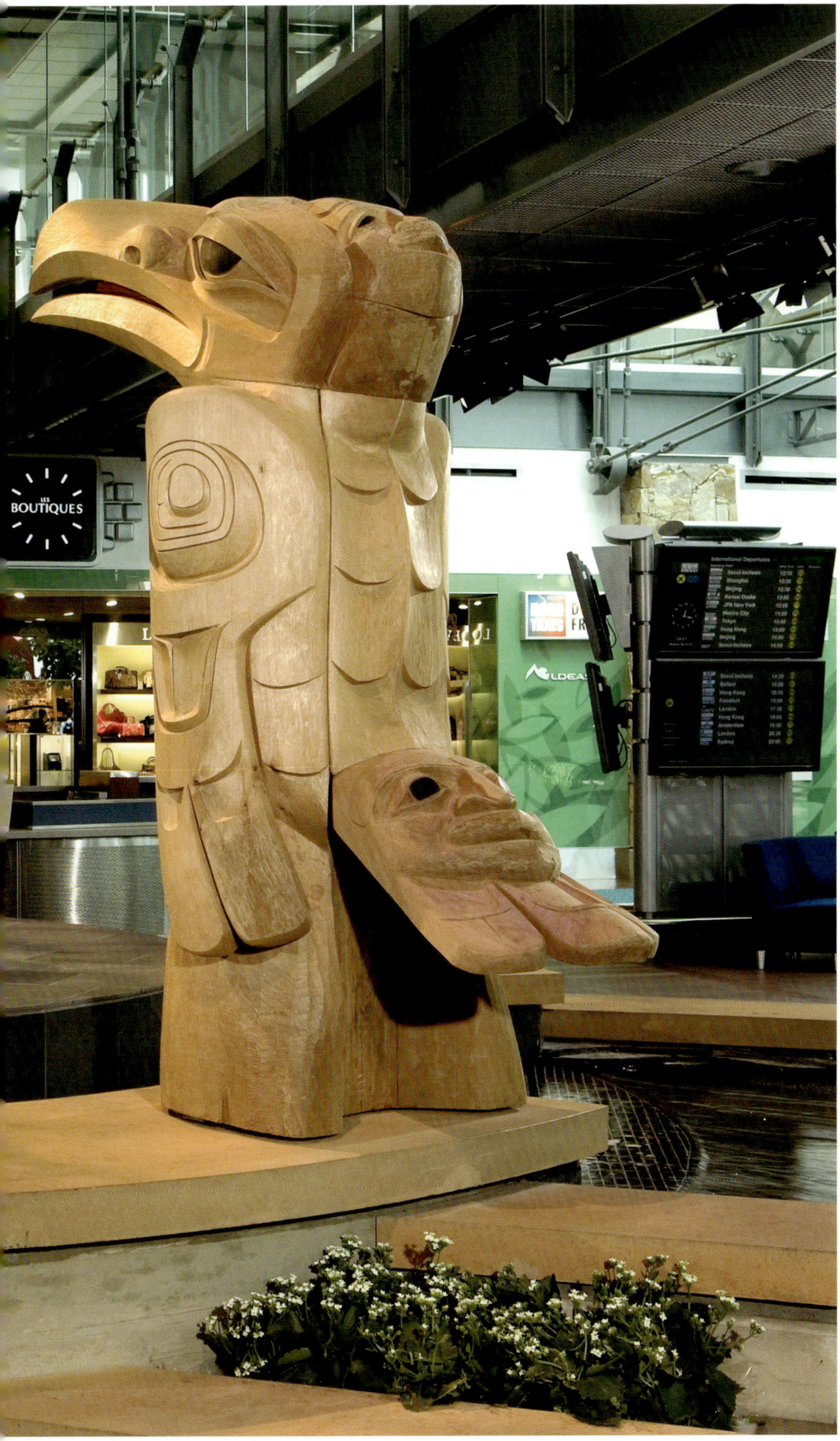
LES BOUTIQUES

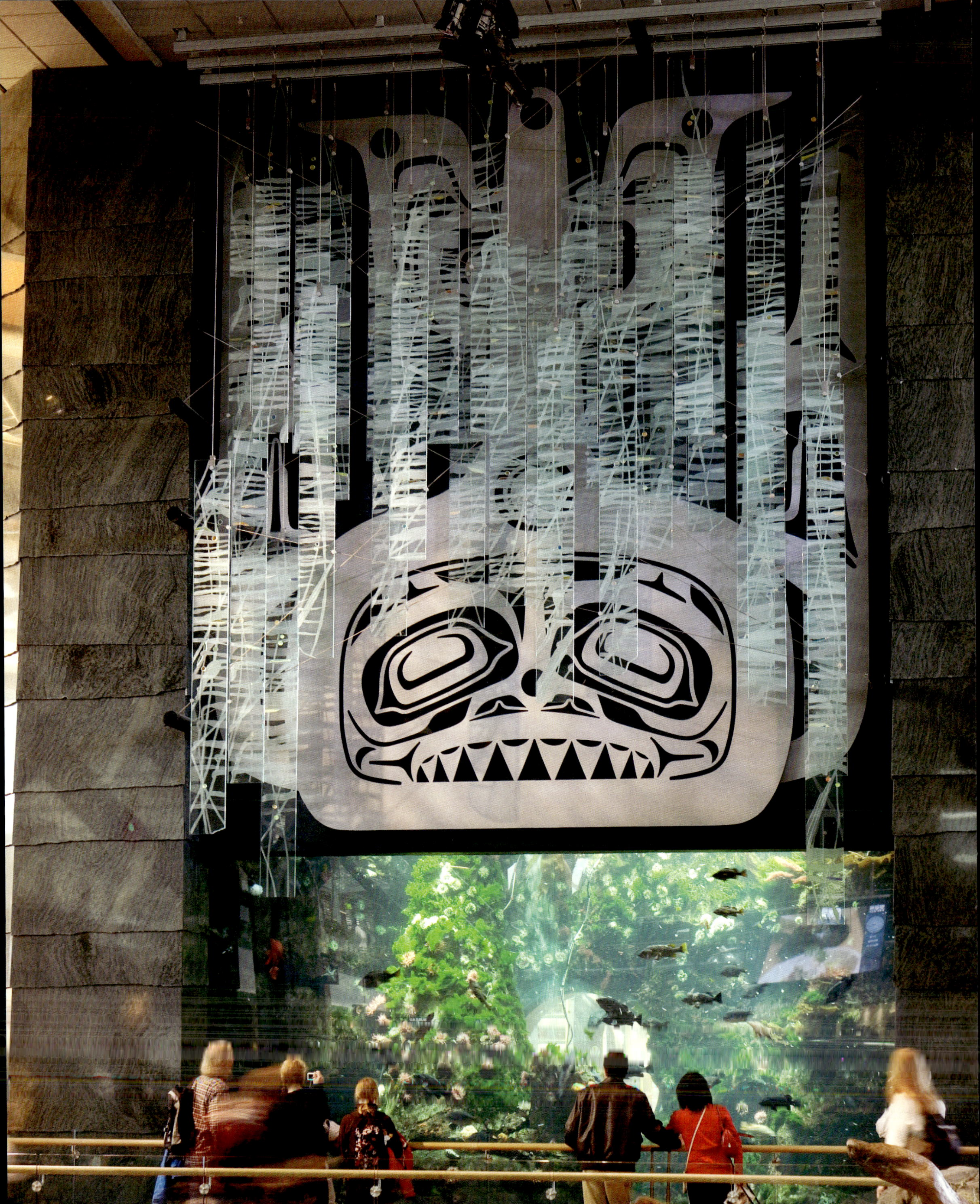

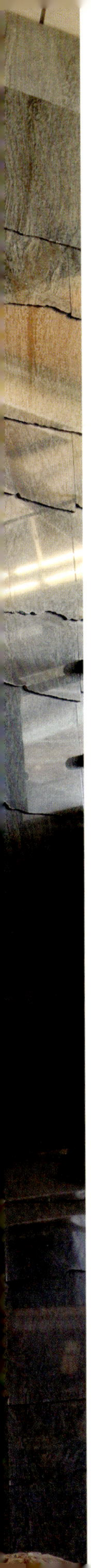

ORCA CHIEF AND THE KELP FOREST

Lyle Wilson and John Nutter

2007 aluminum, glass | ORCA CHIEF 5.59 × 5.99 × 0.91 m | KELP FOREST 4.98 × 0.56 m | INDIVIDUAL GLASS 0.02 m

This spectacular installation is a collaboration between Haisla artist Lyle Wilson and his non-Native friend and fellow artist John Nutter. Together they have responded to the work's location, above and in front of the enormous aquarium in the departures area of YVR's International Terminal. Wilson and Nutter created a mixed-media piece that speaks to the animals and plants that dwell in the ocean waters off the Northwest Coast. Their art combines images drawn from the ancient myths and cultural traditions of the Haisla people with contemporary Western materials and technology.

The installation depicts the Orca Chief, ruler of the sea with power over its creatures, swimming through a kelp forest toward the viewer. The Orca Chief is represented by Wilson on a large aluminum panel, and conveys the respect First Nations peoples accord both the mythical being, dwelling in a copper great house beneath the sea, and the naturally occurring orcas (also known as killer whales), observed and encountered in daily coastal life and admired for their size, beauty and intelligence.[1] Killer Whale is an important crest figure among many Northwest Coast groups, and figures actively in many myths.

The kelp forest is represented by Nutter using vertical panels of etched glass, and suggests not only the plants that surround the Orca Chief's great house but also the beauty and biological importance of the kelp that thrives in shallow waters off the Northwest Coast.

Lyle Wilson grew up in Kitamaat Village, where he was influenced by his uncle, Sam Robinson, a full-time carver who helped maintain classic Haisla art forms and traditions. Educated at the University of British Columbia and the Emily Carr College (now University) of Art and Design, Wilson has become one of the most respected Northwest Coast artists of his generation; his work is widely exhibited and collected.

Born in Winnipeg, John Nutter has been a glass artist for some forty years, often working with architects, designers and other artists, including the late Haida artist Bill Reid. Nutter has focused on large-scale works in stained, leaded, cast and sandblast-carved glass.

1 Lyle Wilson, artist's statement, 2007.

NET WORK

Eric Robertson

2007 cast aluminum, steel |
#1 (WEST) approx. 3.58 × 2.64 × 9.13 m
#2 (EAST) approx. 5.54 × 2.64 × 10.16 m
#3 (MIDDLE) approx. 1.48 × 2.64 × 6.96 m

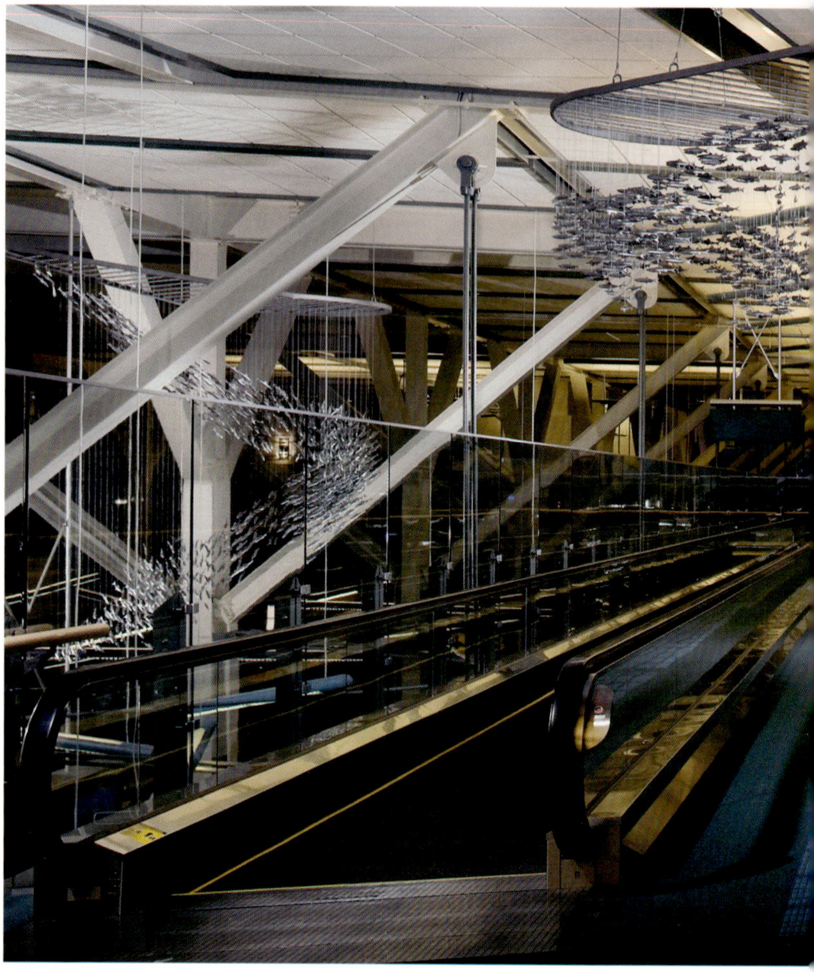

This engaging installation, with a title that is a play on words, represents three big herring balls, which are defensive formations created by groups of herring as they burst away from their schools when threatened by predators. Such swirling balls of form and movement act as a diversion; at the same time, they create a powerful visual pattern that speaks to the communal motion of a multitude of creatures acting of one mind. This work also expresses the importance of herring in the complex marine ecosystem of the North Pacific Coast, and the impact of human beings on the balance of nature. Each of the three groupings of silver-coloured fish is suspended from a large, abstracted form representing a dip net.

For First Nations peoples on the Northwest Coast, the arrival of the herring in the spring to spawn in near-shore waters has long represented the renewal of life, prompting a season of fishing and feasting. Humankind, along with crowds of sea birds, marine mammals and larger fish such as salmon, hake, cod and halibut, has long harvested herring as part of what artist

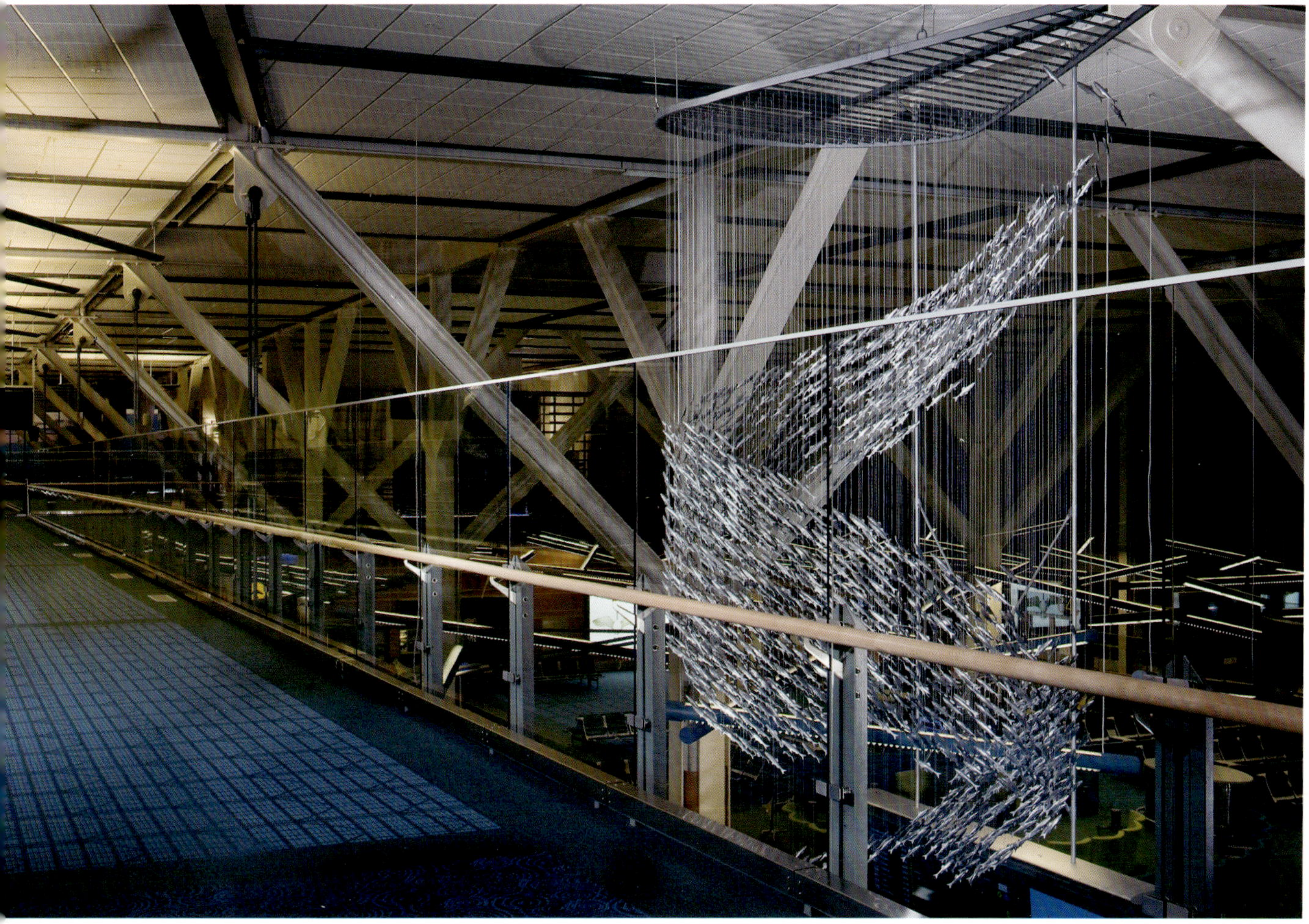

Eric Robertson describes as the "life-sustaining wealth" of the sea.[1] In recent decades, however, Pacific herring (and other fish species) appear to have declined in numbers, and controversies have erupted about commercial overfishing, environmental changes and the management of herring stocks. Robertson's installation encompasses both wonder at the beauty and collective power of these important fish, and concern over their future—and ours.

Eric Robertson's art draws upon his mixed Gitxsan and European heritage, as well as his background working in fisheries and forestry. Based in Vancouver, Robertson holds an MFA from Concordia University and has created a number of important public artworks displayed throughout the region. Often juxtaposing traditional Northwest Coast and Western art forms and materials, his sculptures and installations address the interface between indigenous and non-indigenous histories and cultures.

1 Eric Robertson, artist's statement, 2007.

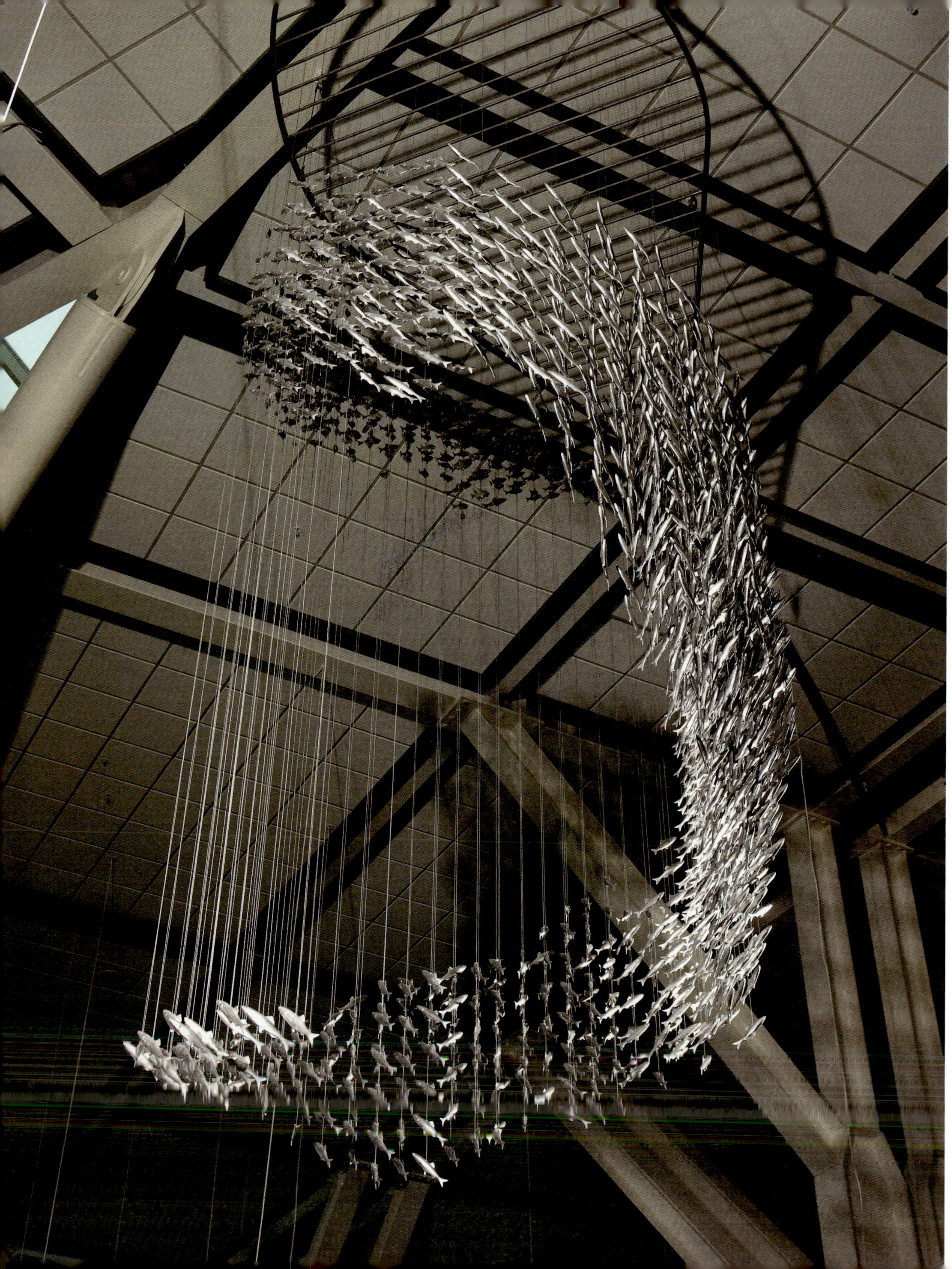

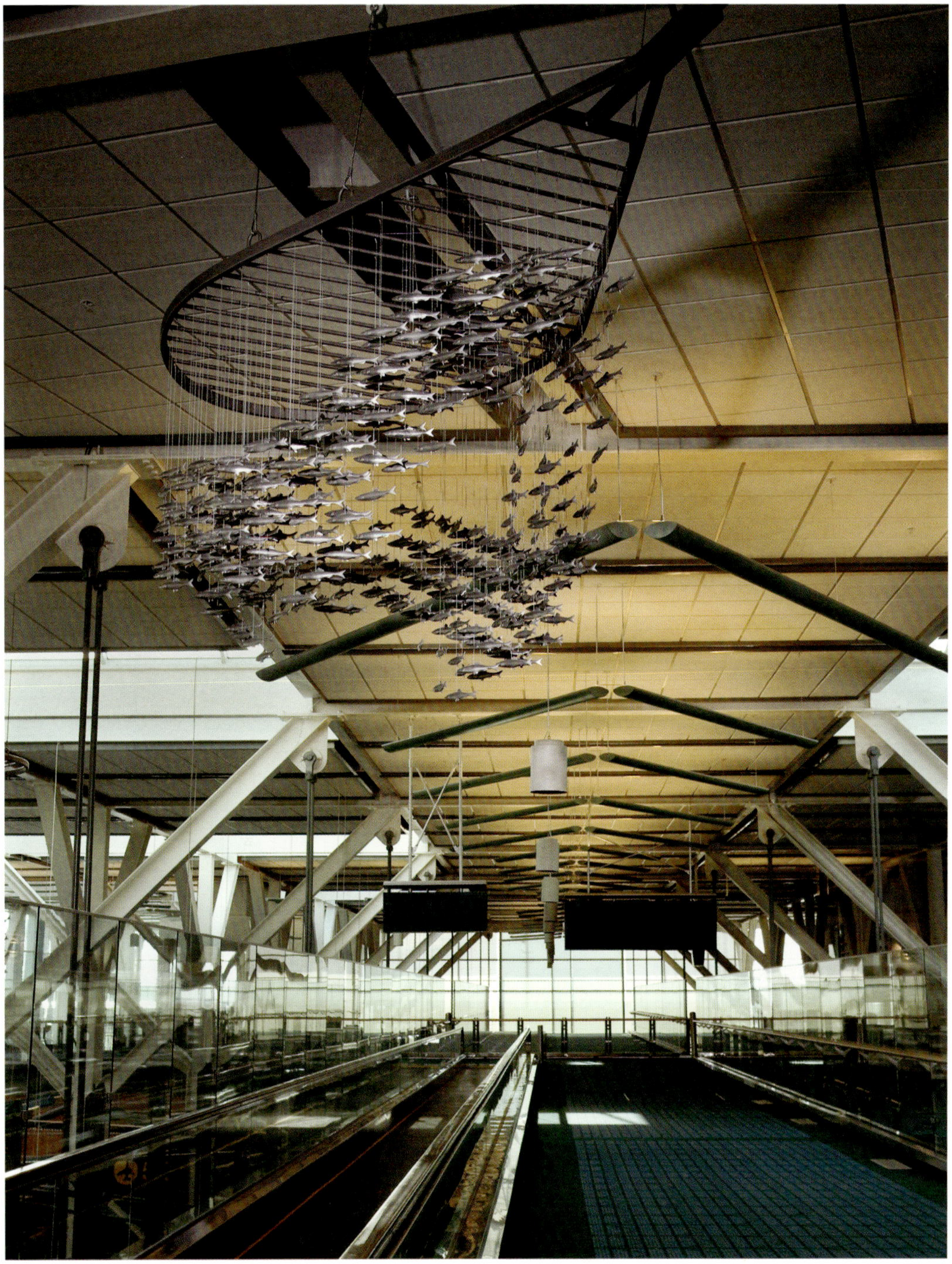

KING SALMON HOUSEFRONT

Roy Henry Vickers
(Tsimshian, Haida, Heiltsuk)

c. 1990 carved and painted cedar |
PANELS 2.9 × 2.9 m
CENTRE COLUMN 3.3 × 0.9 × 0.4 m
OUTER COLUMN 2.9 × 0.9 × 0.3 m

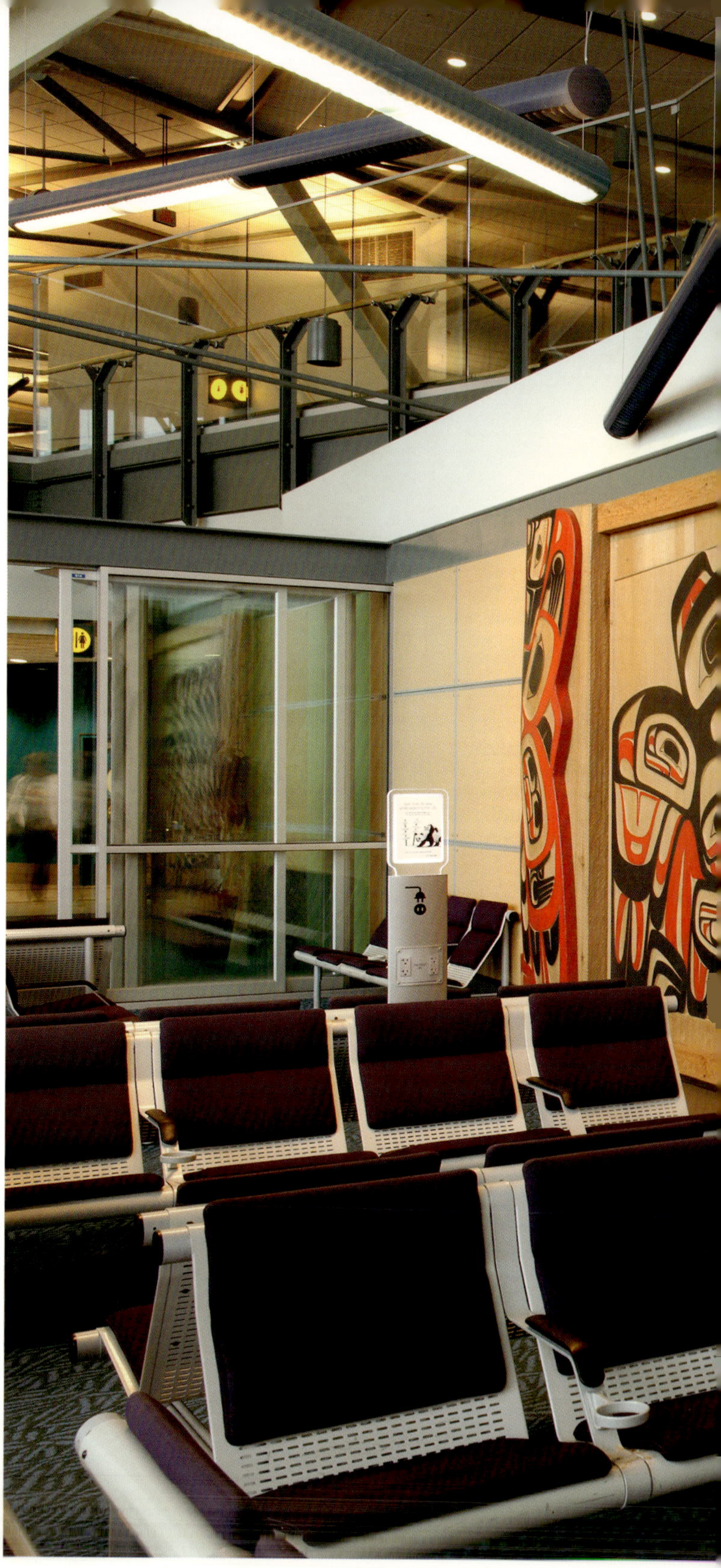

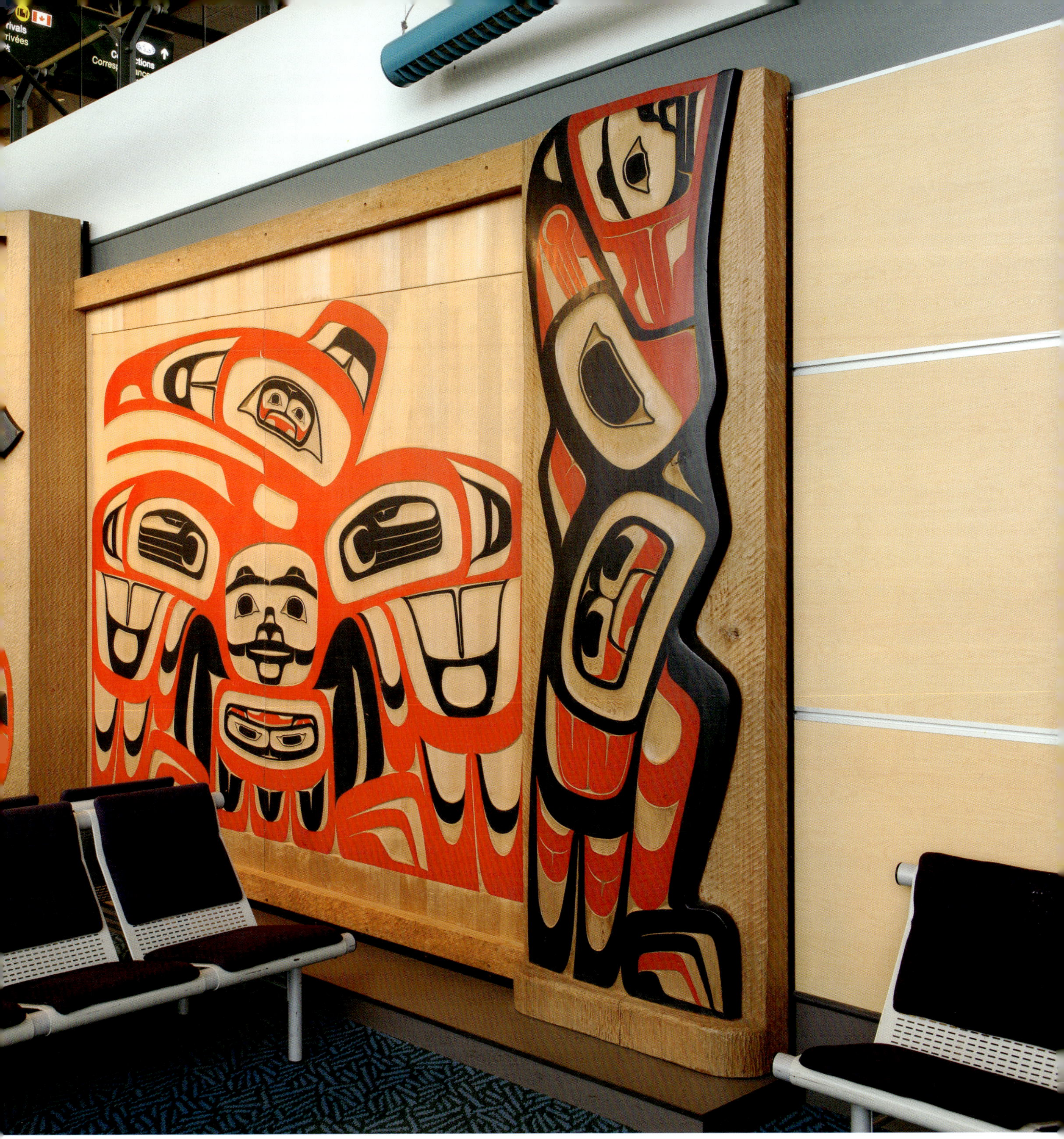

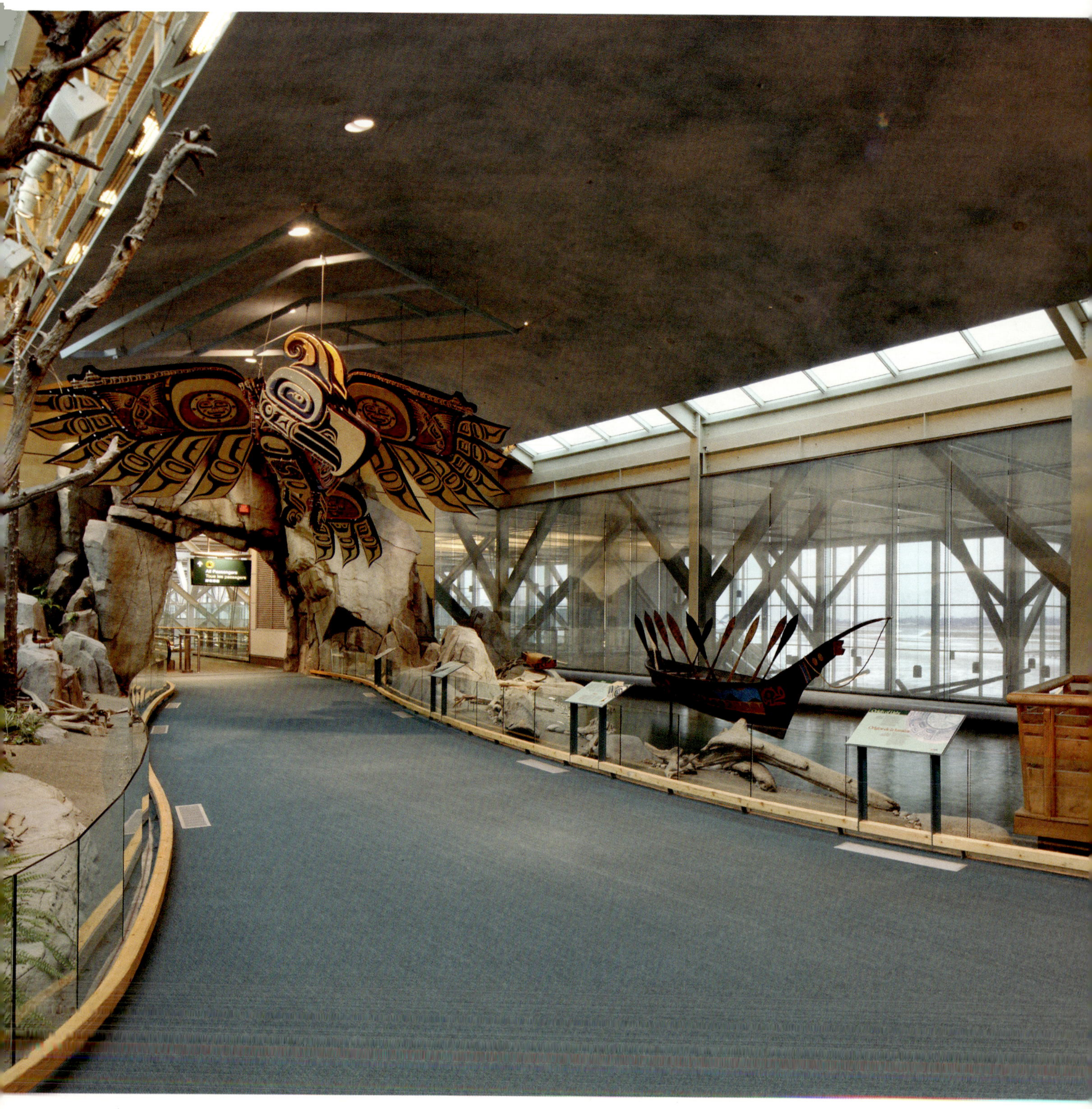
All Passengers
Tous les passagers

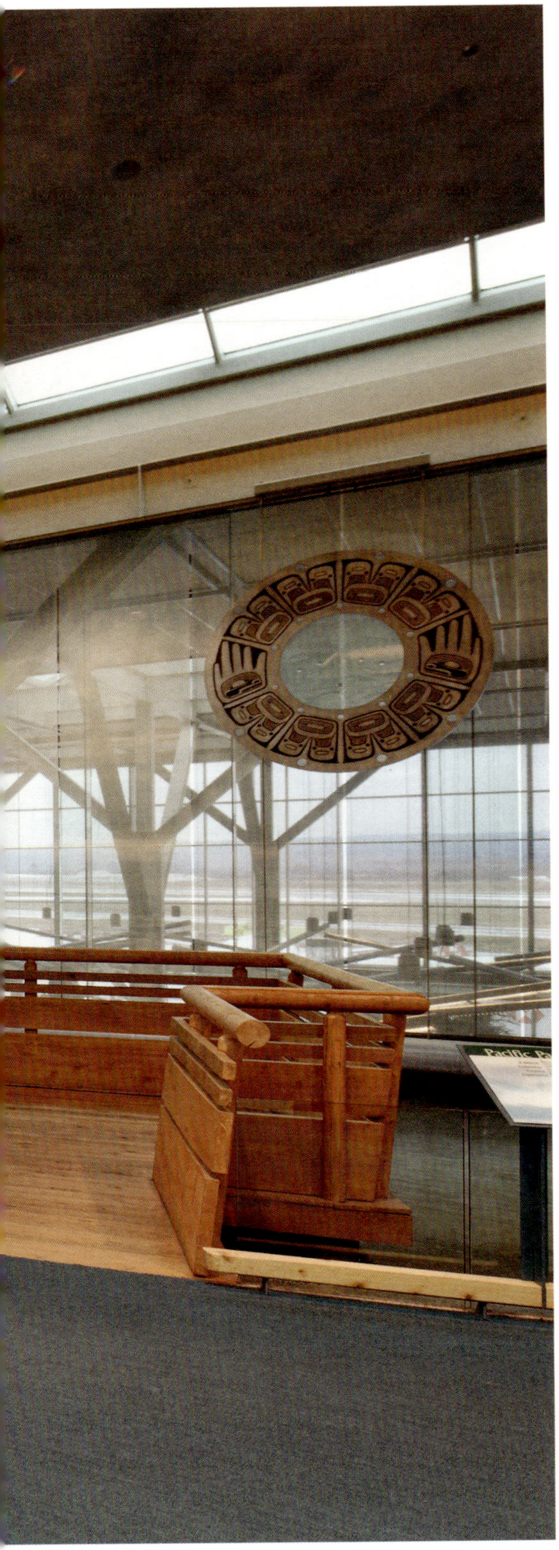

4

THE PACIFIC PASSAGE

U.S. ARRIVALS

(POST-SECURITY)

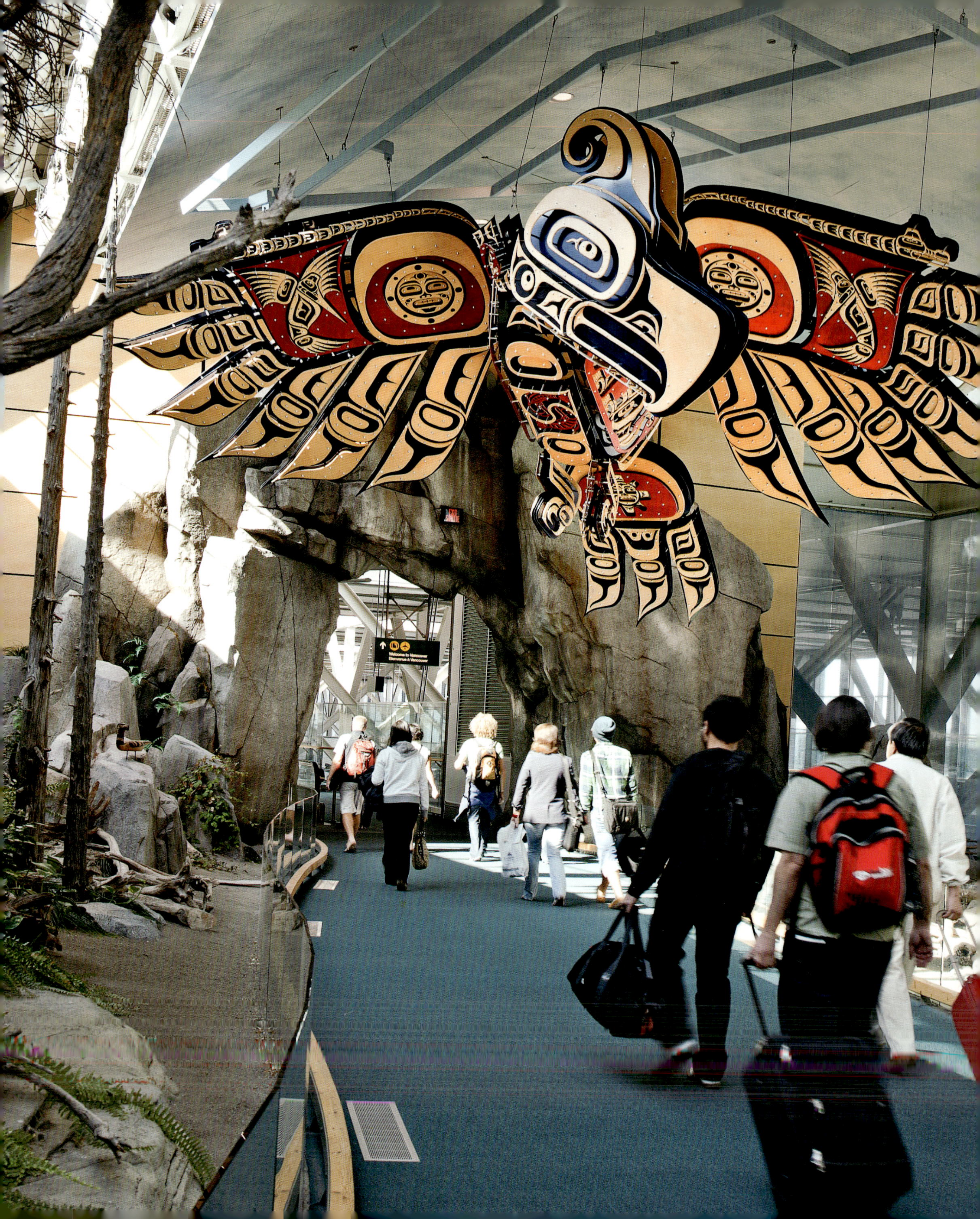
Welcome to Vancouver

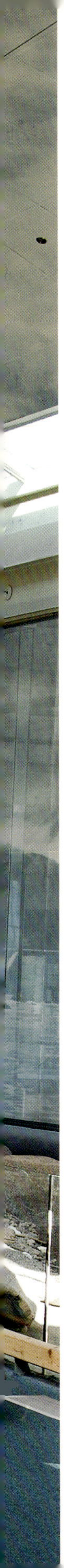

HETUX

Connie Watts

2000 aluminum, Baltic birch, stain | 6.5 × 4.2 × 4.6 m

This big, dramatic, thoroughly modern Thunderbird, created from powder-coated aluminum and stained birch panels, looms above travellers as they walk through YVR's Pacific Passage. The innovative approach to forms and materials it displays, and the contemporary recasting of the elements of classic Northwest Coast art, are exemplary of the practice of its maker, mixed-media artist Connie Watts. Of Nuu-chah-nulth, Kwakwaka'wakw and Gitxsan descent, Watts reshapes First Nations cultural references with her knowledge of Western design and media arts, and with her eclectic approach to fusing "past, present and future" in a single artwork.[1]

Thunderbird is a powerful and important crest figure among a number of Northwest Coast groups; a giant, supernatural bird, it is characterized as the keeper of the sky, the source of thunder and lightning, and a fearsome hunter of large prey such as Killer Whale. Watts, however, has imbued Thunderbird with the personality of her grandmother, Hetux, whom she describes as determined, creative and generous.[2] Smaller animals and celestial bodies, depicted on Thunderbird's body, wings and tail, signify other aspects of Hetux's character. The wolves represent intensity and determination; the male and female salmon, generosity and prosperity; the hummingbird, joy and energy; the wren, magic and fortuity; the moon, intuition and perceptiveness; and the sun, logic and power.[3]

Based in Port Alberni and West Vancouver, Connie Watts has degrees from the University of Manitoba and the Emily Carr Institute (now University) of Art and Design. She brings a wide range of disciplines to her interest in cultural identity, language, family relations and the tension between tradition and modernity.

---

1 Connie Watts, on her website www.conniewatts.com.
2 Connie Watts, artist's statement, 2000. 3 Ibid.

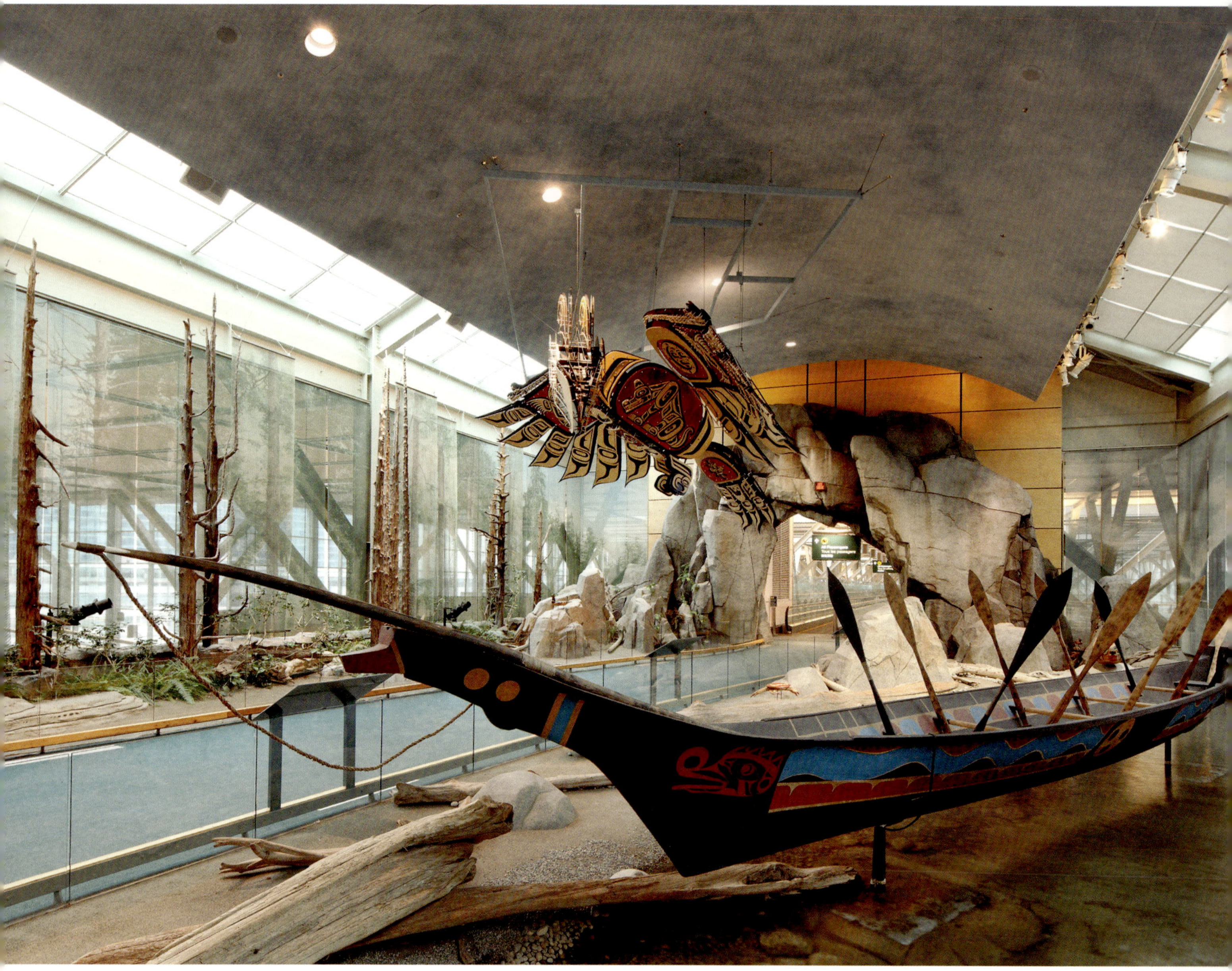

ABOVE

RAINBOW OFF THE BEACH

Tim Paul (Hesquiat Band, Nuu-Chah-Nulth)

[illegible]

OPPOSITE

ORIGIN OF LIGHT

Lyle Wilson (Haisla)

2000 polished aluminum, etched glass | 2.5 m in diameter

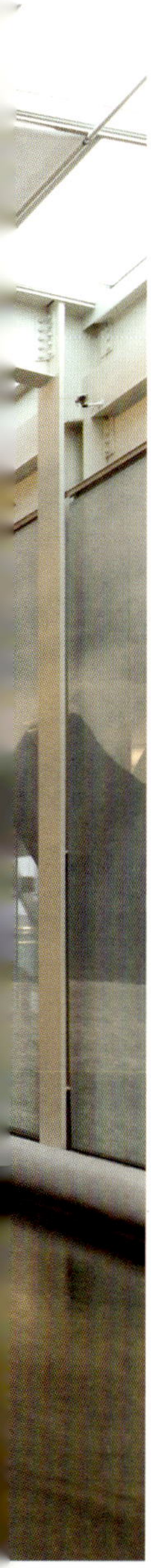

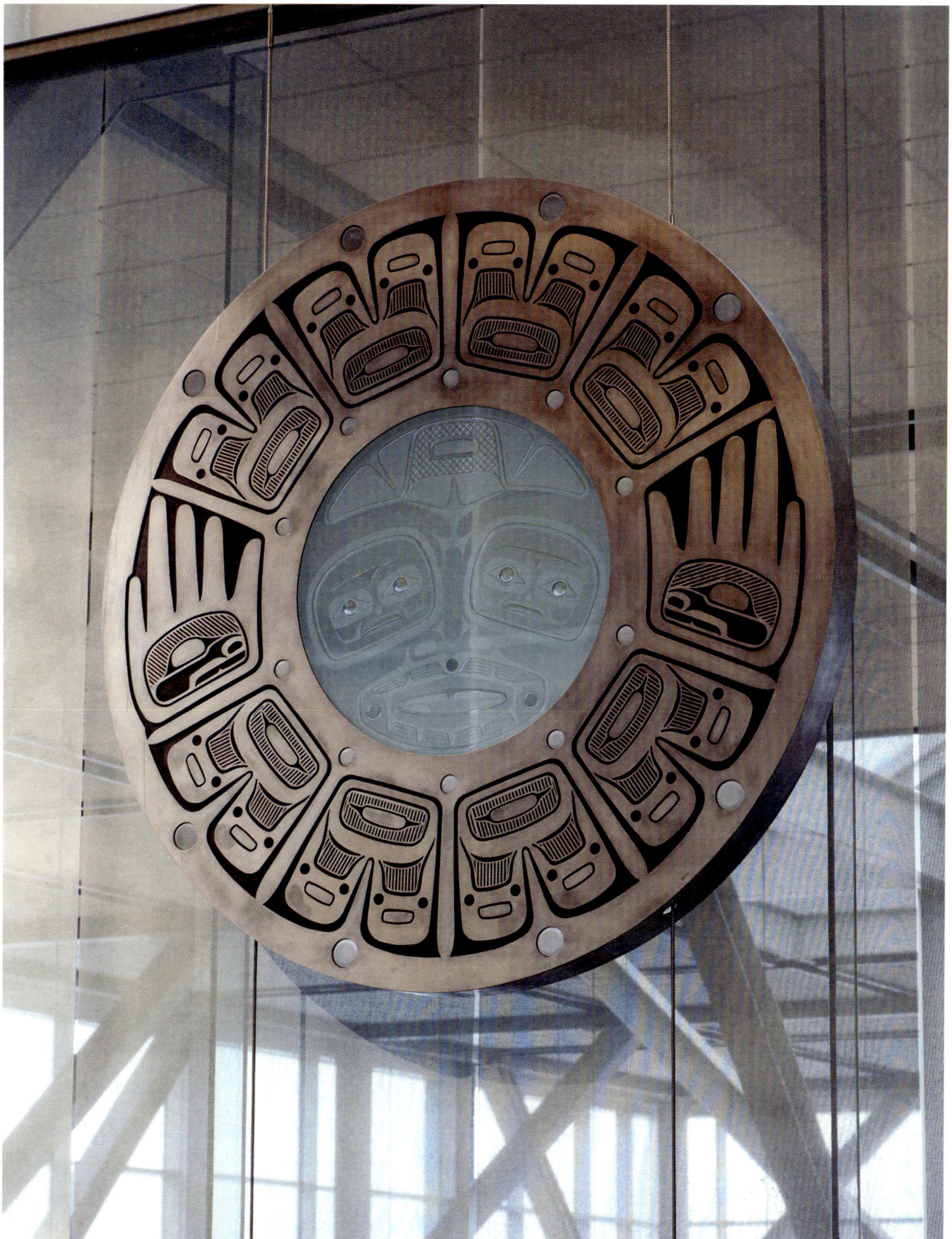

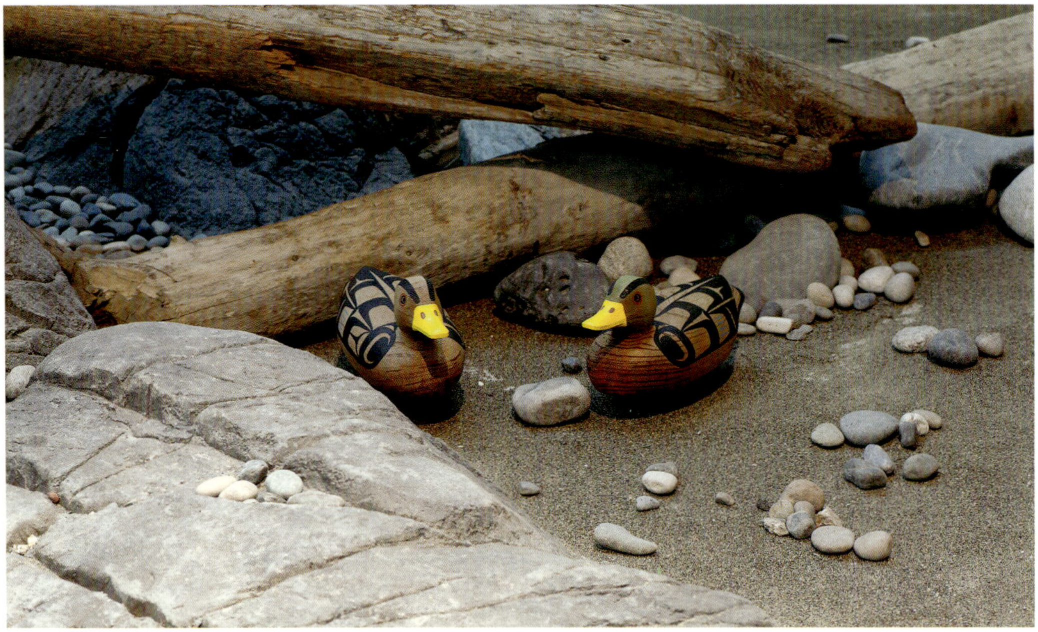

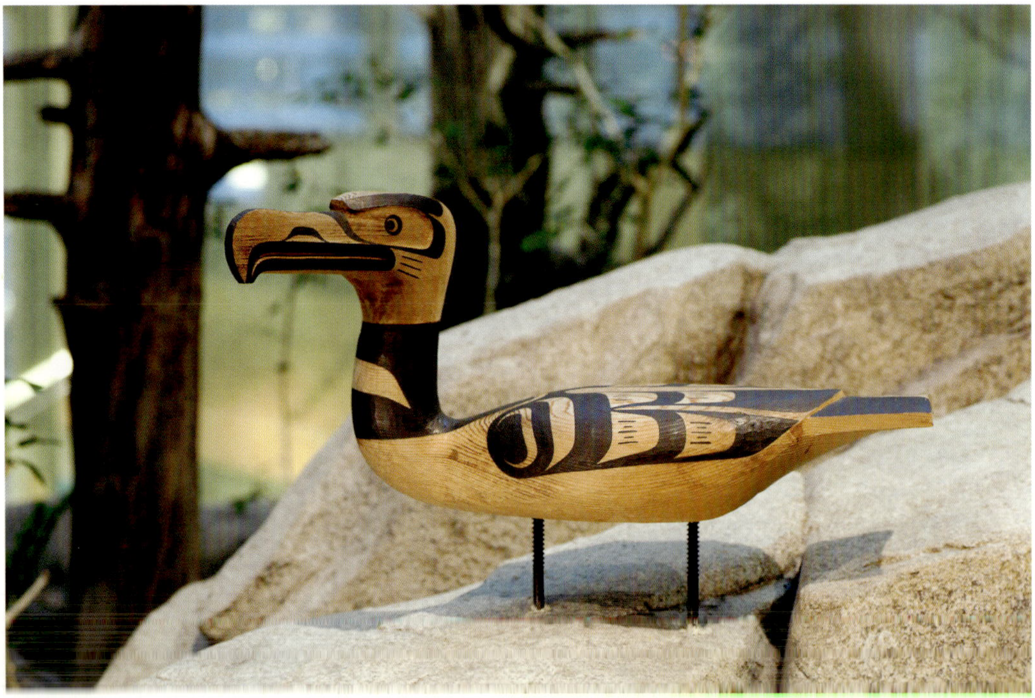

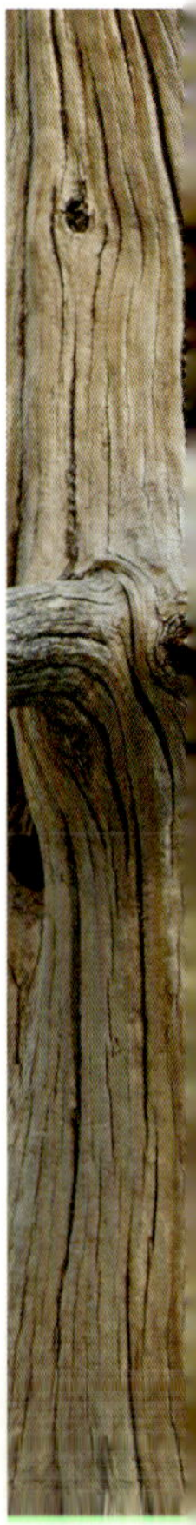

OPPOSITE

Stephen Bruce (Kwakwaka'wakw)

ANIMAL CARVINGS

Ducks

2000 painted red cedar |
LEFT DUCK 18 × 18 × 46 cm
RIGHT DUCK 13 × 13 × 30 cm

Cormorant

2000 painted red cedar | 25 × 18 × 53 cm

BELOW

Eagle

2000 painted red cedar | 64 × 97 × 25 cm

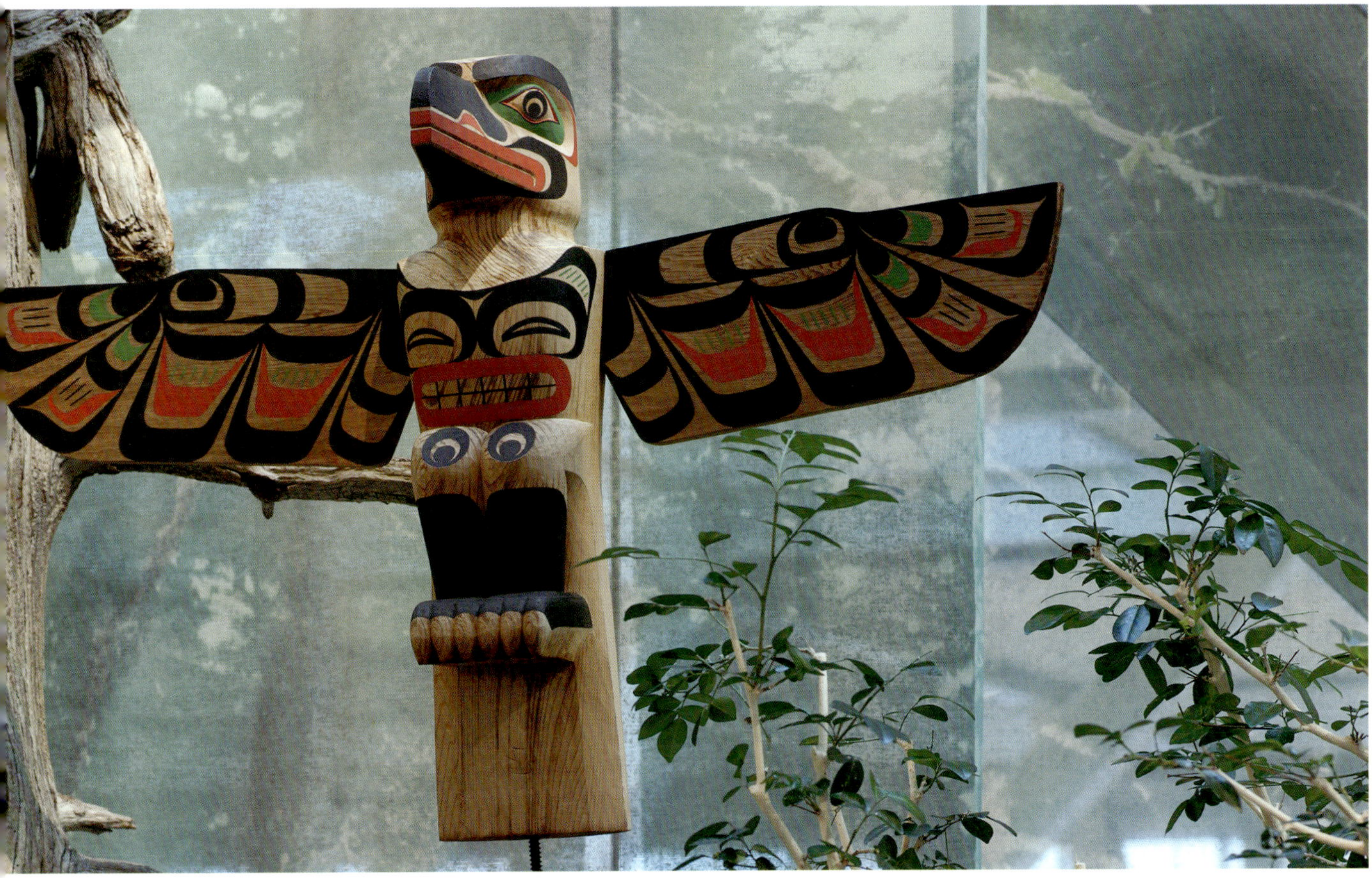

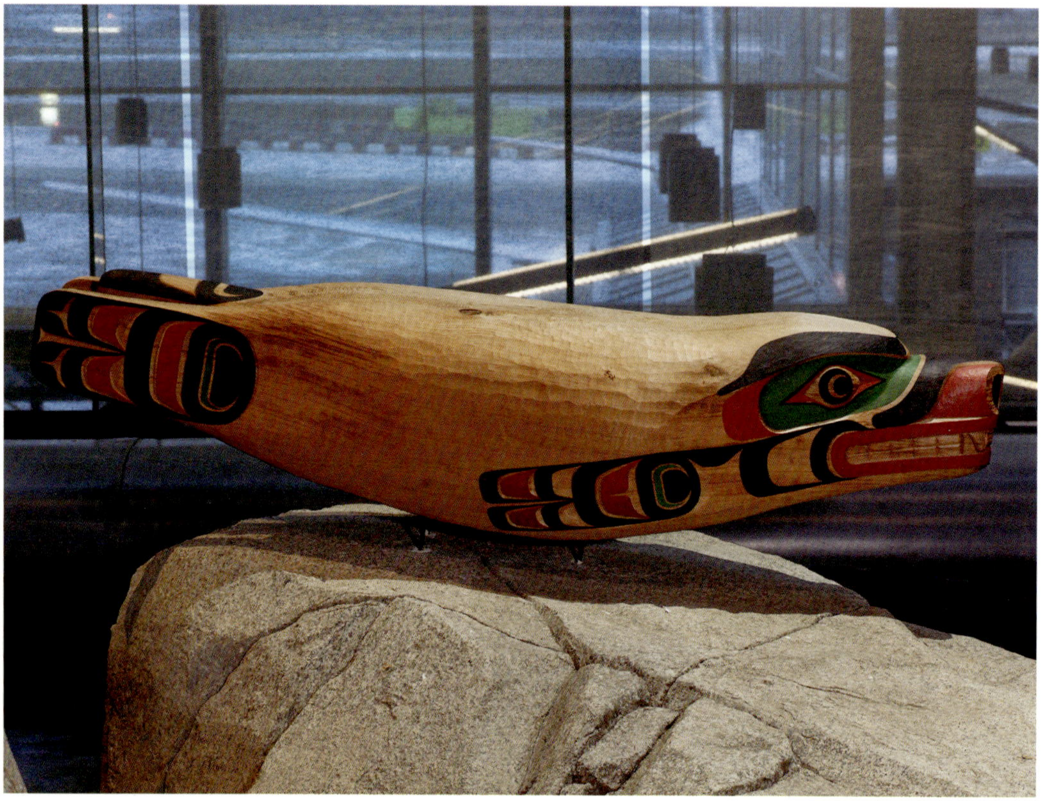

ABOVE

Stephen Bruce (Kwakwaka'wakw)

Seal

2000 painted red cedar | 46 × 38 × 163 cm

OPPOSITE

Crab

2000 painted red cedar | 25 × 74 × 56 cm

Sea Bird

2000 painted red cedar | 16.5 × 11.4 × 33.0 cm

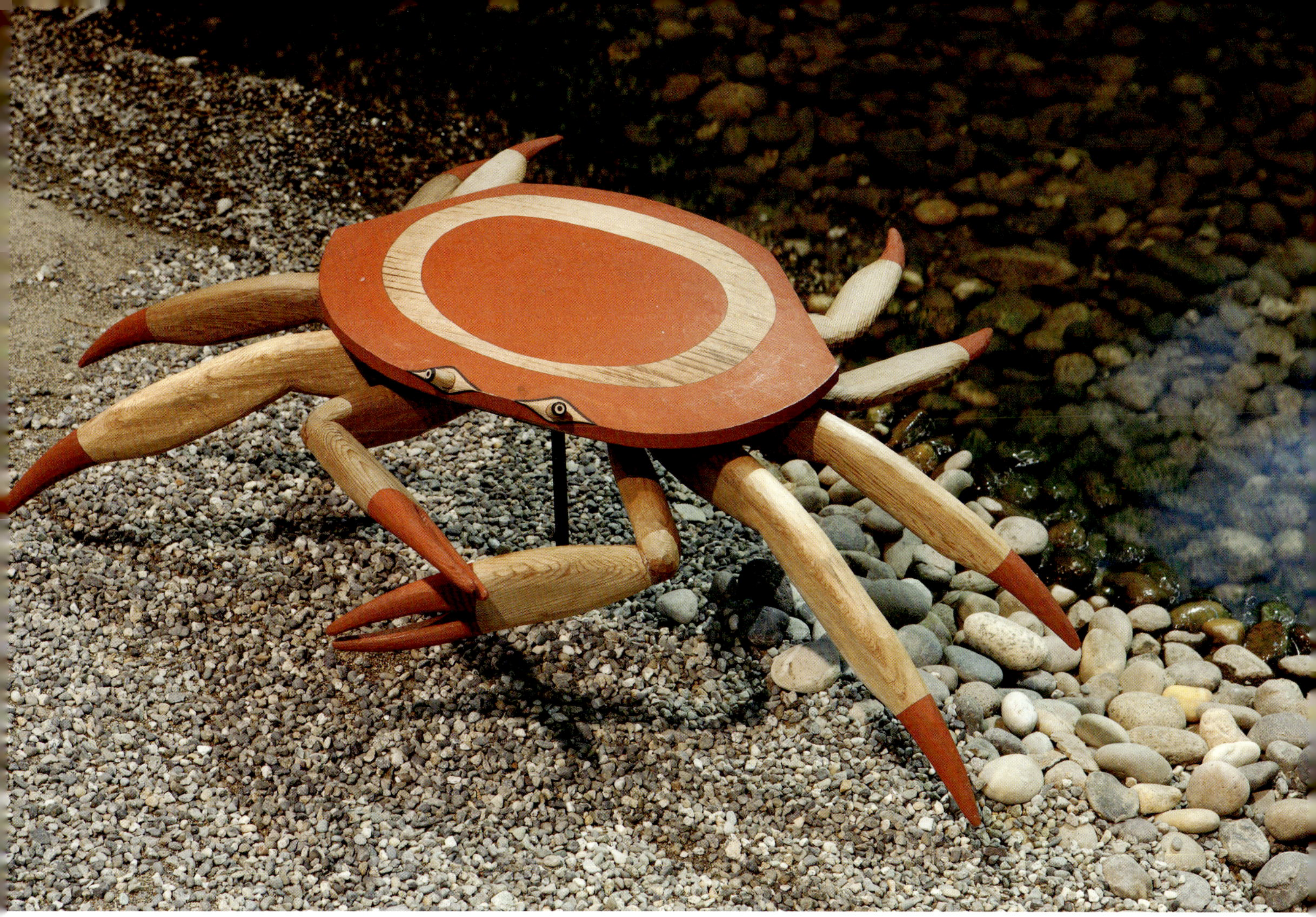

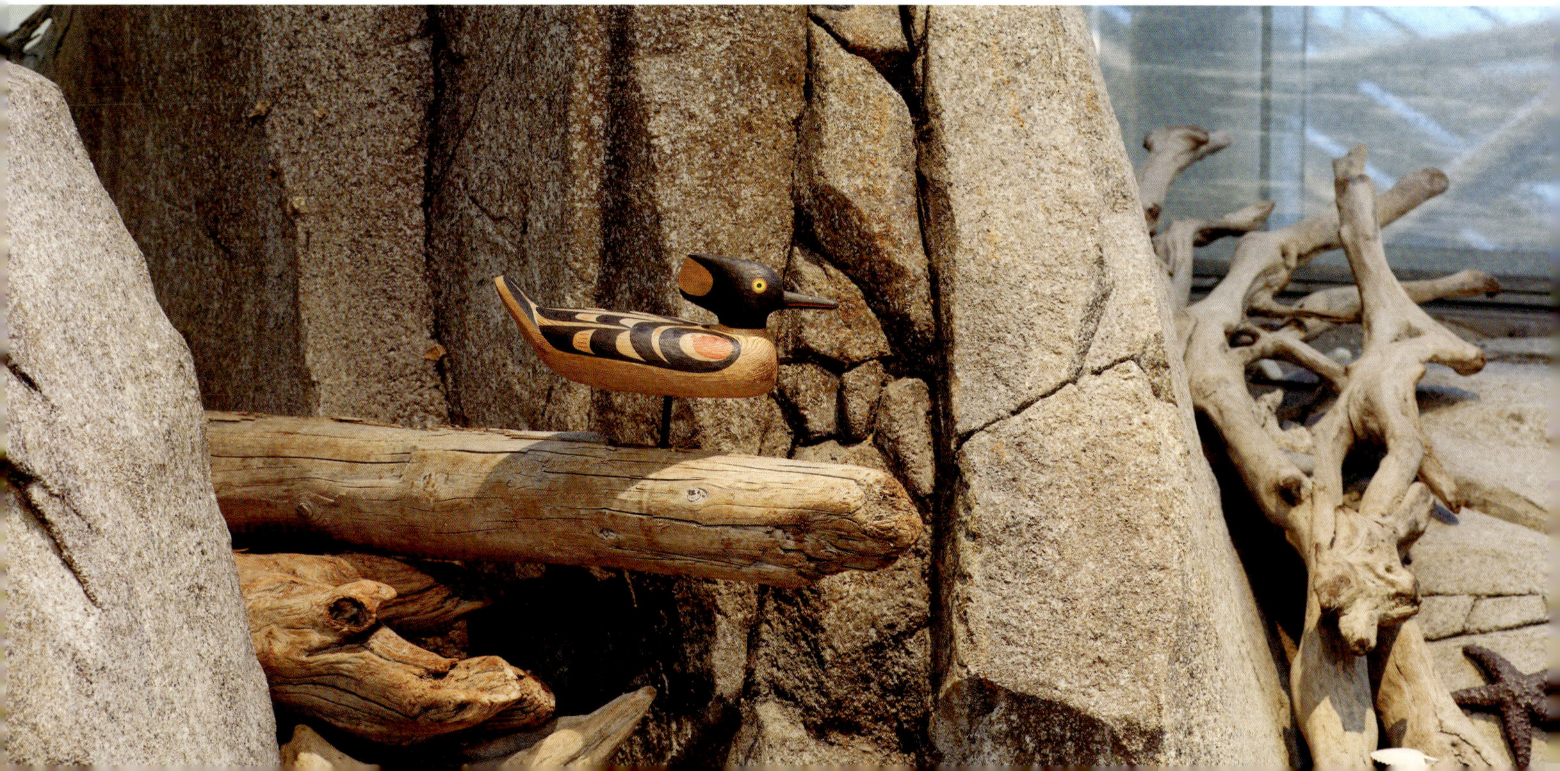

TRANSFORMATION MASK

Stan Wamiss

2000 red cedar, acrylic paint, horse hair | 104 × 89 × 97 cm

The large and dramatic transformation mask created by Kwakwaka'wakw artist Stan Wamiss depicts Raven, culture hero and Trickster, as its outer being, visible when the mask is in its closed position, and the fearsome-looking Bak'was as its inner being, revealed when the mask is open. A malevolent spirit commonly known as Wild Man of the Woods, Bak'was is recognized among all Northwest Coast groups. (Among the Kwakwaka'wakw, his name translates as "man of the ground embodiment.") He is "the keeper of drowned souls," and he "causes loss of reason and sanity; he lures those seeking escape into the night woods with faint firelight."[1] In art, his attributes include deep-set eyes, prominent cheekbones, a hooked nose, a toothy grimace and an overall skeletal appearance, as befits his status as chief of the ghosts.

Transformation masks, whose inner and outer faces vary widely according to the story being enacted, are worn by ceremonial dancers. They convey, in a dynamic and theatrical way, the act of transforming from one being or condition of existence to another. The hinged parts of the outer masks are designed to open and spread by the pull of a cord or by the dancer's whirling movements.

Acclaimed Kwakwaka'wakw artist Stan Wamiss, a member of the Quatsino First Nation, apprenticed with his father, master carver and chief Tom Patch Wamiss. His art, which ranges from masks, paddles and talking sticks to monumental poles and canoes, reveals his careful attention to the style and cultural traditions of his ancestors.

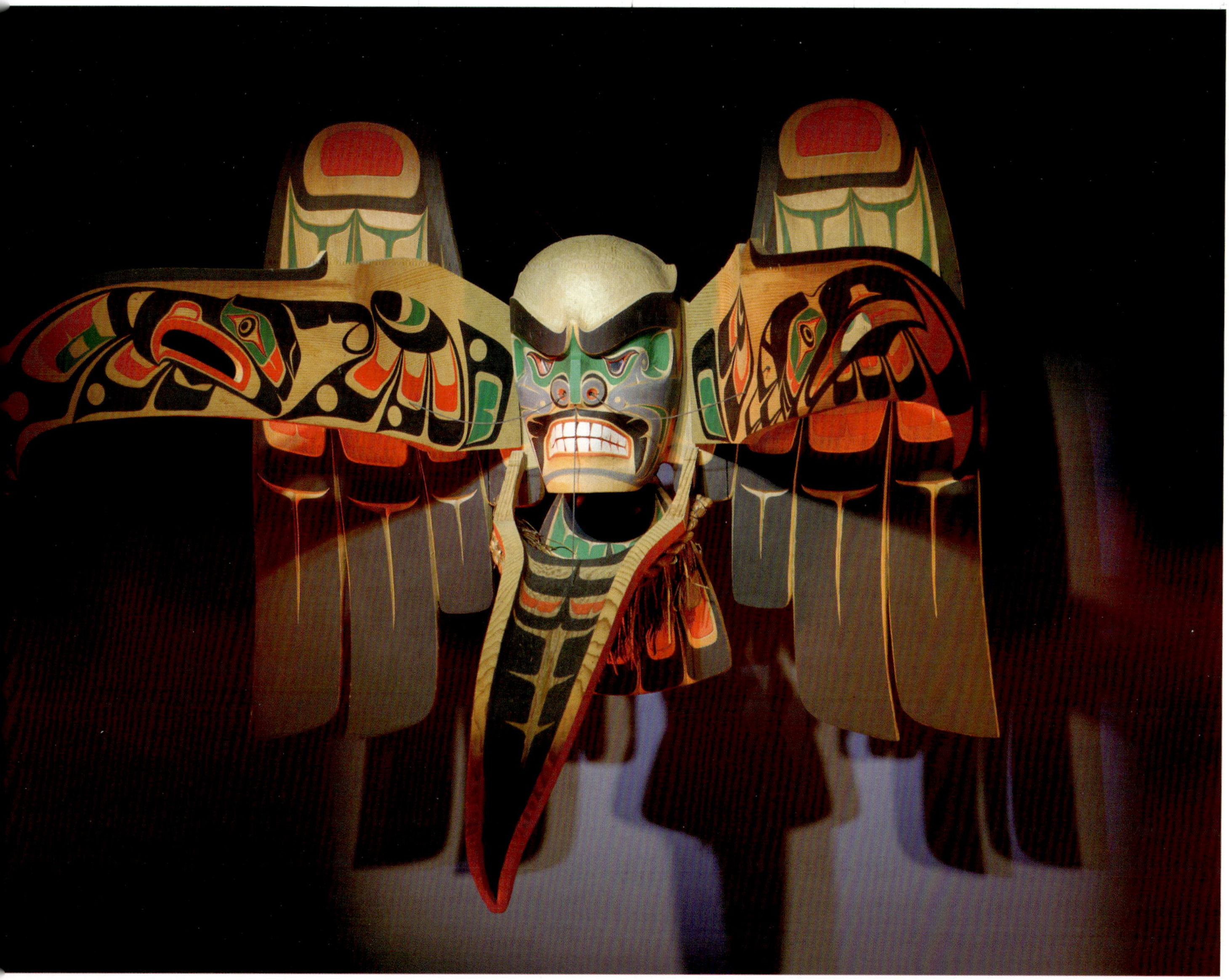

1 Peter McNair, "Power of the Shining Heavens," in Peter McNair, Robert Joseph and Bruce Grenville, *Down from the Shimmering Sky* (Vancouver: Vancouver Art Gallery; Vancouver/Toronto: Douglas & McIntyre; Seattle: University of Washington Press, 1998), p. 169.

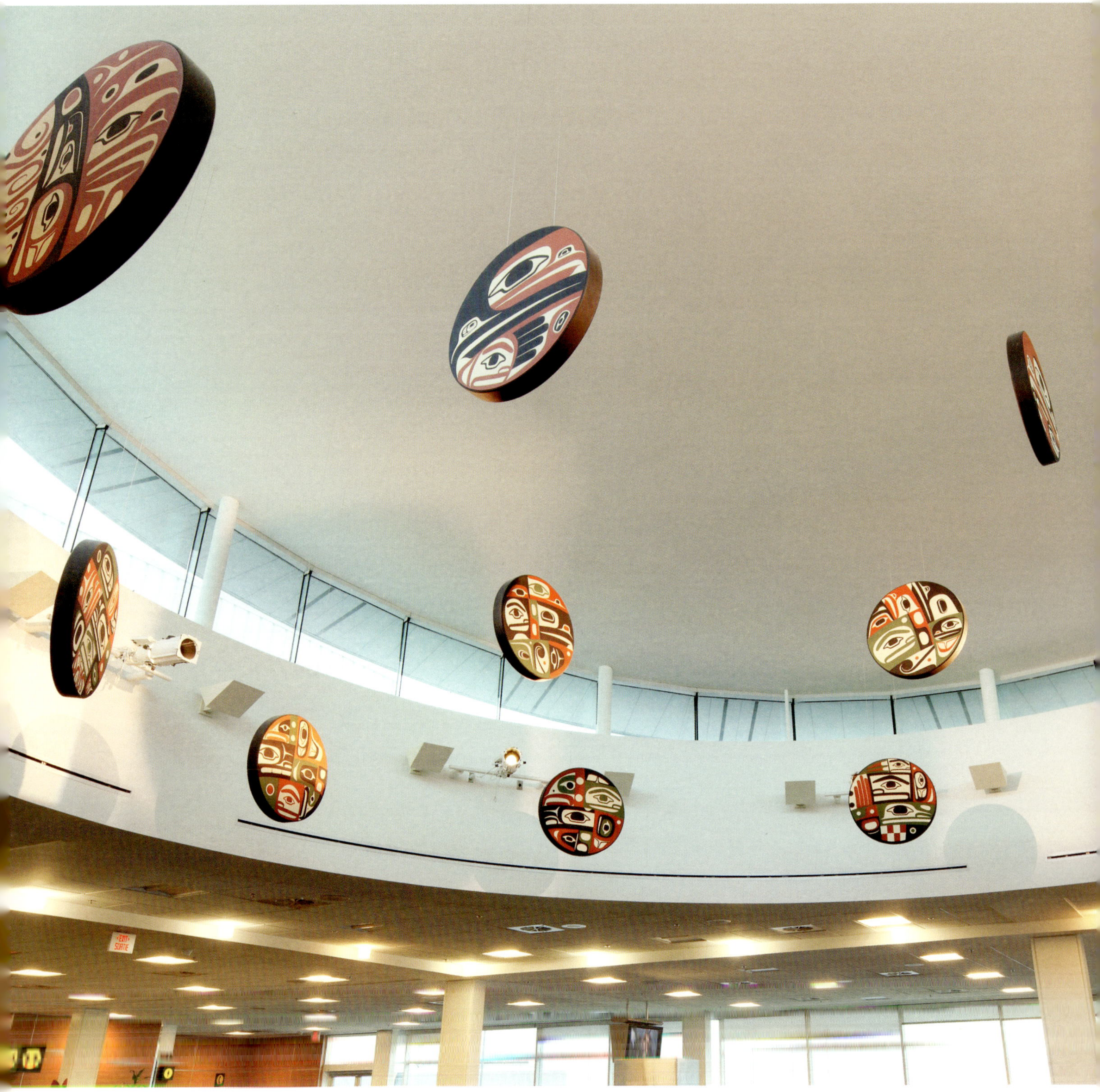
EXIT
SORTIE

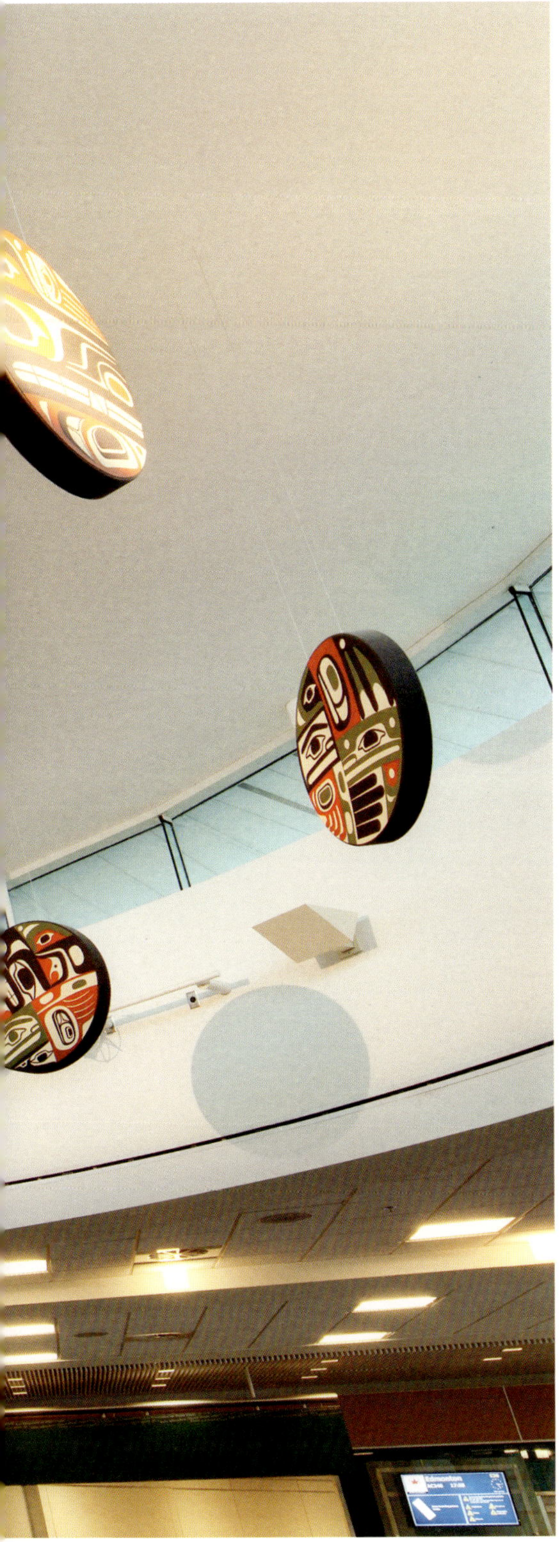

5

SEA TO SKY

DOMESTIC TERMINAL BUILDING

(POST-SECURITY)

THE RIVERS MONUMENT

Marianne Nicolson "Tayagila'ogwa" (Kwakwaka'wakw)

2015 glass, stainless steel, red cedar and acrylic paint | 8.57 m tall | glass columns from 1.42 m at the bottom to 1 m at the top |

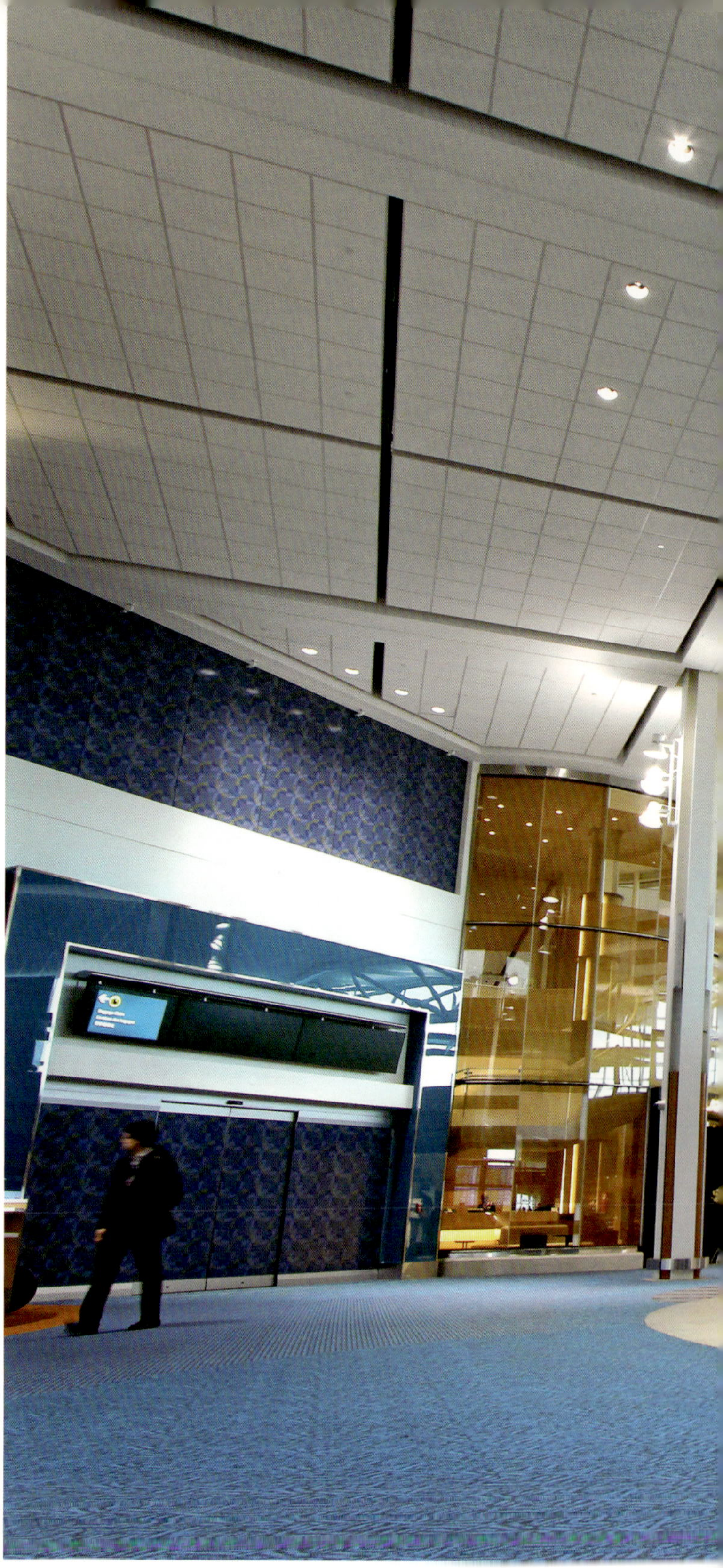

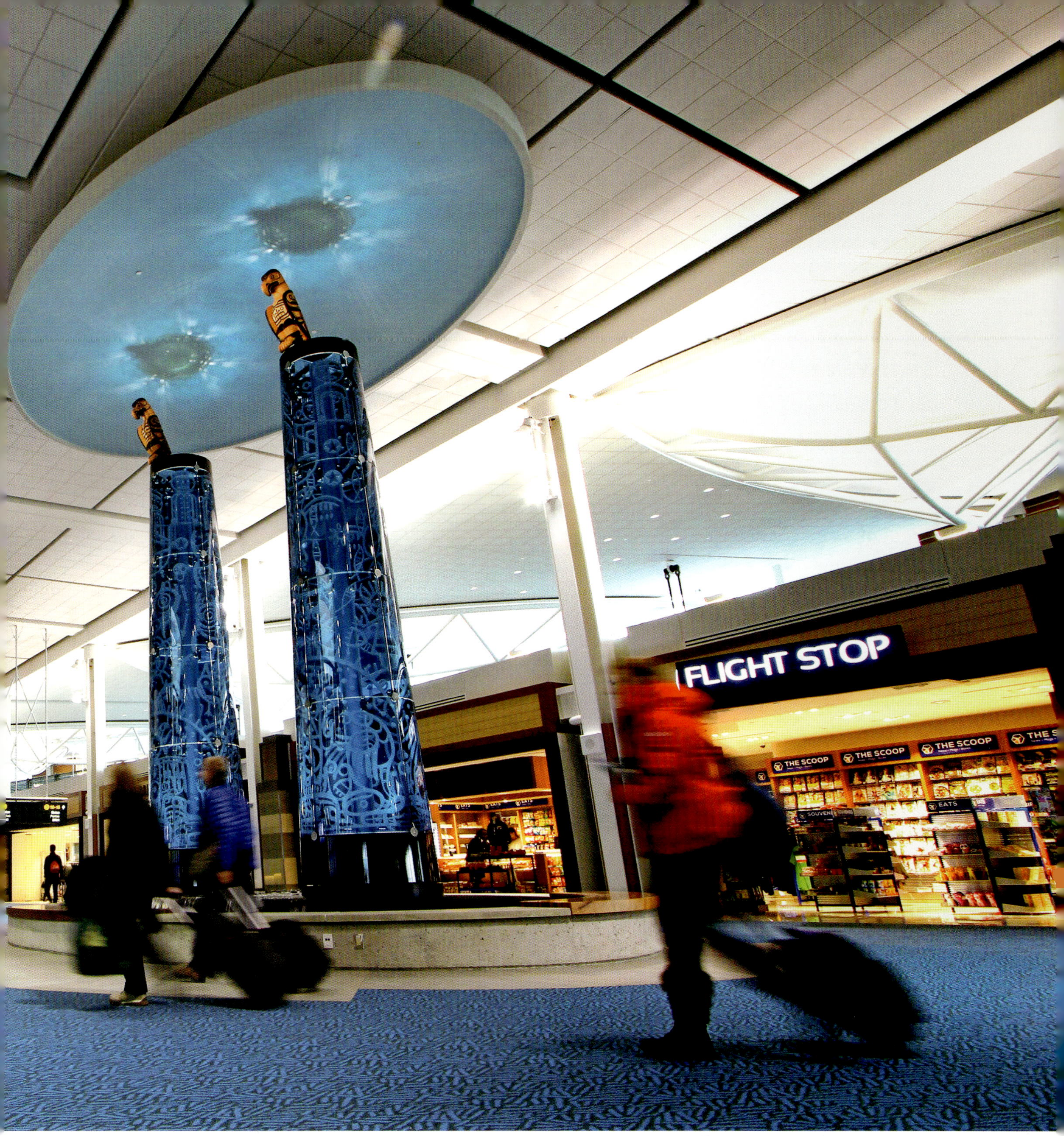
FLIGHT STOP
THE SCOOP
THE SCOOP
THE SCOOP
EATS

SNUW'UY'ULTH

John Marston (Qap'u'luq)

2009 yellow cedar, acrylic paint, glass, cedar bark rope, abalone shell, operculum | 187.76 × 22.86 cm each, with the exception of the steersman paddle, at 213.4 × 22.86 cm

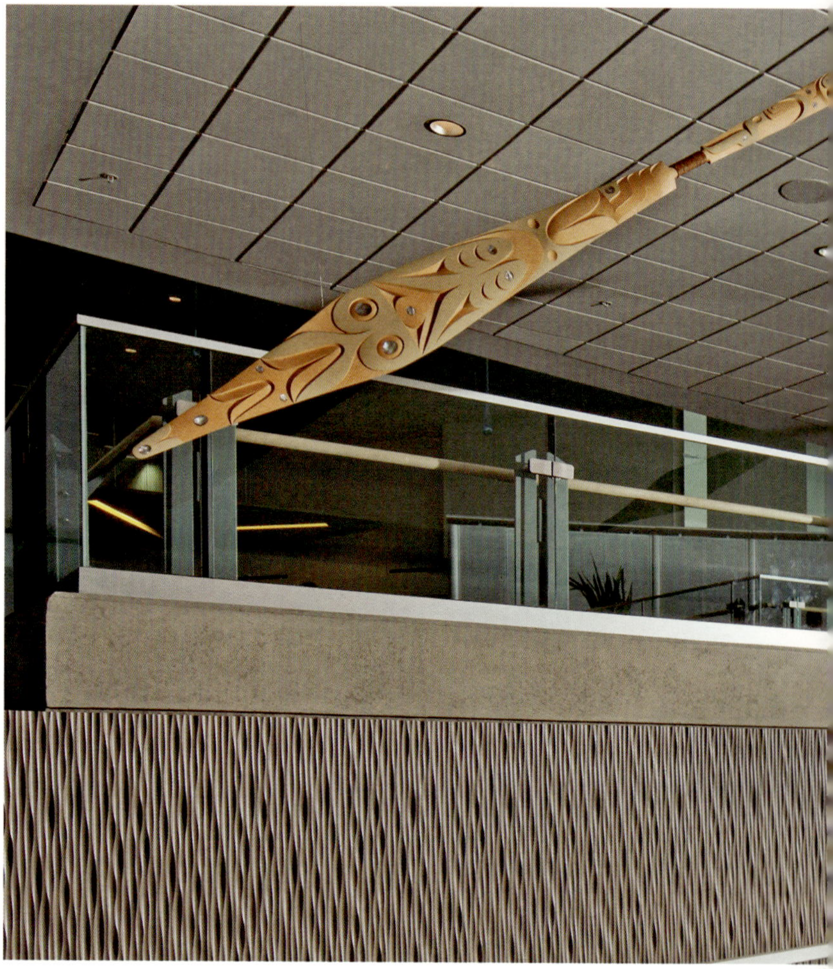

This striking installation of carved and painted canoe paddles exists very comfortably within its setting as a metaphor of travel and a symbol of the sea, one of the defining elements within the overall land, sea and sky theme of YVR's art and architecture. More specifically, the work alludes to the immense importance of the dugout cedar canoe to the indigenous peoples of the Northwest Coast, for whom it was the principal means of transportation for thousands of years. Coast Salish artist John Marston (whose First Nations name is Qap'u'luq) recounts that each canoe was endowed with its own spirit, protecting the people it conveyed as long as they honoured and cared for it.[1] Labour intensive in their creation and essential in their function, canoes were extremely valuable possessions of individuals or families.

Marston's paddles also symbolize the canoe's protective spirit and represent "snuw'uy'ulth," meaning "the teachings of our nation." Their installation, hanging in the air as if poised by ghostly paddlers to propel an

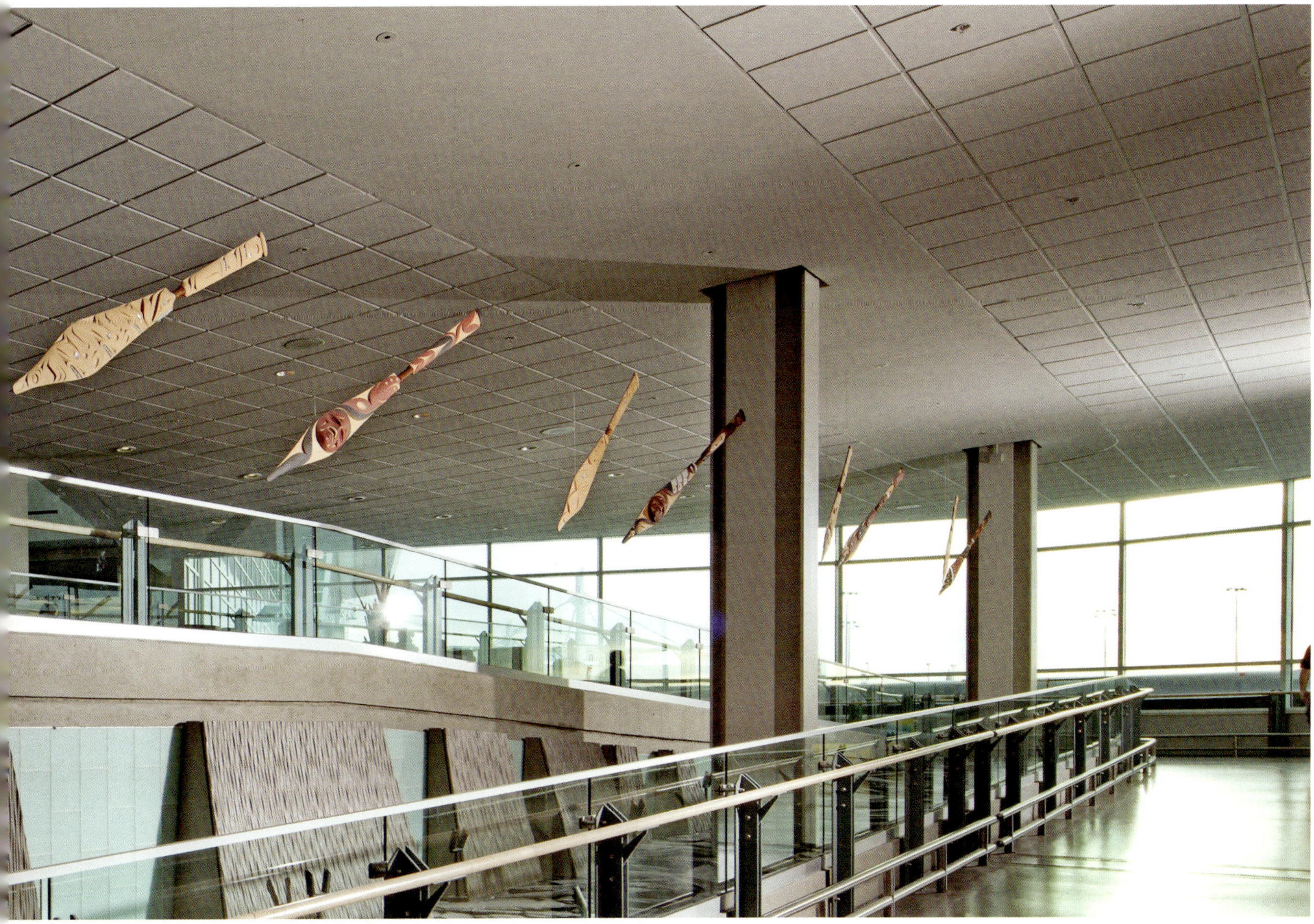

invisible canoe through offshore waters, adds an almost supernatural mood to the work. The paddles are deeply carved and richly painted with stories from the artist's people, the Chemainus First Nation, and each portrays a different animal of importance to the culture. Marston's style is unique among Coast Salish artists and reveals not only his knowledge of classical forms and designs but also the impact of cross-cultural exchanges that took him to Papua New Guinea in 2006 and Japan in 2009.

1 John Marston, artist's statement, 2009.

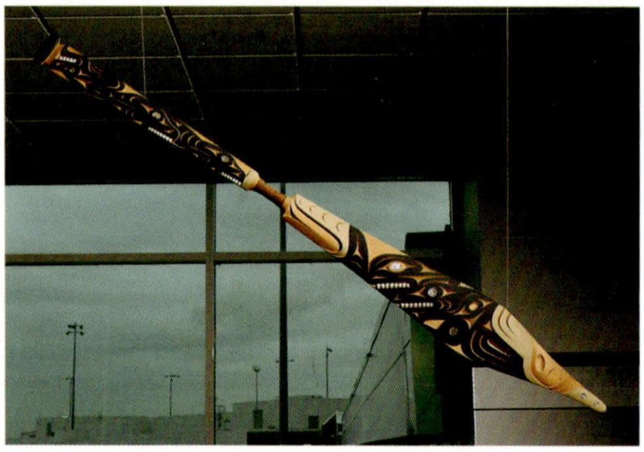
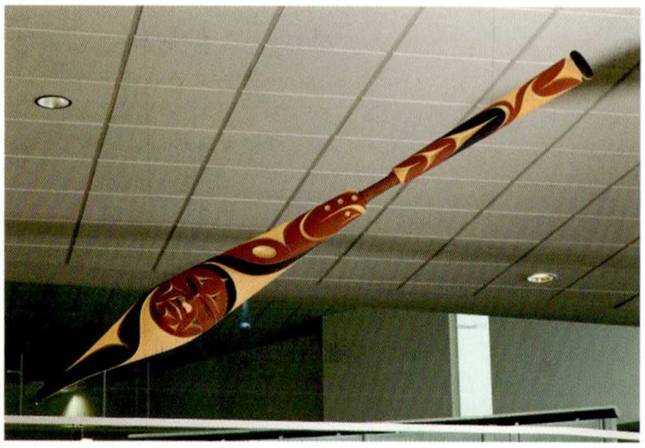
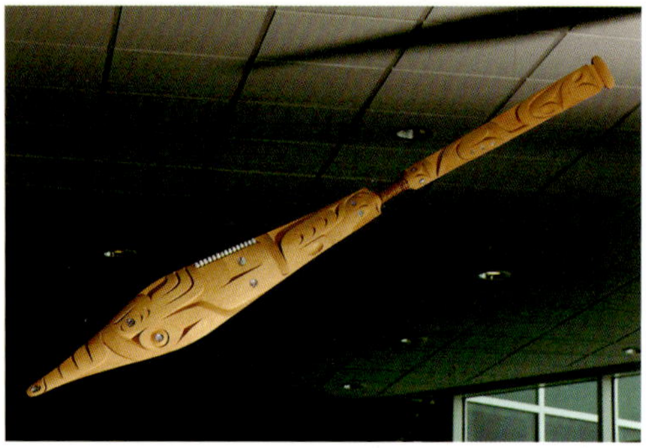
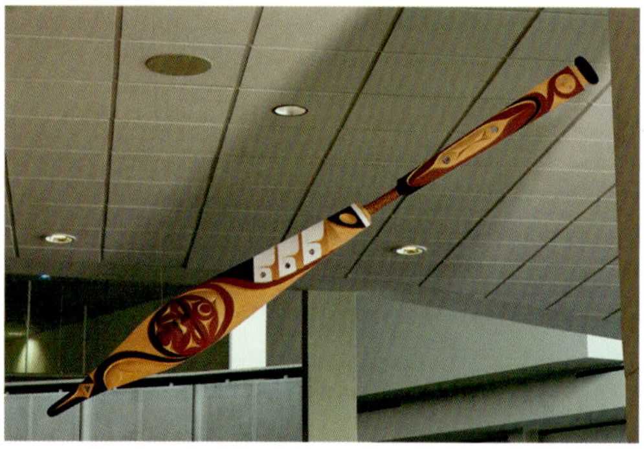

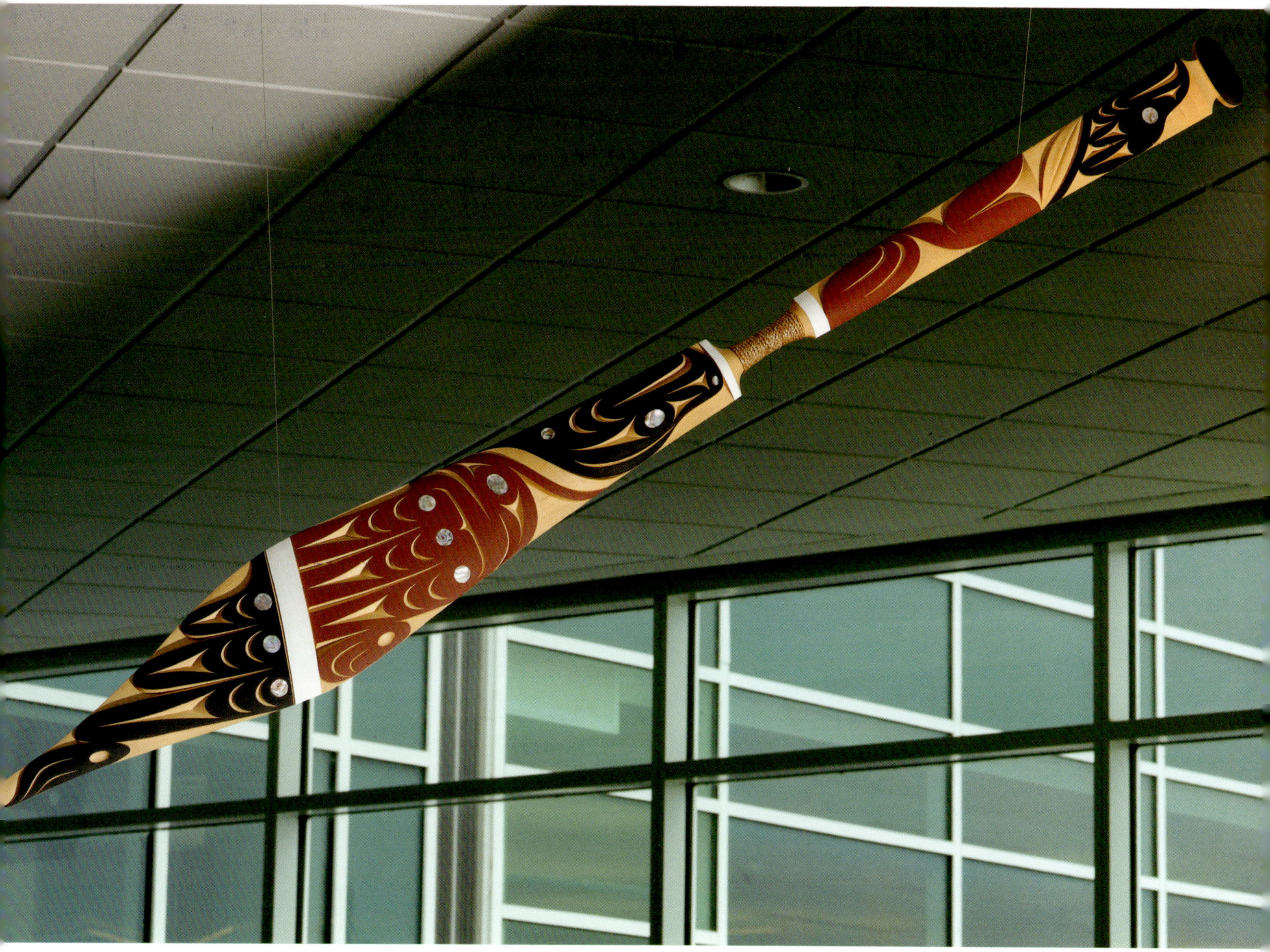

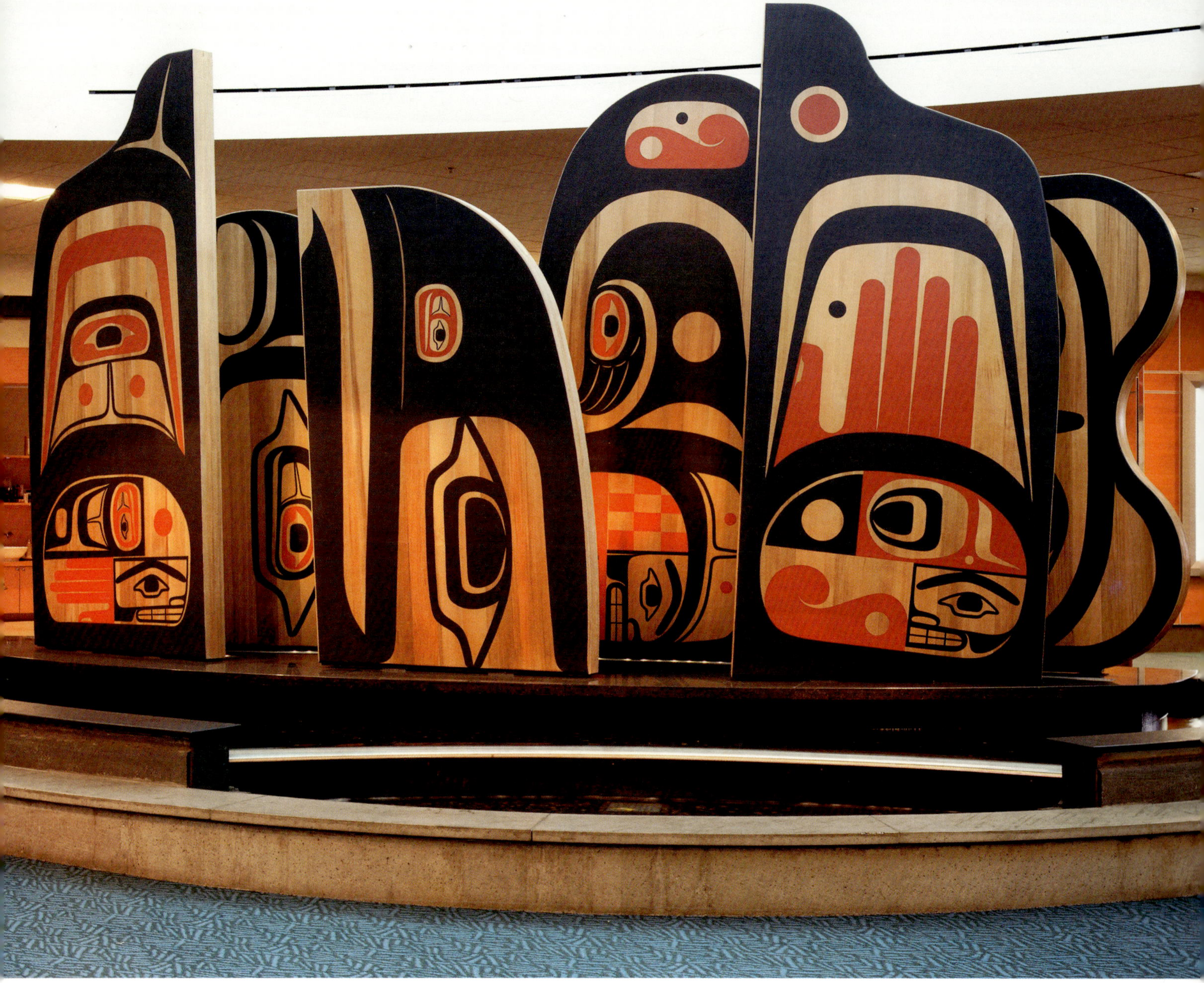

FREEDOM TO MOVE

Steve Smith

2009 laminated red cedar, acrylic paint | 6.3 × 1.4 × 3.25 m overall

In creating this arresting work, set on a black granite platform above a pool of water, Kwakwaka'wakw artist Steve Smith sought to encourage air travellers to "slow down, contemplate and acknowledge their surroundings; to experience a change of pace, physically and spiritually."[1] Filled with stylistic innovations, yet still alluding to Northwest Coast beliefs and graphic design conventions, *Freedom to Move* is composed of six large, laminated red cedar panels. Worked on both sides, they represent a host of crest and story creatures in a state of transformation. Their vertical orientation suggests they are rising up out of the dark water—emerging from a time and place of creation.

Viewed from one side of the installation is Raven, identified by the shape of its beak and characterized here as "Transformer and Creator."[2] Raven is complemented by Killer Whale, identified by its dorsal fin and tail, into which are set secondary designs of a human figure, an upright human hand and Eagle. Together these motifs represent "friendship and freedom."[3] Eagle, Killer Whale and Grizzly Bear, representing strength and authority, can all be viewed from the other side of the installation, realized on the flip sides of the shaped and painted cedar panels. The head of Bear is depicted in Killer Whale's tail, and its claw is seen on the dorsal fin.

As a young man, Steve Smith studied Kwakwaka'wakw carving, painting and design principles with his father, Harris Smith. He has since evolved his own distinctive style, characterized by innovation in forms and materials. He breaks up and isolates classic design components, and interjects unexpected patterns and motifs into age-old ways of working. The Kwakwaka'wakw name with which he signs his work is Dla'kwagila, which means "made to be copper." ■

---

1 Steve Smith, artist's statement, 2009. 2 Ibid. 3 Ibid.

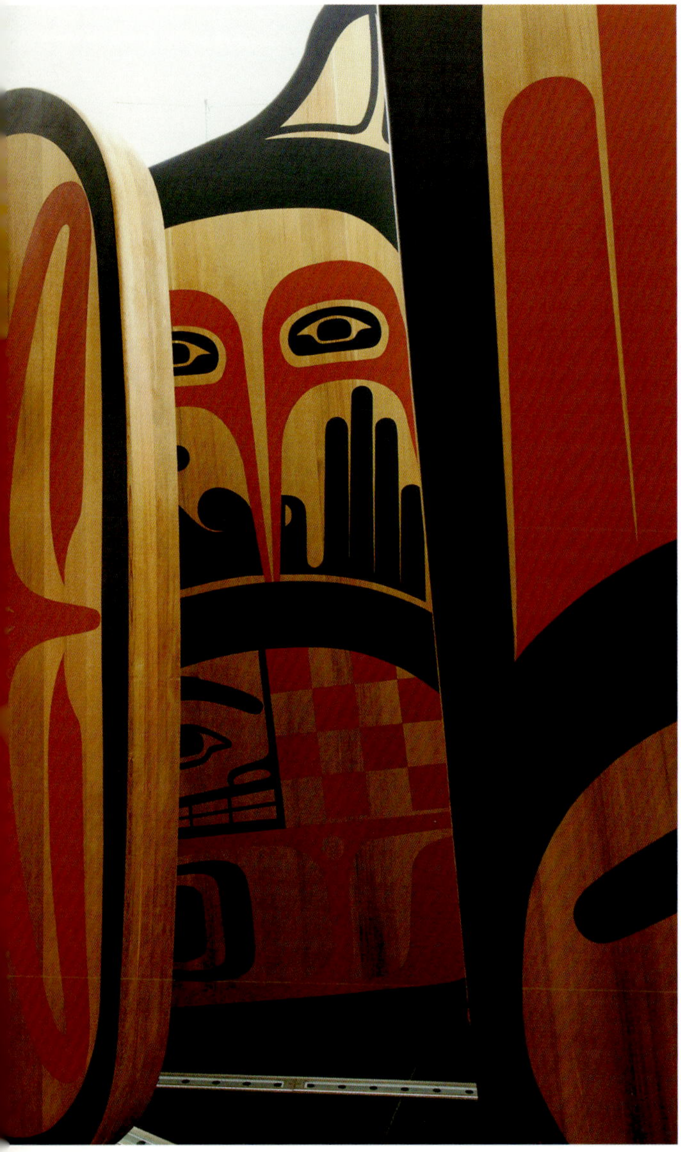

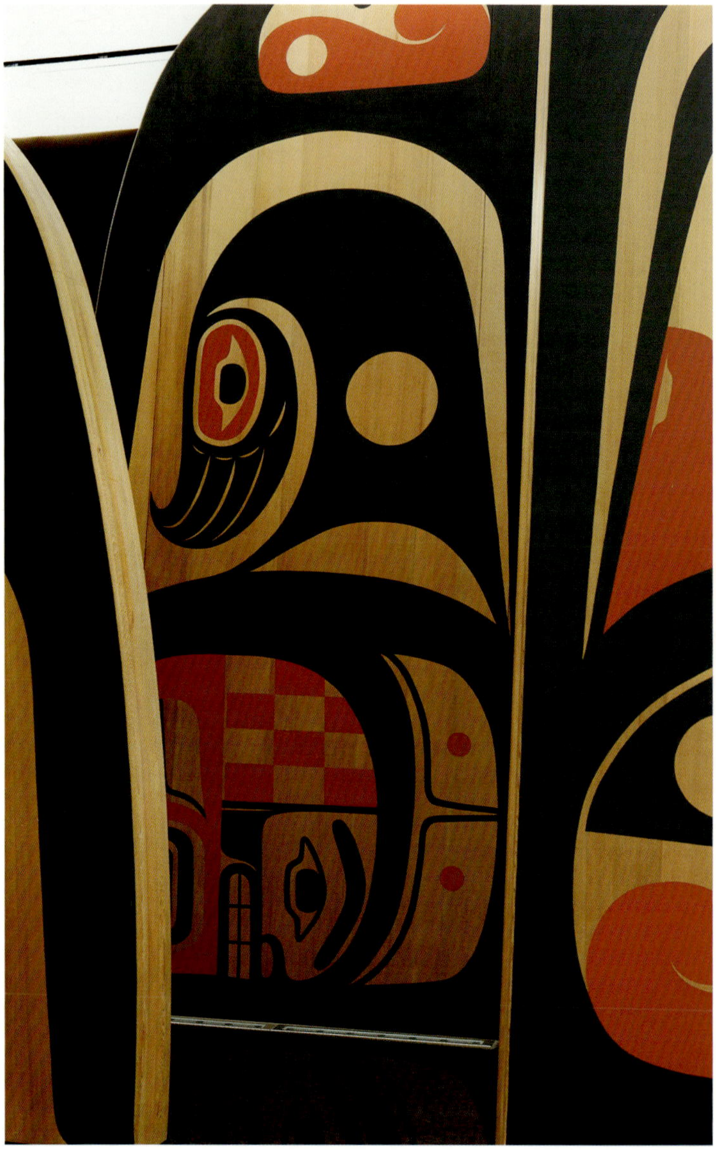

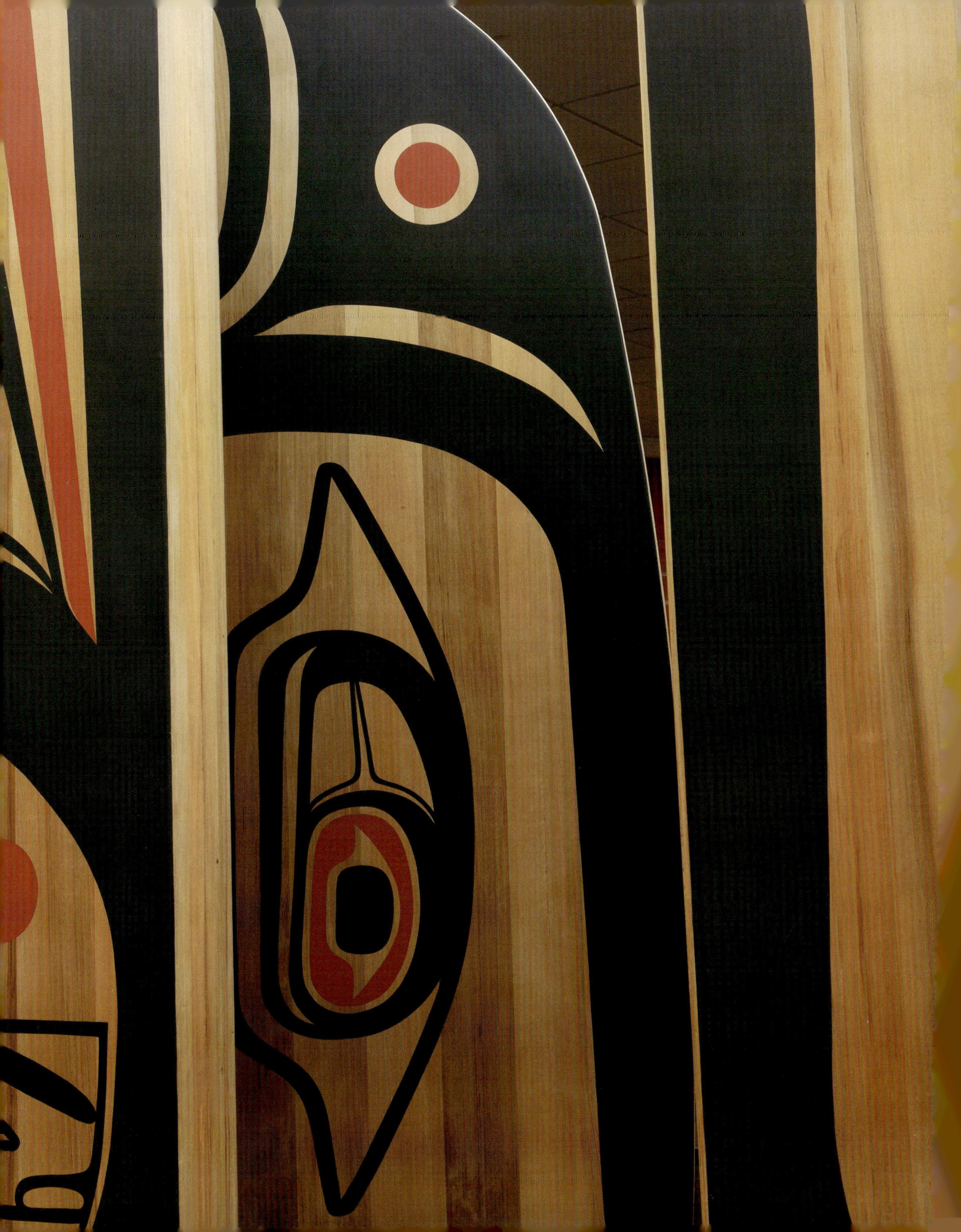

SEA TO SKY

Steve Smith (Kwakwaka'wakw, Oweekeno)

2011 mahogany plywood, medium-density fibreboard, acrylic paint | 91 cm in diameter

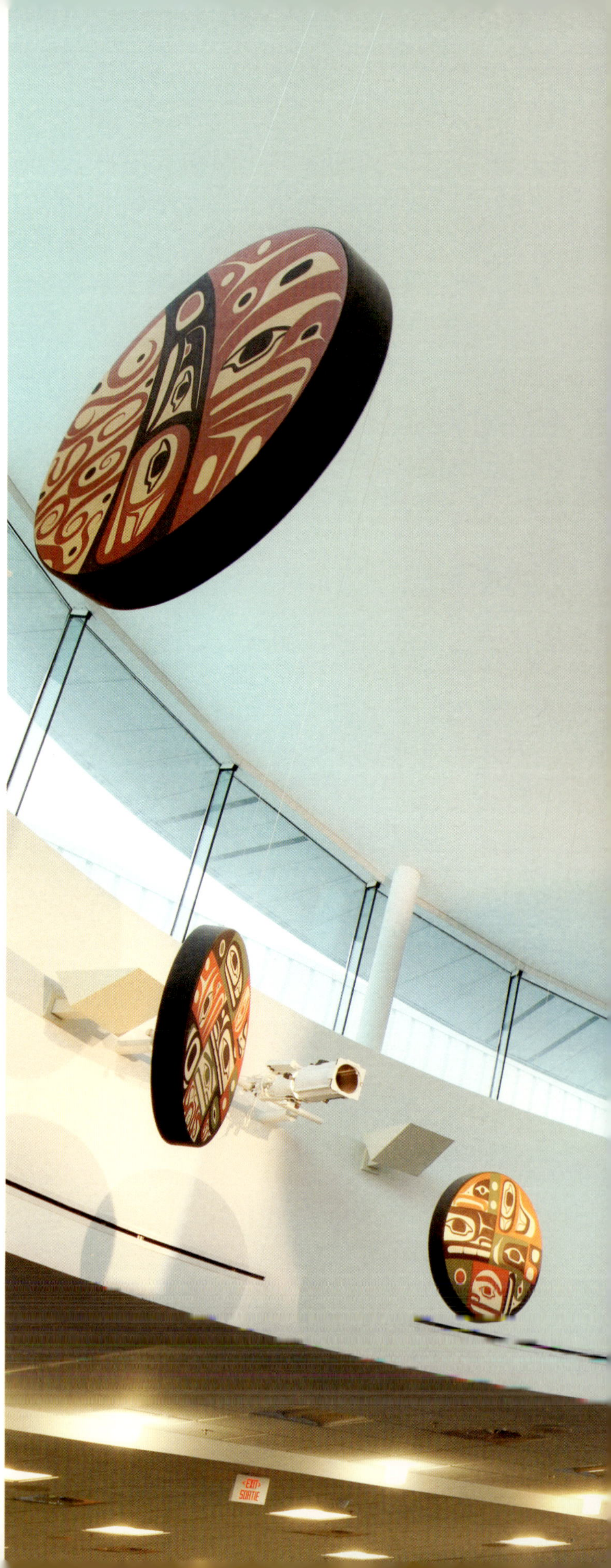

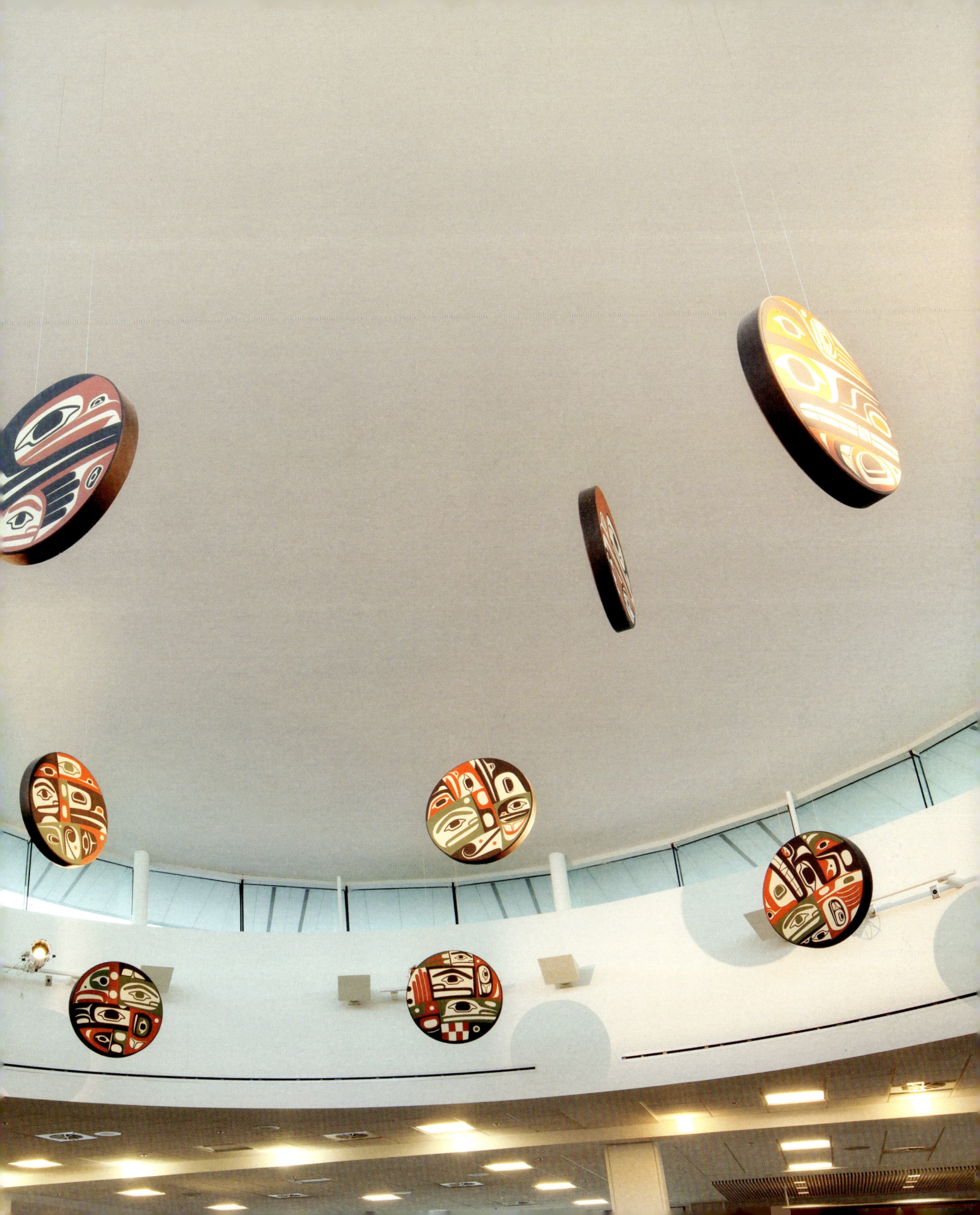

BELOW

Roy Henry Vickers
(Tsimshian, Haida, Heiltsuk)
SPLIT BEAR PANEL

c. 1990 painted red cedar | 2.1 × 6.3 m

OPPOSITE

THUNDERBIRD PANEL

c. 1990 painted red cedar | 2.1 × 6.3 m

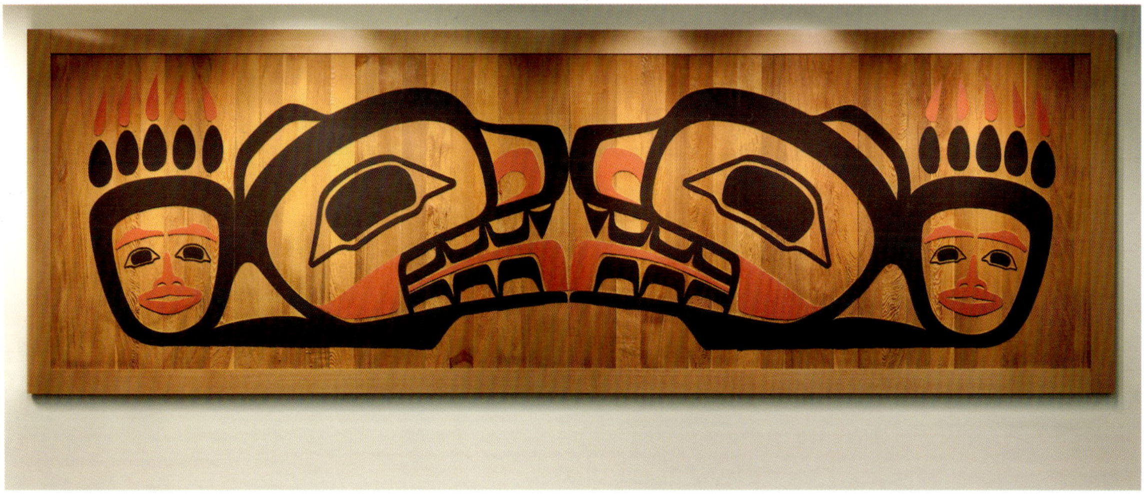

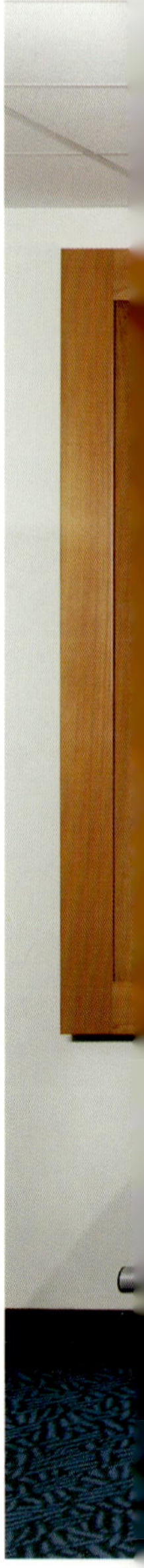

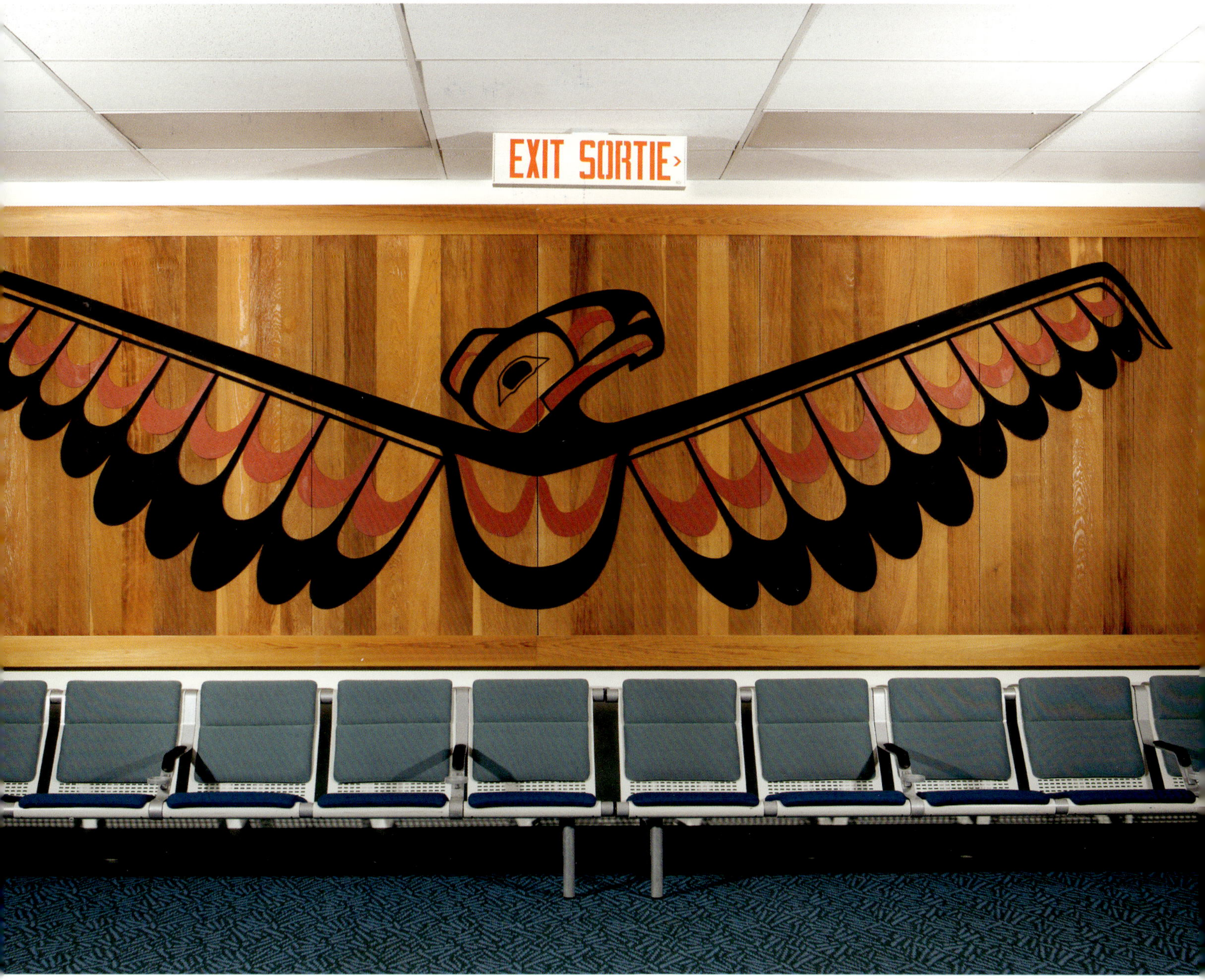
EXIT SORTIE

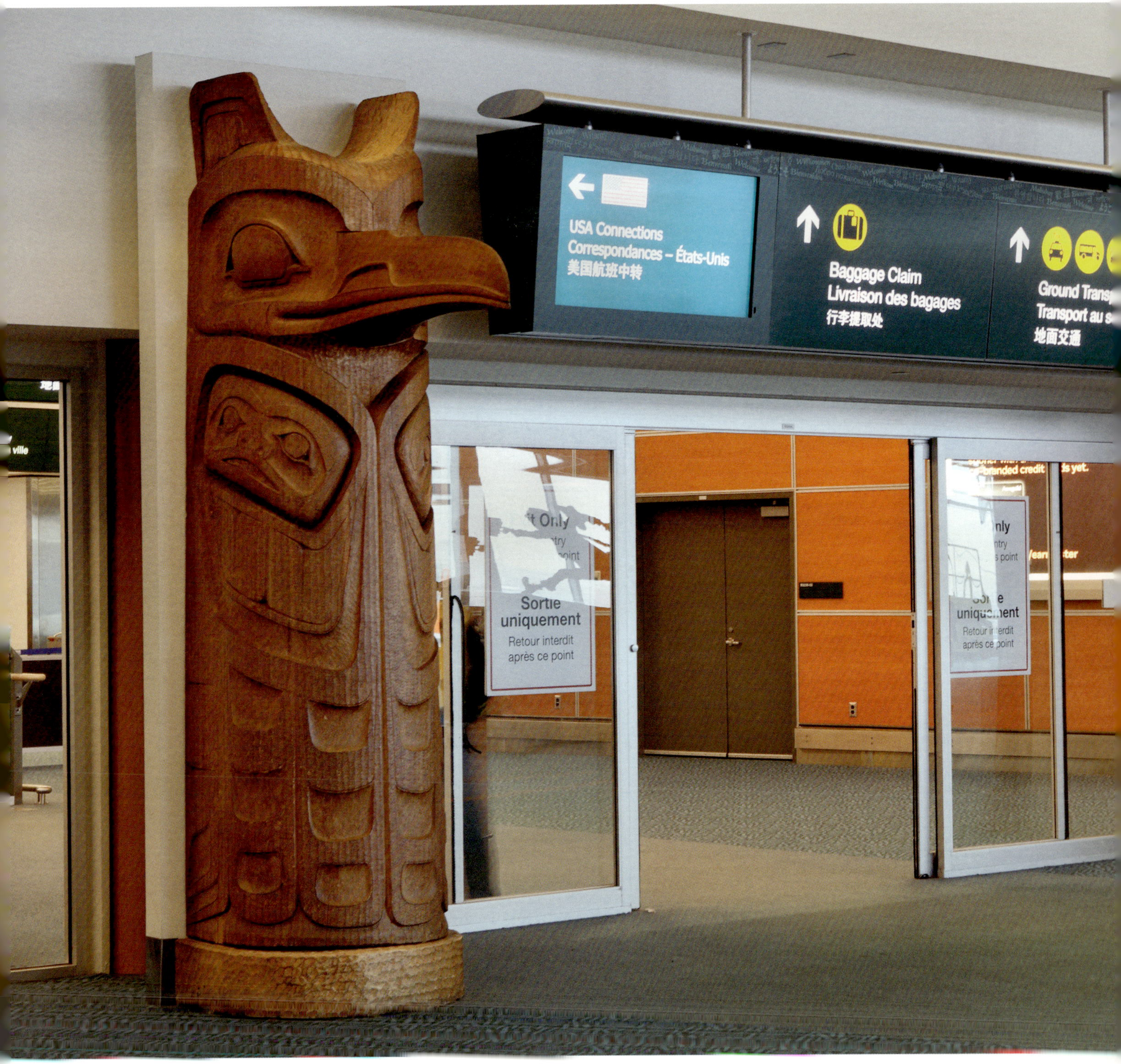
USA Connections
Correspondances – États-Unis
美国航班中转
Baggage Claim
Livraison des bagages
行李提取处
地面交通
Sortie uniquement
Retour interdit après ce point

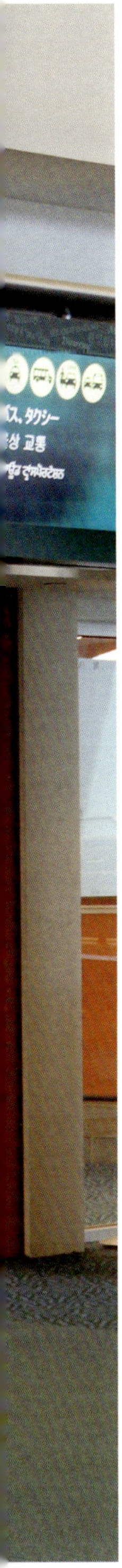

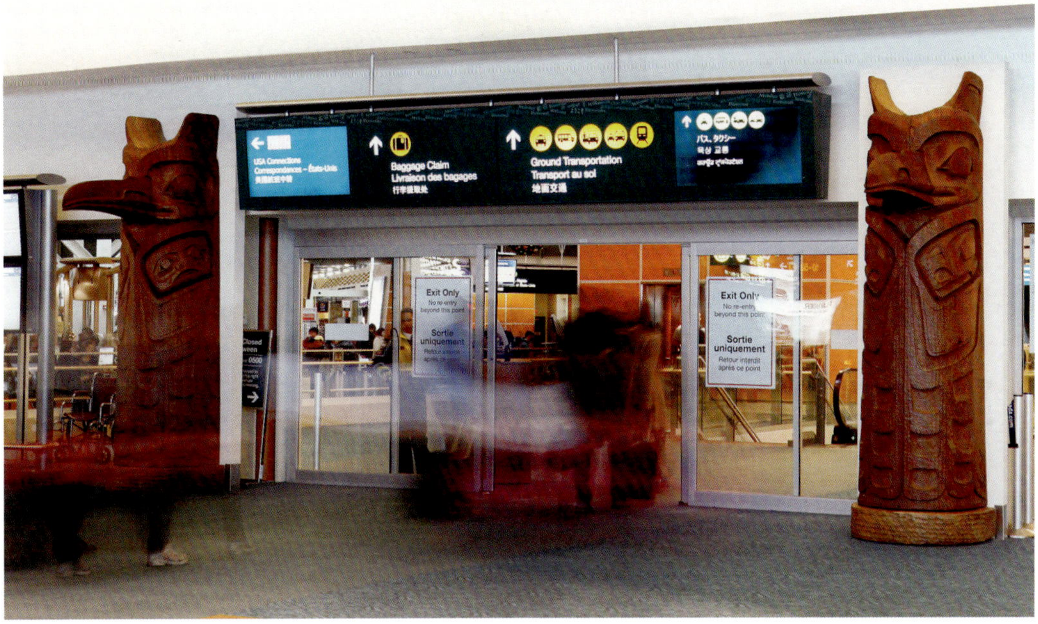

RAVEN HOUSE POSTS

Roy Henry Vickers
(Tsimshian, Haida, Heiltsuk)

c. 1990 painted red cedar | 3.3 × 0.9 × 1.5 m

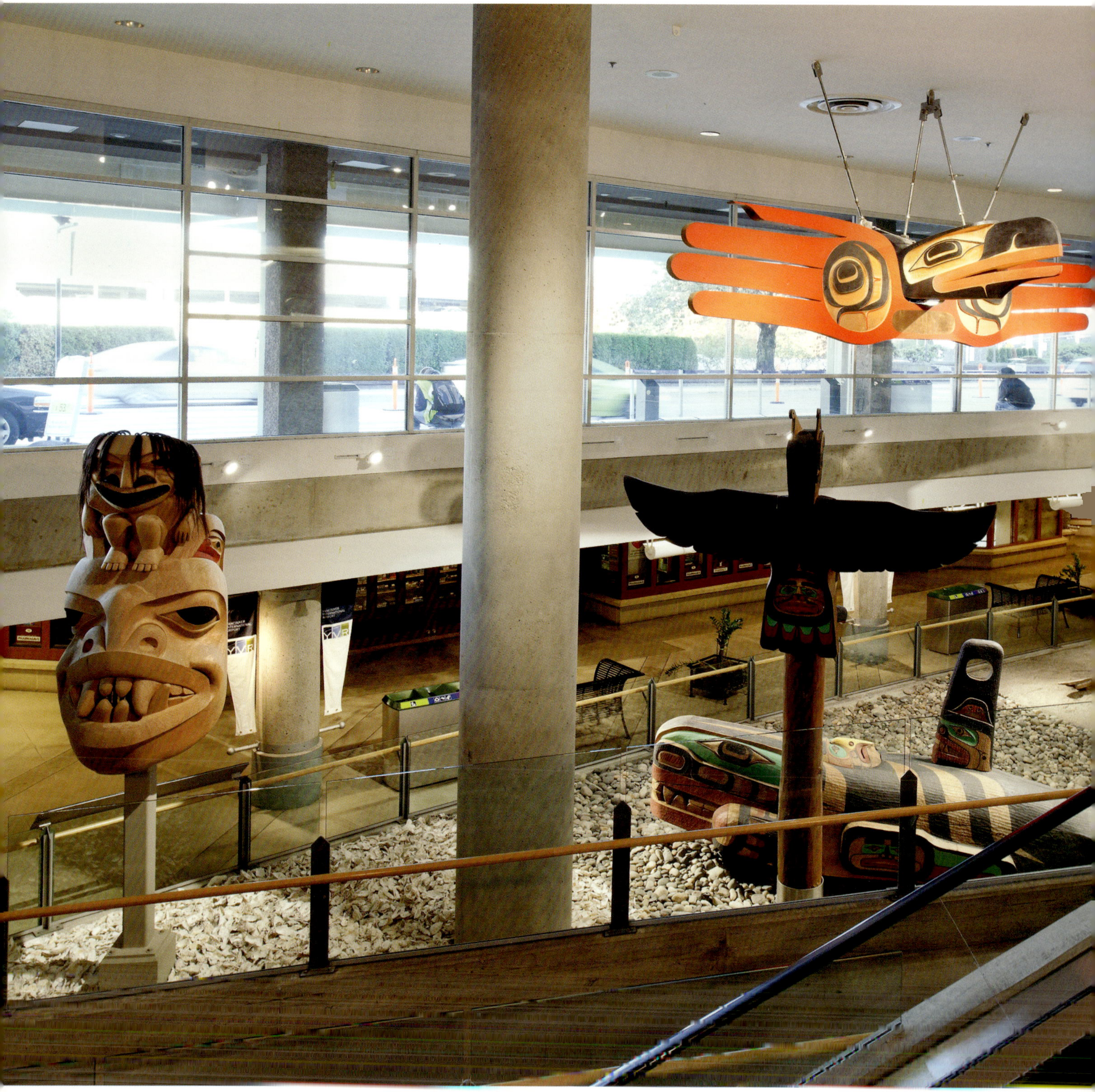

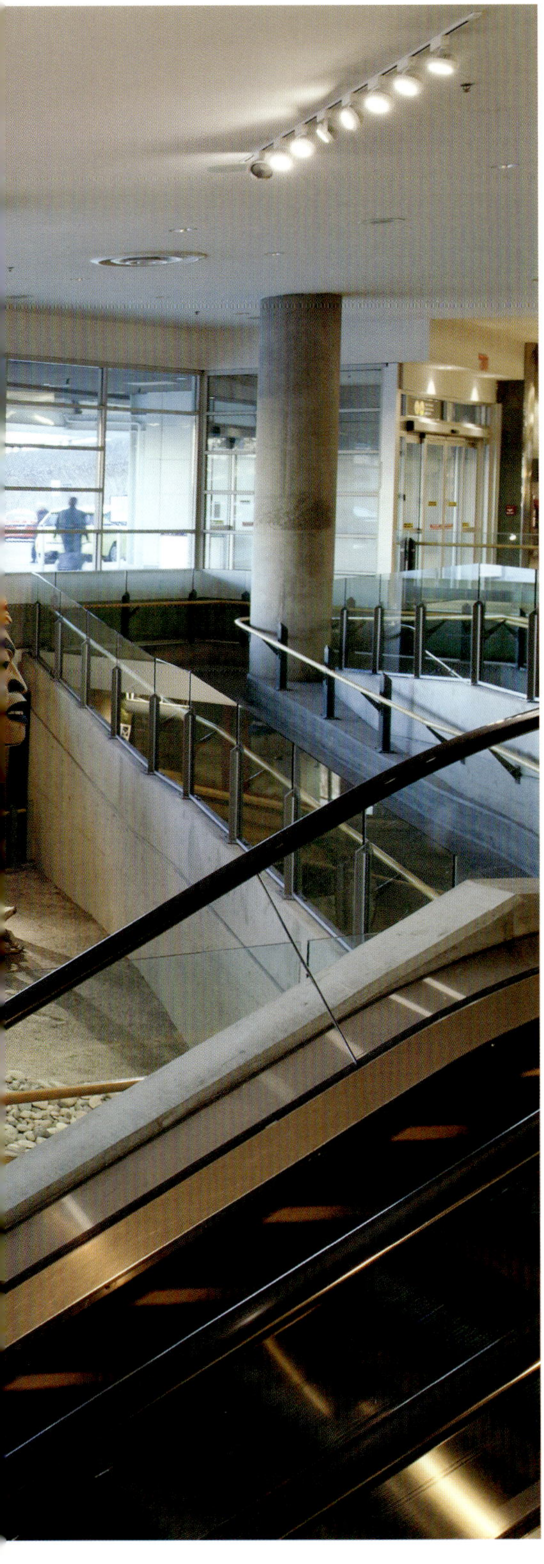

6

SUPERNATURAL WORLD

DOMESTIC TERMINAL BUILDING

(PRE-SECURITY)

HUGGING THE WORLD

Robert Davidson

1999 red cedar, acrylic paint, copper | 2.7 × 4 × 1 m

Robert Davidson's depiction of the two principal crests of the Haida people, Eagle and Raven, has been designed to occupy a difficult space of transition. Located in the grouping of works titled Supernatural World, it is suspended from the ceiling between two towering architectural pillars and addresses travellers passing by on the sidewalk outside the Domestic Terminal, and on the escalators, ramp and concourse inside the building. Davidson has said that he was interested in creating a piece of public art "that complements the setting rather than competes with it"[1] and this is evident in the work's unusual form and execution.

Carved like large dance masks mounted back to back, the work speaks to the importance of Eagle and Raven in Haida spiritual belief and social structure. In stories about them, they may be characterized as either rivals or close friends. Raven may be seen as cultural hero or as Trickster, and Eagle is admired for its hunting prowess and its intelligence. Here, the birds share the same pair of flat, outstretched wings, fashioned to resemble open human hands, which suggest either creation or friendship. As Davidson portrays them, Eagle looking outward, Raven looking inward, they seem to signify "two halves of the great whole."[2]

Robert Davidson is one of the most esteemed artists working on the Northwest Coast. He is the great-grandson of the revered nineteenth-century Haida artist Charles Edenshaw, and has been inspired and influenced by him. At the forefront of the resurgence of First Nations art and culture, Davidson was only twenty-five in 1969 when he carved the first totem pole to be raised in Haida Gwaii in more than ninety years. Since then, his career has soared and his work is highly sought after, locally, nationally and internationally.

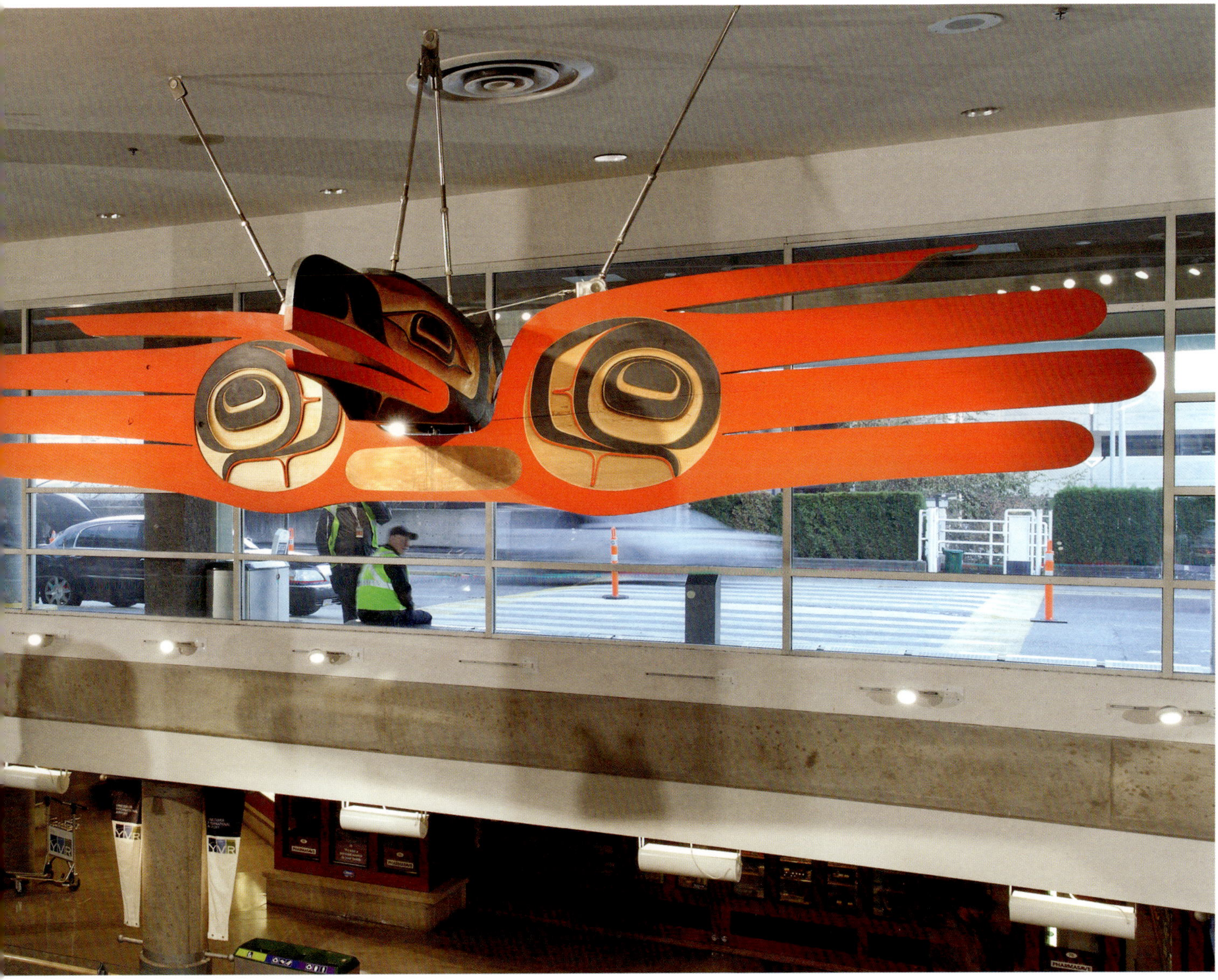

1 Robert Davidson, artist's statement, 1999. 2 Cheryl Shearar, *Understanding Northwest Coast Art* (Vancouver/Toronto: Douglas & McIntyre; Seattle: University of Washington Press, 2000), p. 44.

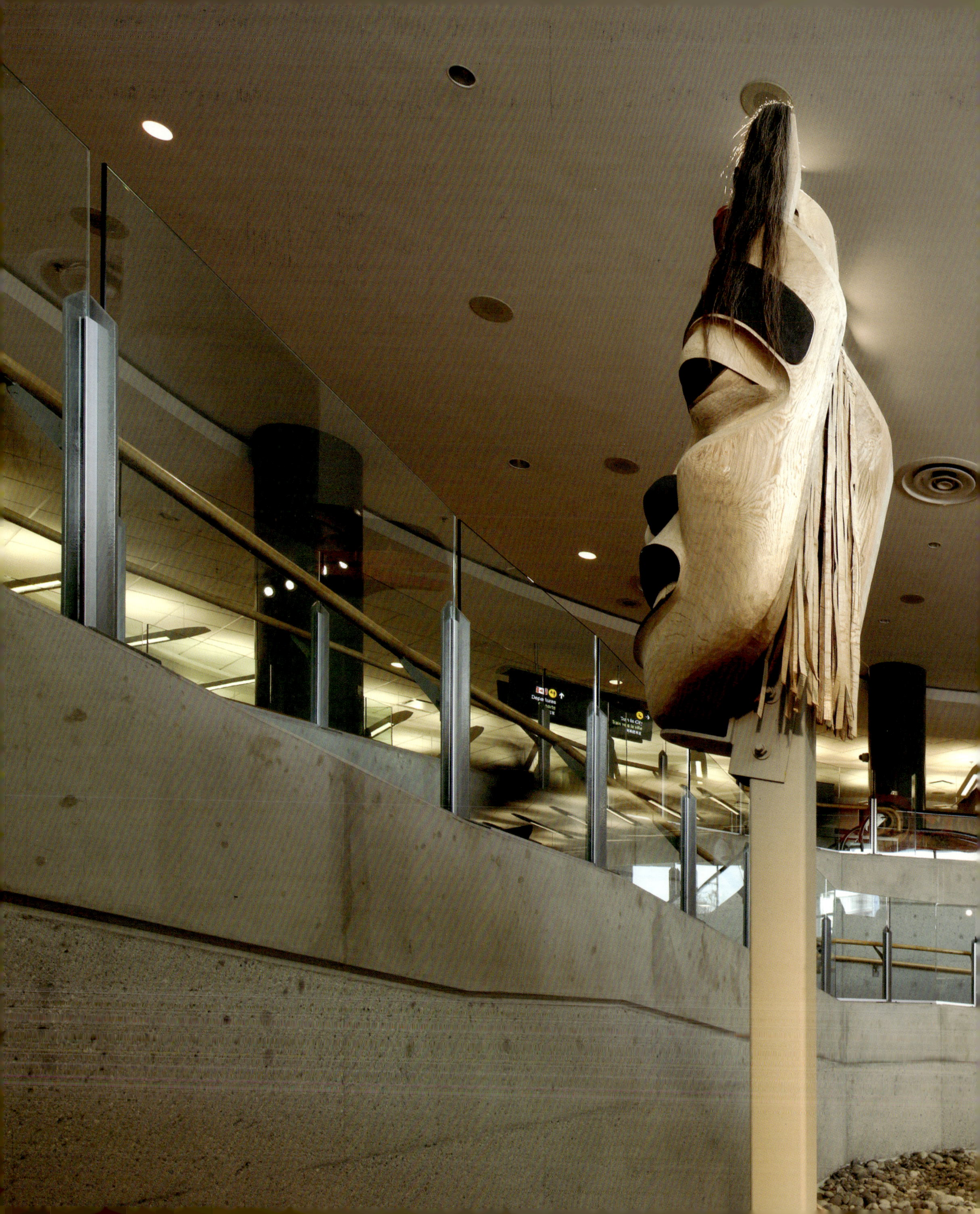
Departures

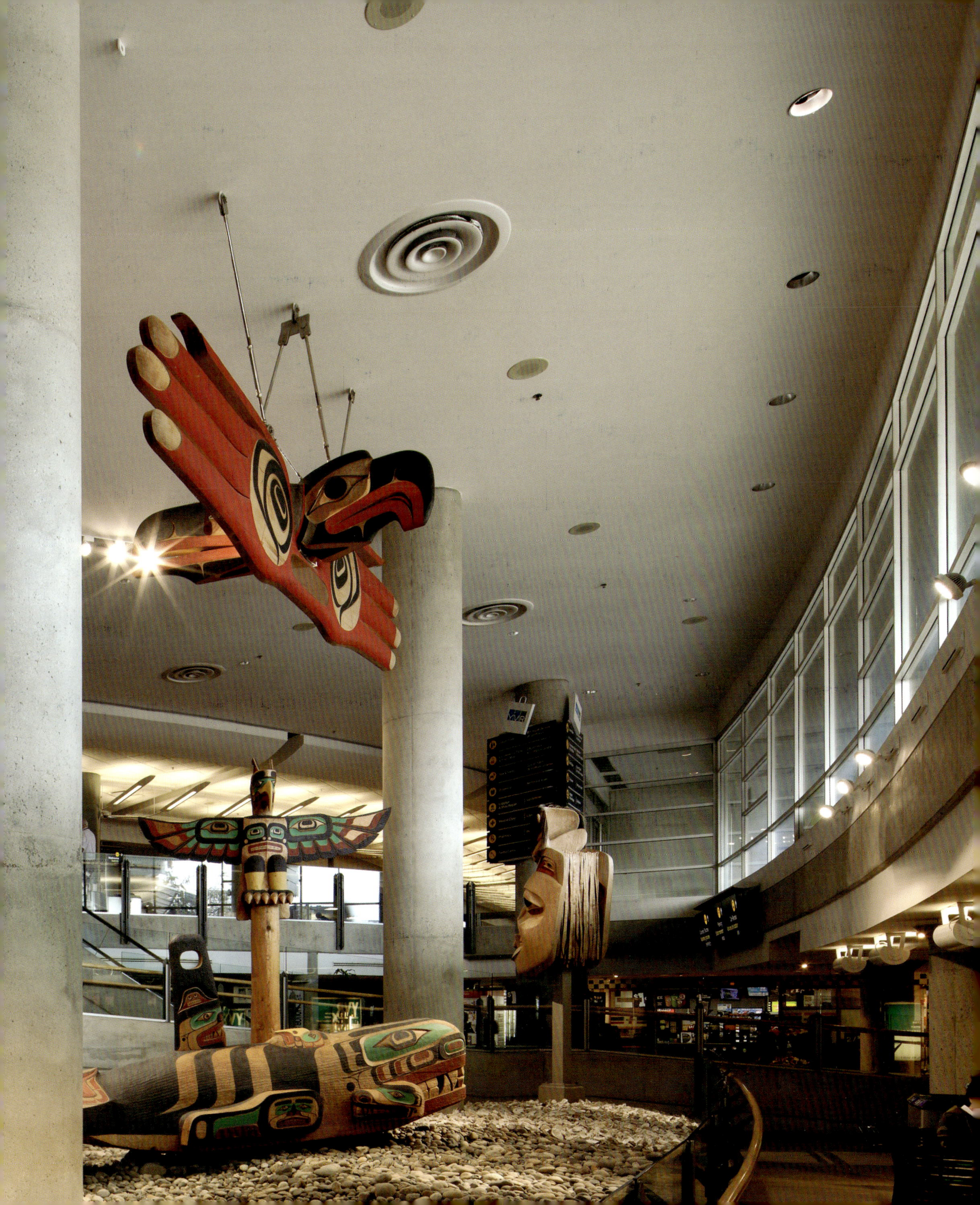

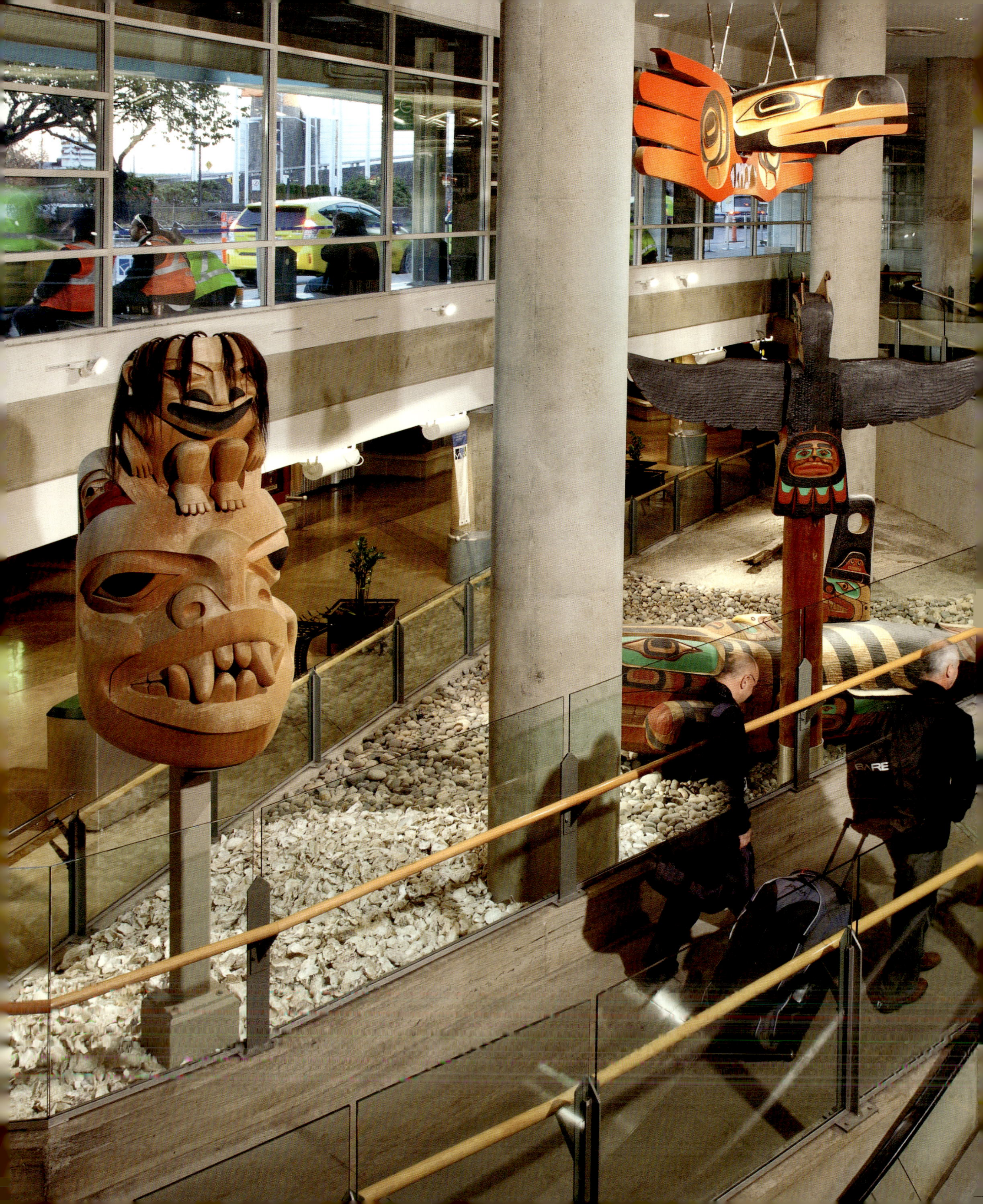

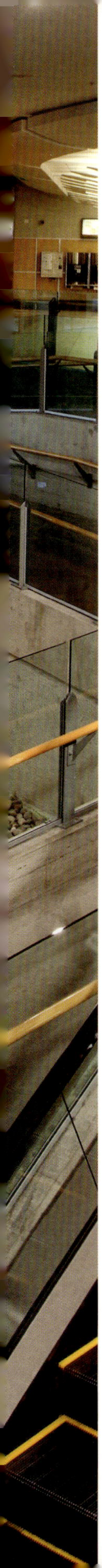

HUMAN/BEAR MASK

Dempsey Bob

1999 red cedar, horse hair, acrylic paint | 152 × 76 × 61 cm

Two monumental masks by Tahltan-Tlingit artist Dempsey Bob reveal this artist's distinctive style, which is sleek yet muscular with large, expressive, half-hooded eyes. Carved in red cedar and selectively painted, these works declare the artist's family connection with the Bear clan while also expressing the Tlingit belief that "people and animals are relatives who can cross into each others' worlds."[1] The masks acknowledge a special kinship between bears and human beings, defined by the ways in which they share the same natural environment and seek out the same food sources (such as salmon and wild berries). Bears also have the capacity to stand on their hind legs, consolidating their likeness to humans, and myths of marriage between women and bears who assume human form are prevalent through much of the northern and central Northwest Coast.

In one of the sculptures, a small human figure with long black hair crouches between the ears of a huge-fanged bear; in the other, the small face of a bear, with human teeth and extended tongue, is perched on the forehead of a human portrait mask. Bob, who is both an acclaimed artist and an honoured teacher, recounts in his artist's statement a childhood memory of salmon fishing among grizzlies and black bears: "My grandmother would speak to them in our language and explain that we were from the Bear clan, and that we wouldn't harm them. The bears always left us alone."[2] Bob also builds a cautionary note into these artworks, emphasizing human connection to the land and advising us that "whatever happens to the bear happens to the environment around us."[3]

---

1 Carnegie Museum of Natural History, *American Indians and the Natural World — Tlingit* (http://www.carnegiemnh.org/online/indians/tlingit/transformations.html)
2 Dempsey Bob, artist's statement, 1999. 3 Ibid.

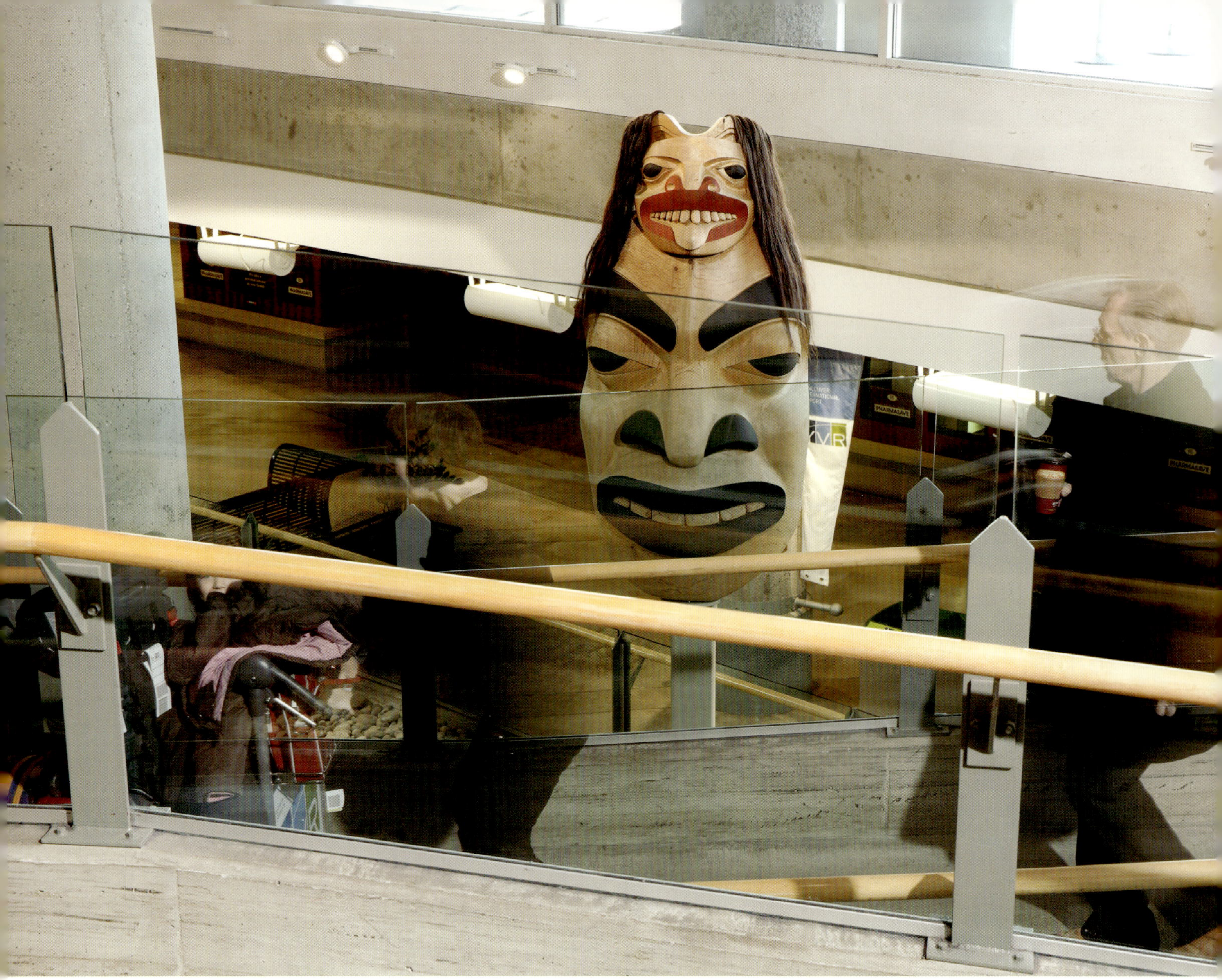

BEAR/HUMAN MASK

Dempsey Bob

1999 red cedar, horse hair, acrylic paint |
213 × 91 × 61 cm

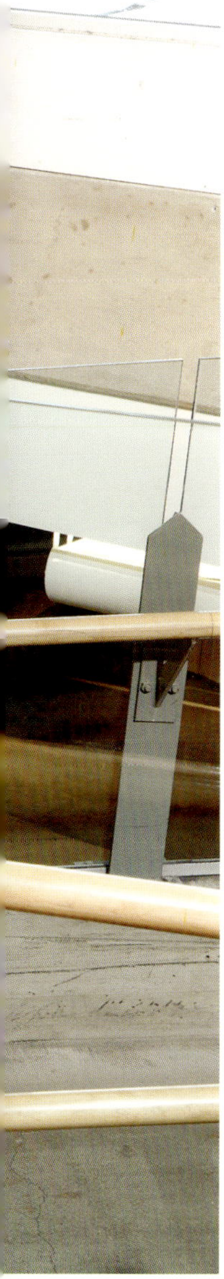
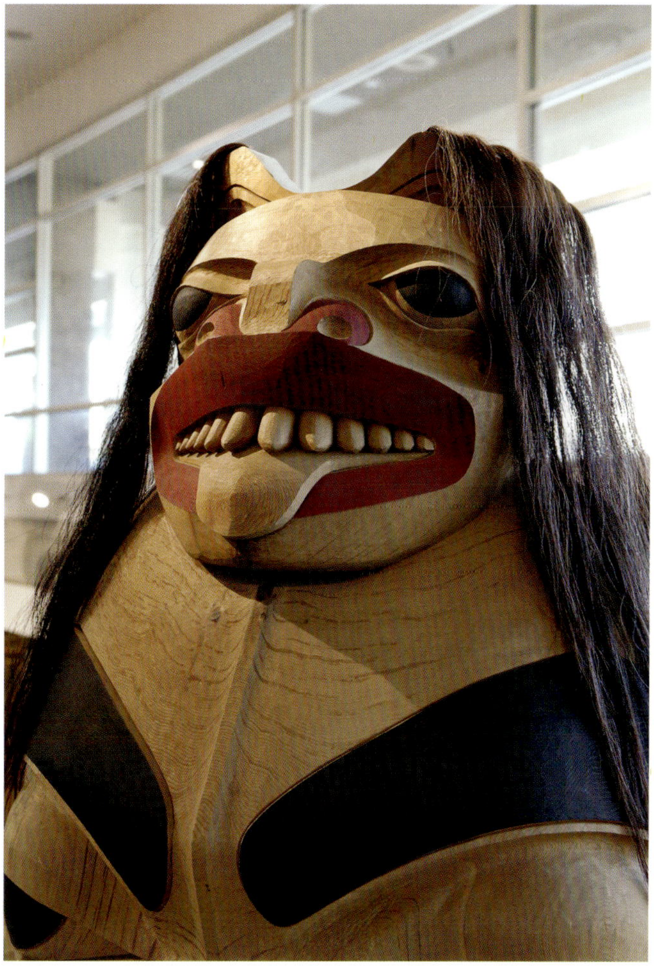
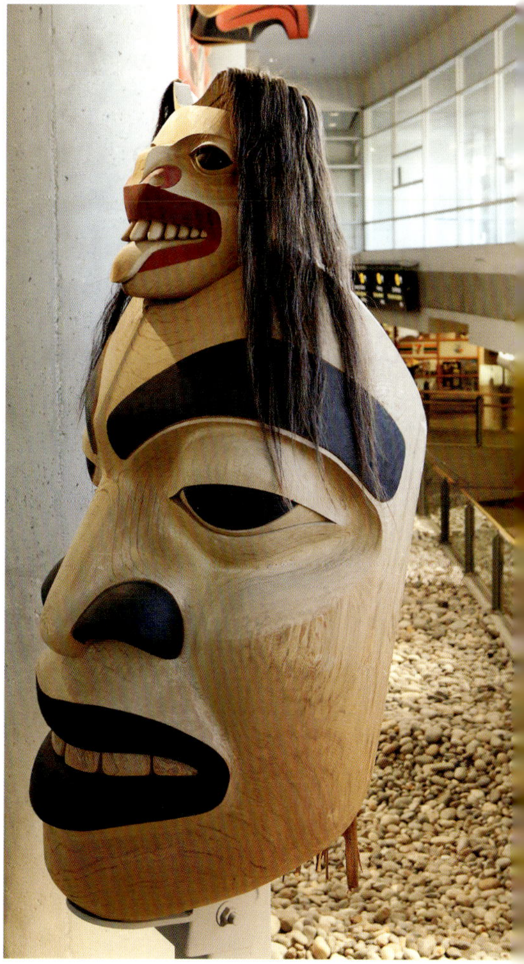

THUNDERBIRD AND KILLER WHALE

Richard Hunt

1999 red cedar, acrylic paint | KILLER WHALE 2.1 × 1.2 × 4.9 m | THUNDERBIRD 2.7 × 4 × 6 m

Located in the Supernatural World grouping in YVR's Domestic Terminal, this two-part sculpture by Kwakwaka'wakw artist Richard Hunt shows Thunderbird with wings spread as it is about to swoop down on its prey, Killer Whale. Killer Whale is a hunter, too, and is depicted with a seal in its mouth; human faces are painted on its side fins, a Bear on its dorsal fin and an Eagle on its tail and in its blowhole. Thunderbird's tail displays a human face. All the beings represented are crests of the Kwakwaka'wakw people, the Eagle being the principal crest of Hunt's clan in Fort Rupert, British Columbia, while the Thunderbird was bestowed upon Hunt during a family potlatch.

Many Northwest Coast legends recount the violent battles between the supernatural Thunderbird, whose enormous, flapping wings produce thunder and whose great blinking eyes create lightning, and Killer Whale, its favourite food. In these stories, which explain the crashing and flashing of electrical storms, Thunderbird attempts to carry Killer Whale away in its talons; after a long, fierce struggle, Killer Whale escapes. Thunderbird is of particular importance to the Kwakwaka'wakw people, who frequently depict it at the top of their crest poles with wings outstretched. Its attributes include a powerful hooked beak and curled ears or horns, symbolic of its supernatural powers.[1]

Based in Victoria, Richard Hunt belongs to an internationally renowned family of artists whose work represents an unbroken chain of creation and mentorship from historic to contemporary times. Both of Hunt's crest figures are carved and painted in the bold and flamboyant style of traditional Kwakawaka'wakw art.

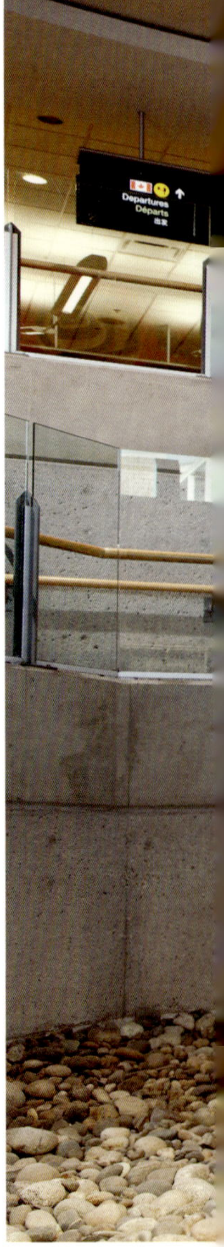

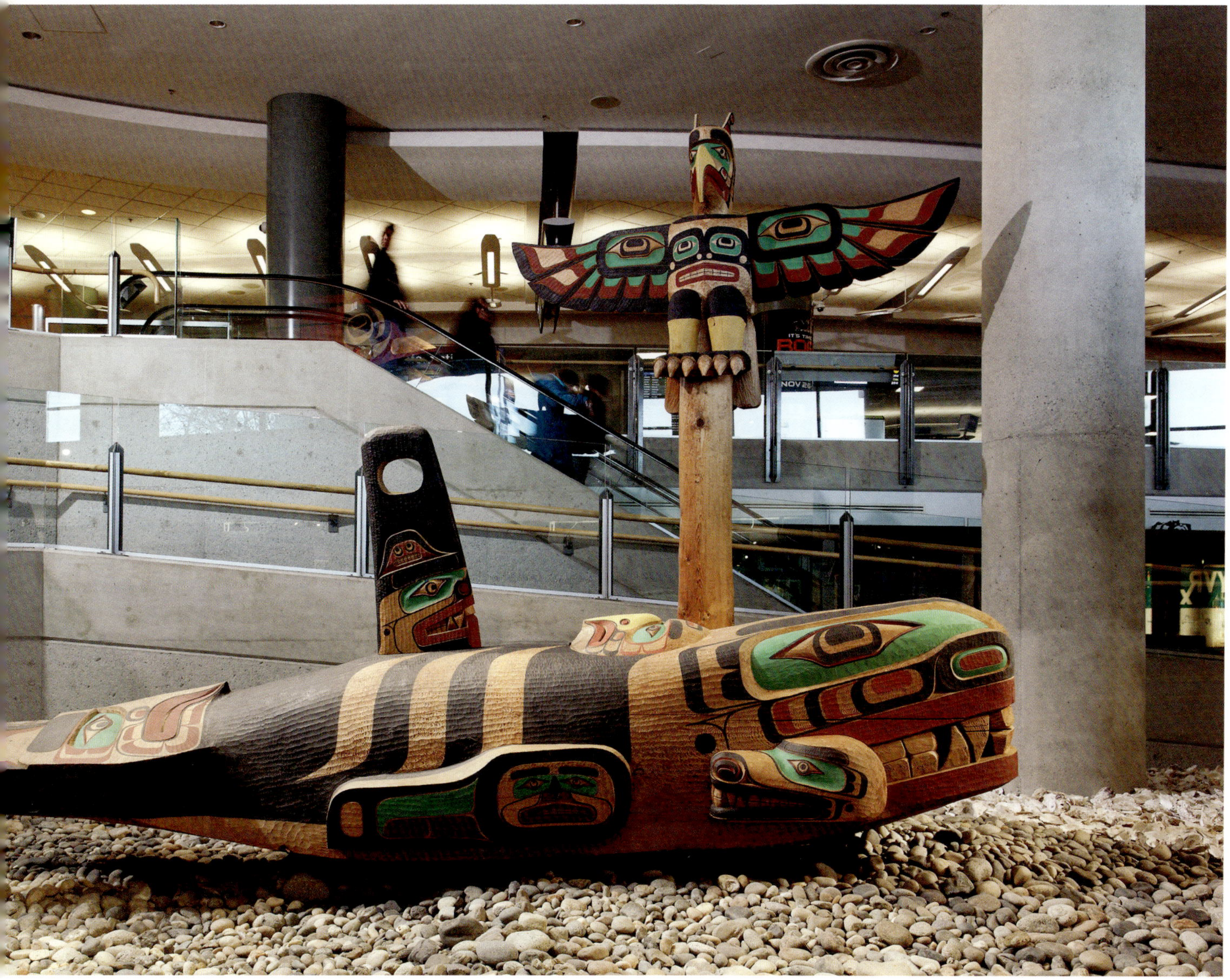

1 Cheryl Shearar, *Understanding Northwest Coast Art* (Vancouver/Toronto: Douglas & McIntyre; Seattle: University of Washington Press, 2000), p. 105.

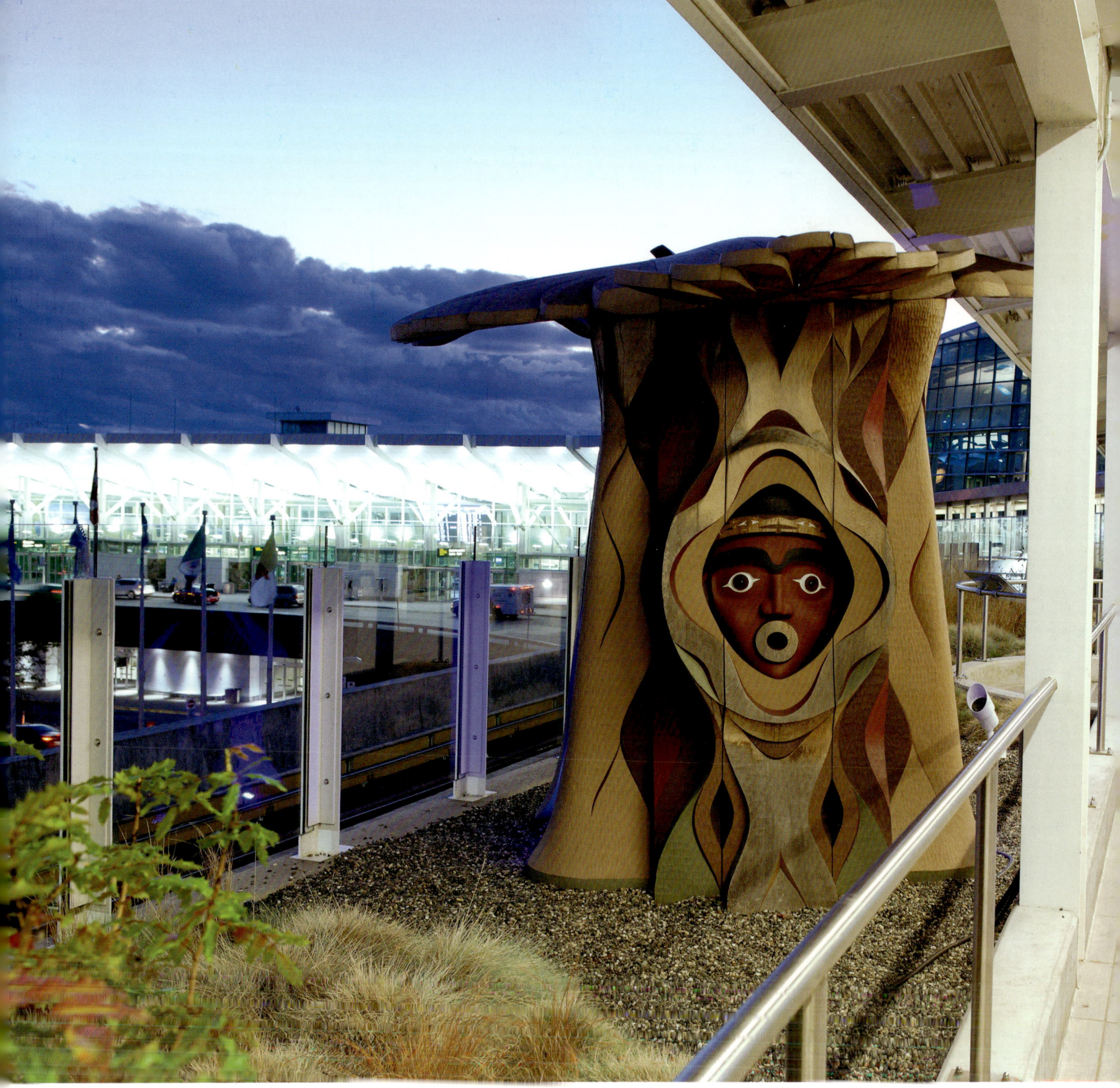

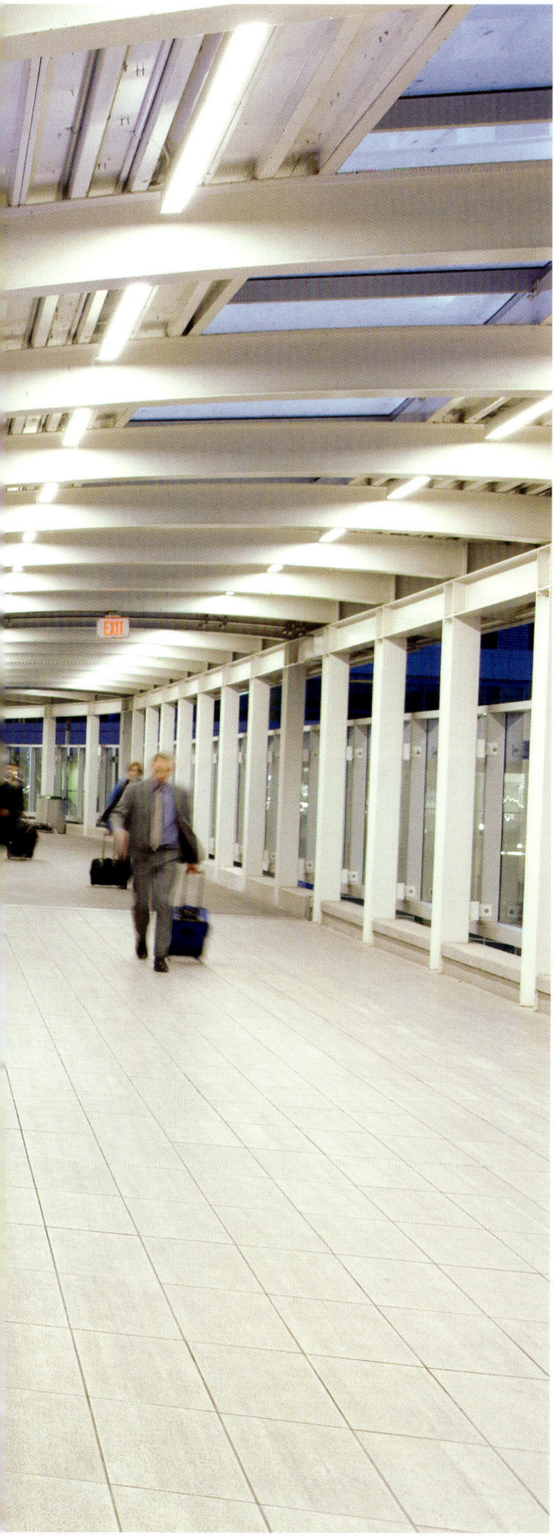

7

LINKING THE WORLD

CANADA LINE

CELEBRATING FLIGHT

Don Yeomans

2007 red cedar, canvas, acrylic paint, LED lights, fibreglass | approx. 10.69 × 4.4 × 3.75 m

The soaring central element of this multi-part installation is a carved and painted pole, one that braids Haida forms and traditions together with cross-cultural references and contemporary allusions. The intention of the pole's artist, Don Yeomans, is to honour humankind for transcending our earthbound existence by creating machines that enable us to fly. At the top of the pole is the Creator Raven and below him is the figure of a man, allotted a high position because of his intelligence and ingenuity.[1] In succession below are Thunderbird, Whale, Eagle, Bear and Frog, each bearing connotations of strength and power in Haida mythology. While these Northwest Coast images help establish a sense of place at YVR, the references to European and Asian cultures that also appear on the pole are especially relevant in a big, busy international airport where people from many nations come together on their journeys. Yeomans has created passages of Celtic knot-work and Chinese characters, the latter denoting "Heaven," "Earth," "Pride" and "Civilization." Rising vertically on either side of the pole are pale green lines of light, drawing our eyes upward, to Trace Yeomans's serene moon mask and a series of curving blue panels representing the aurora borealis.

With his mixed Haida and Metis background, Don Yeomans brings a range of visual and material innovations to his training in classic Northwest Coast art and jewellery-making and his studies in Western-style fine arts. Widely acclaimed and collected, he is known for marrying Haida and non-Haida forms and materials and for employing ancient and contemporary technologies.

1 Don Yeomans, artist's statement, 2007.

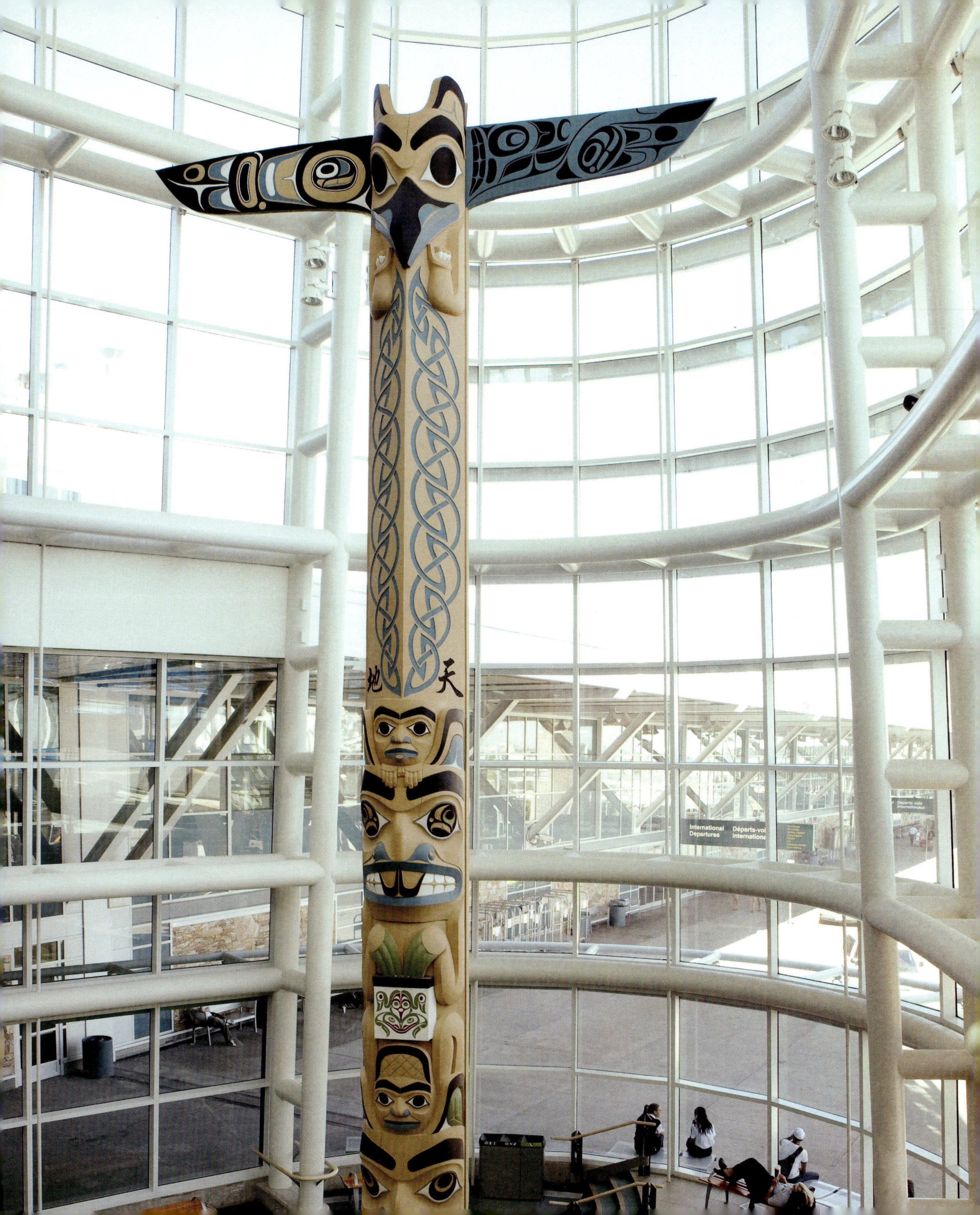
地
天
International
Departures

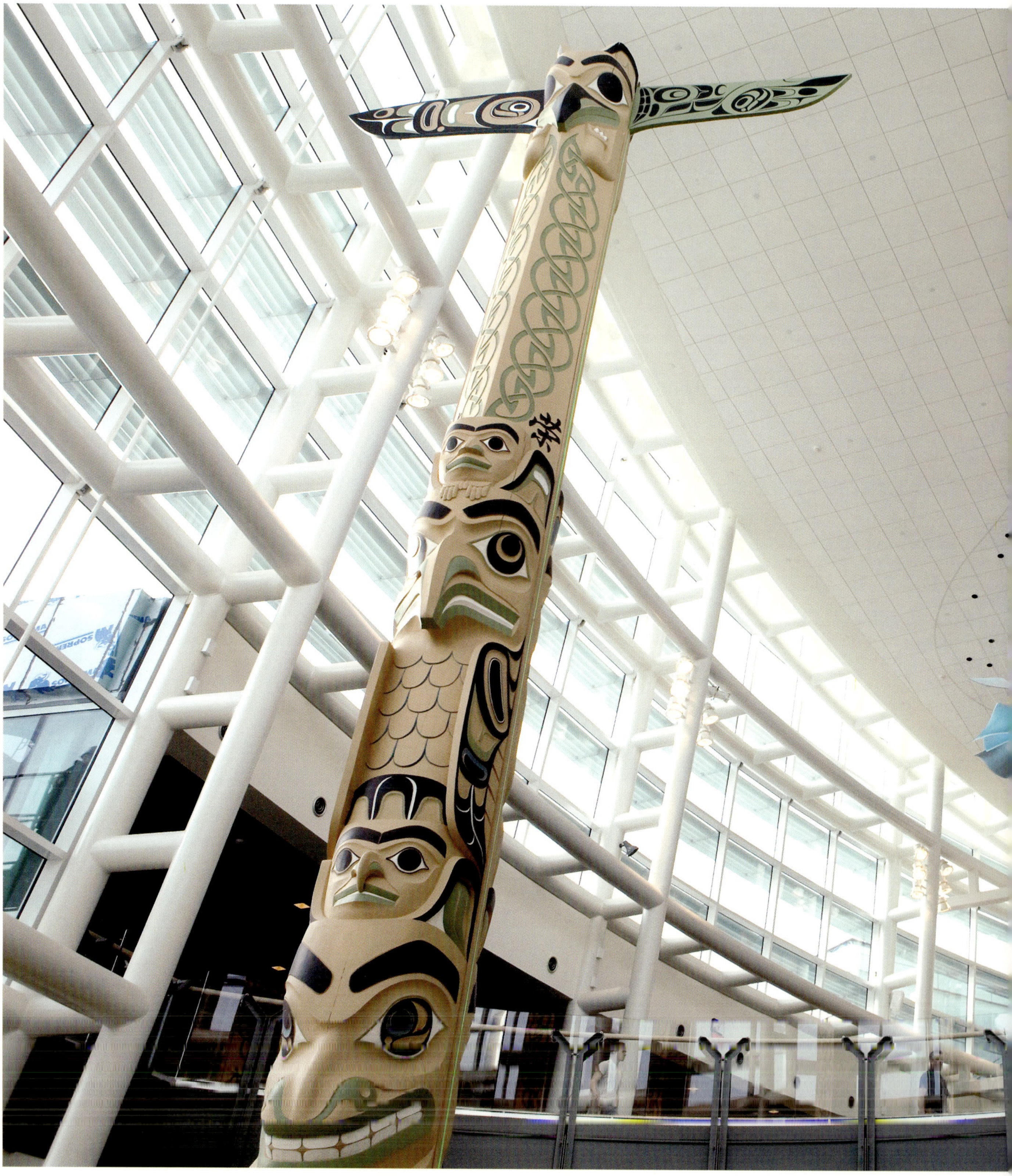

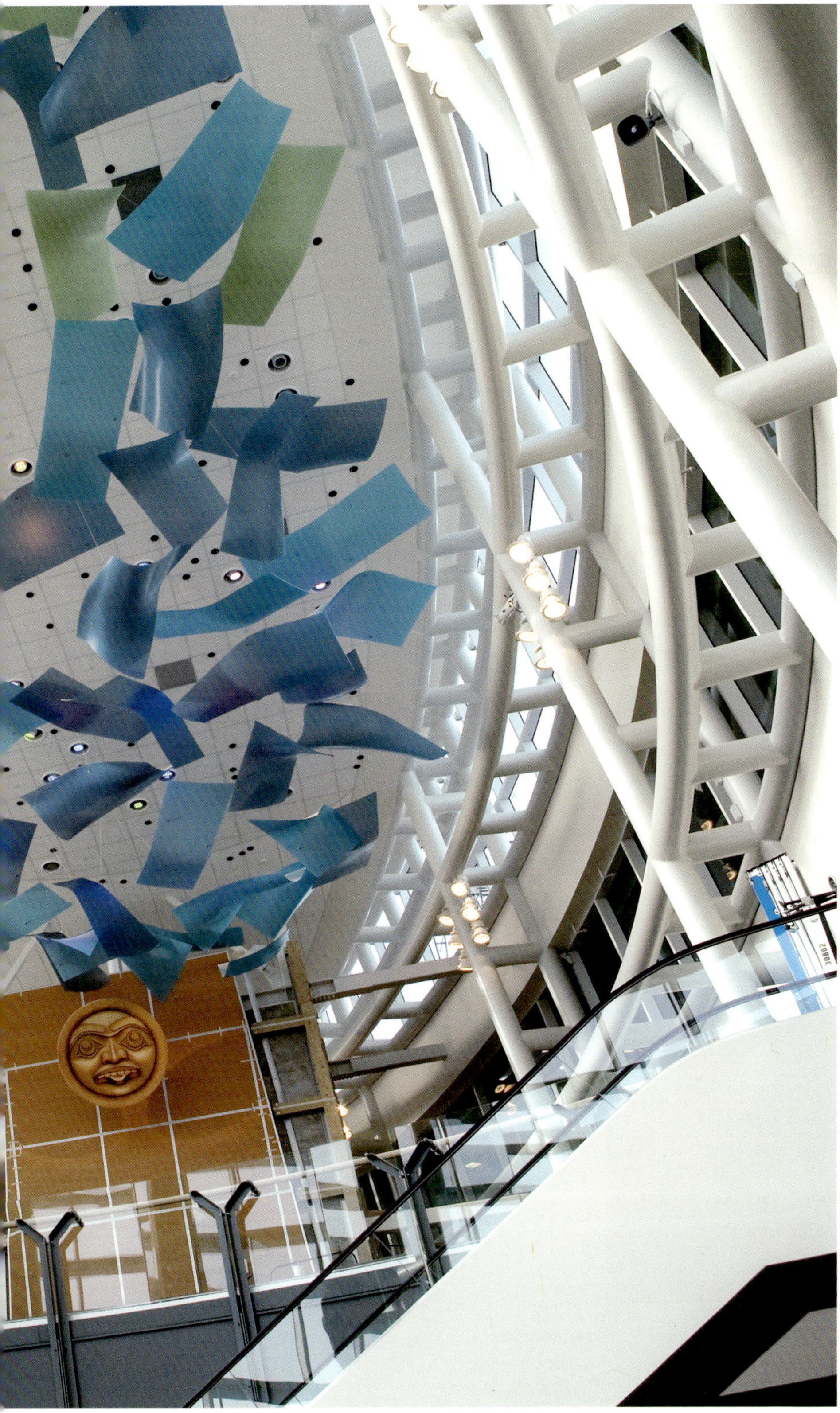

K'SAN TOTEMS

Walter Harris and Earl Muldoe (Gitxsan)

c. 1970 red cedar

LEFT 10.7 × 2.4 × 1.4 m

MIDDLE 13.4 × 0.8 × 1.2 m

RIGHT 11 × 1.3 × 0.8 m

Chester Johnson Park

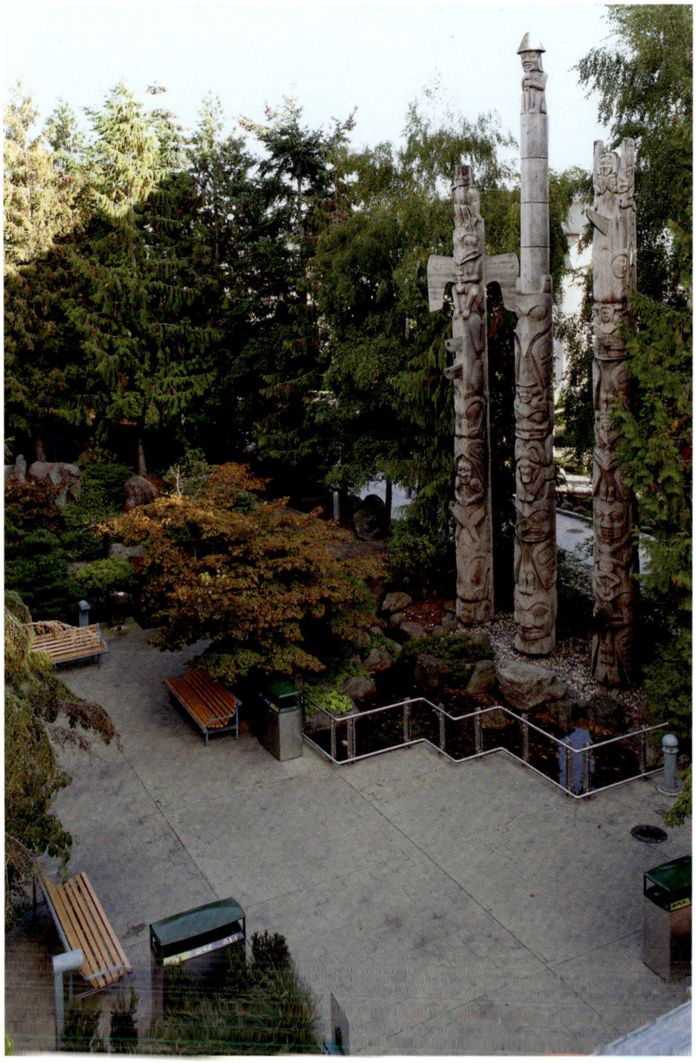

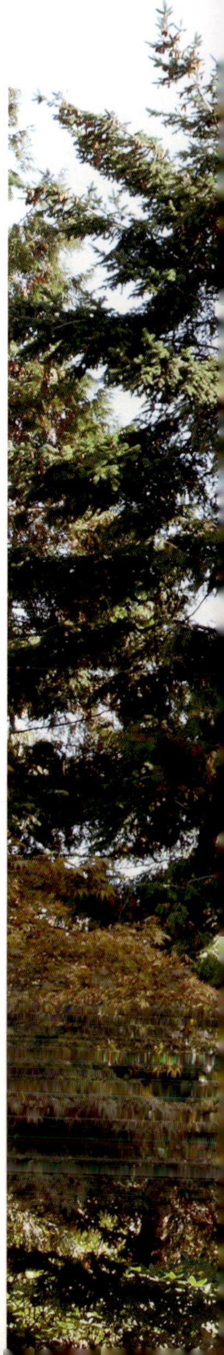

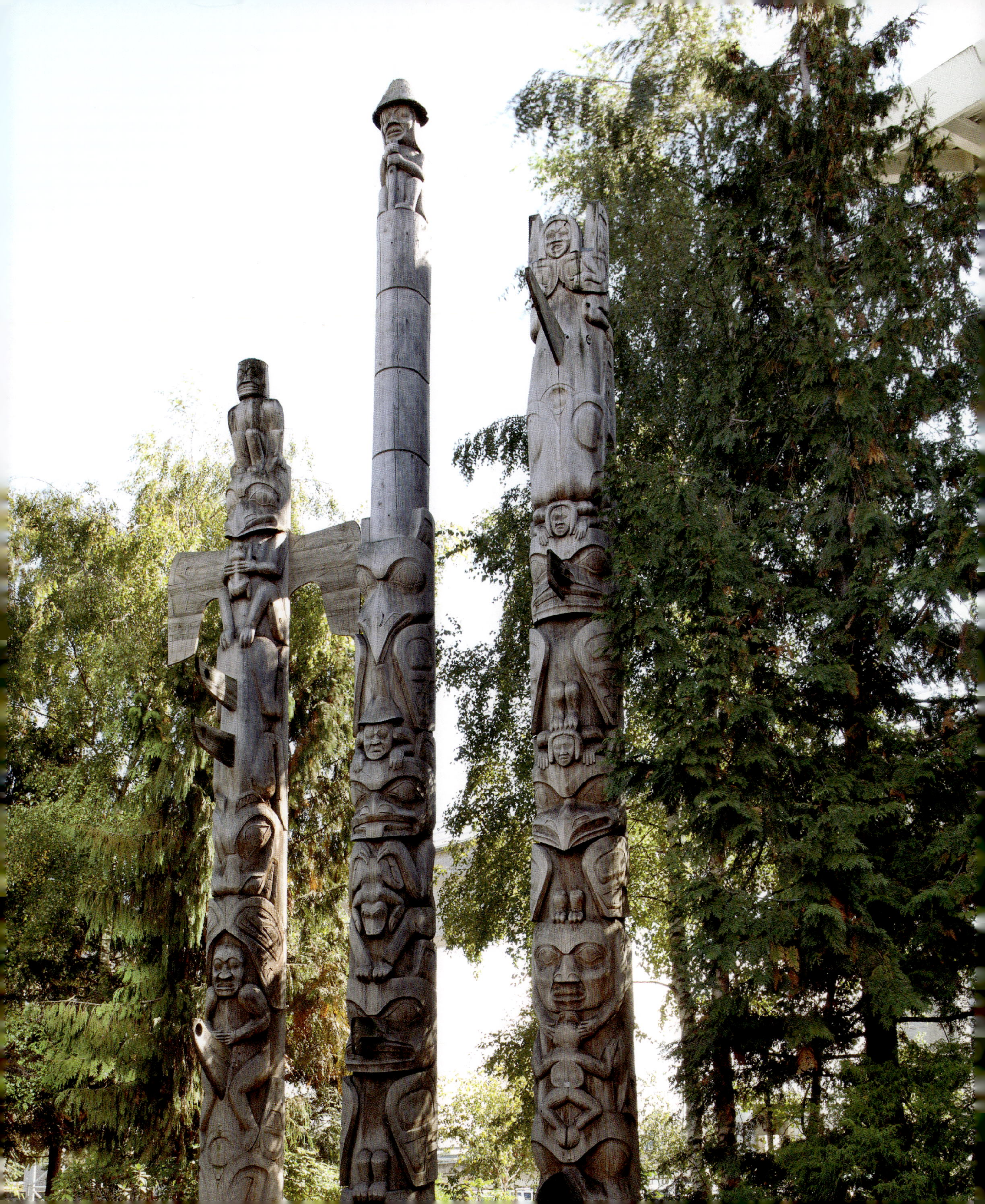

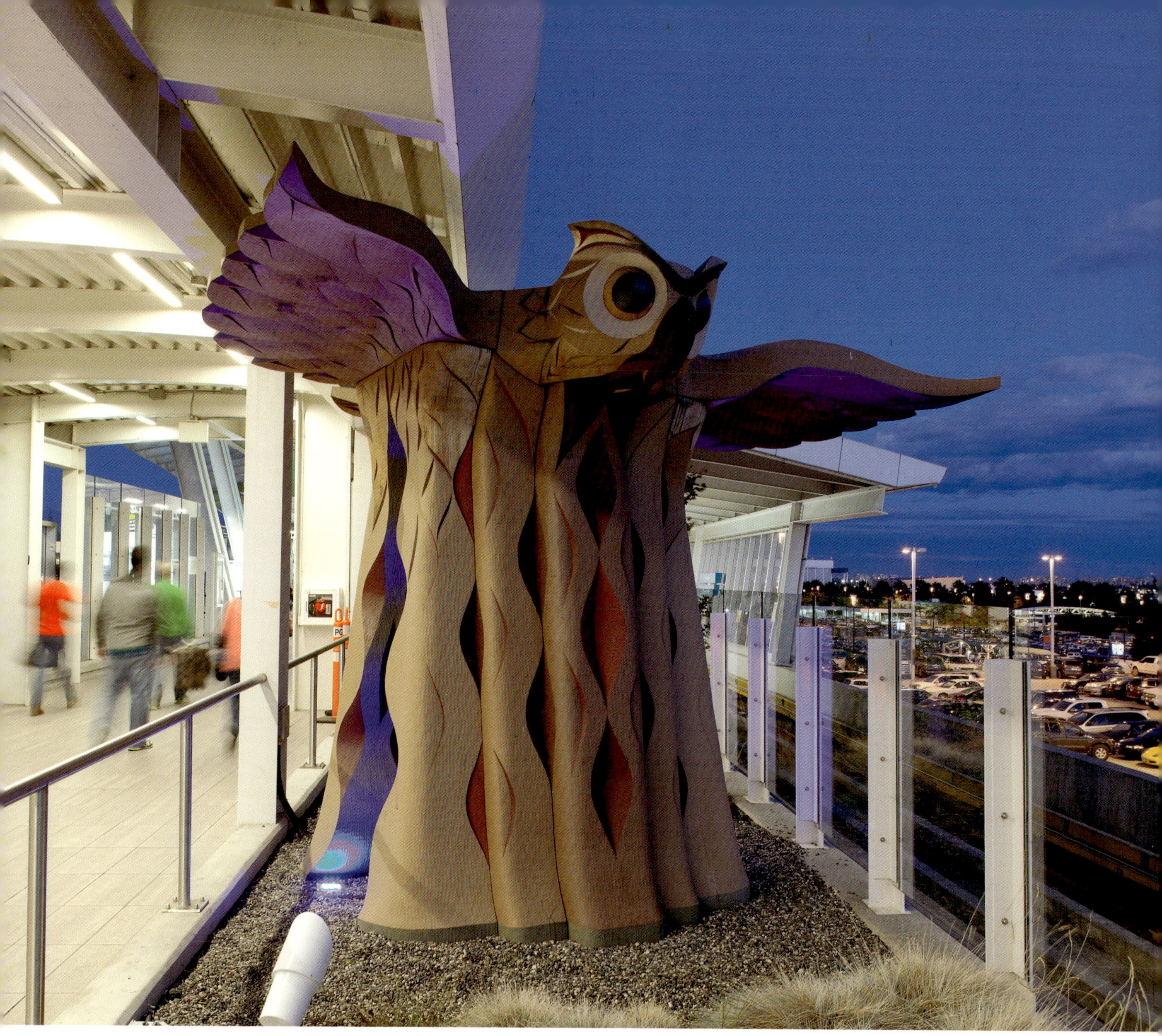

CEDAR CONNECTION

Susan Point

2009 red cedar, acrylic paint | 3.35 × 3.04 × 3.04 m

Carved and painted by leading Musqueam artist Susan Point, this large and complex sculpture evokes the landscape and culture of the area's original people, on whose traditional lands the Vancouver International Airport now stands. The overall shape of the work as a towering, old-growth tree stump suggests the richness of the temperate rainforest and the intensive use of cedar wood in Northwest Coast First Nations art, architecture, implements and canoes. It also honours the natural cycle of life, in which trees sprout upward, mature and eventually fall, their decomposing matter in turn nourishing new growth. *Cedar Connection* is characteristic of Point's dedication to combining cultural, historical and environmental messages in her many-faceted art.

The Fraser River, along which the Musqueam people live and fish, is represented by a flowing waterline motif on the interior of the sculpture. Also visible in the interior of the work is a tufted weaving pattern, symbolizing what Point calls "the tapestry of life."[1] The pattern also represents her people's renowned and longstanding use of cedar bark and other natural materials to weave baskets, mats, hats and clothing.

Looking outward from the tree stump are a human face with a rounded mouth, evoking the oral culture of the Coast Salish people, and Owl, a respected being that functions as both a messenger and a keeper of wisdom. The human face is a tribute to the artist's uncle, Dominic Point, a Musqueam storyteller who educated and inspired Susan Point early in her career.

1 Susan Point, artist's statement, 2009.

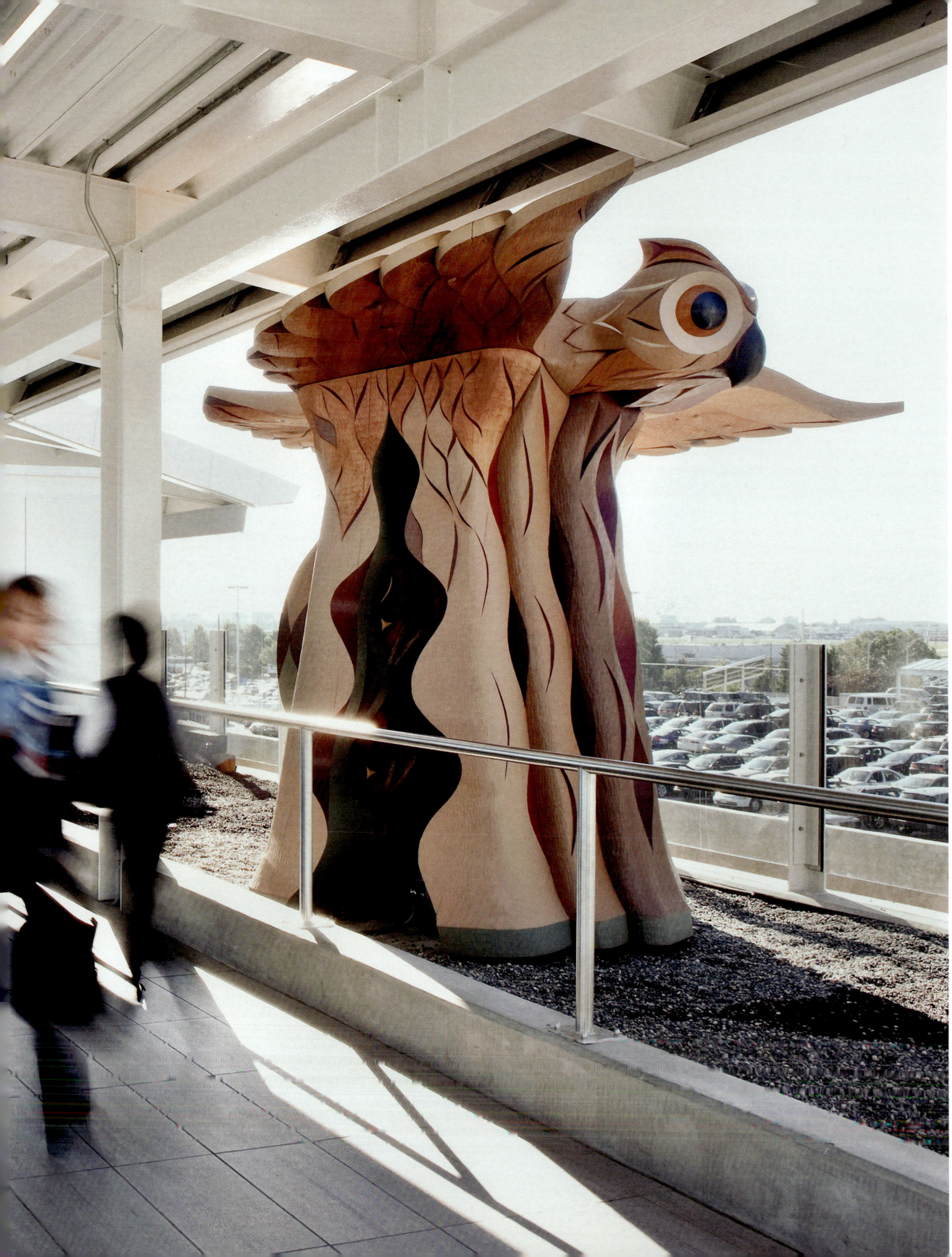

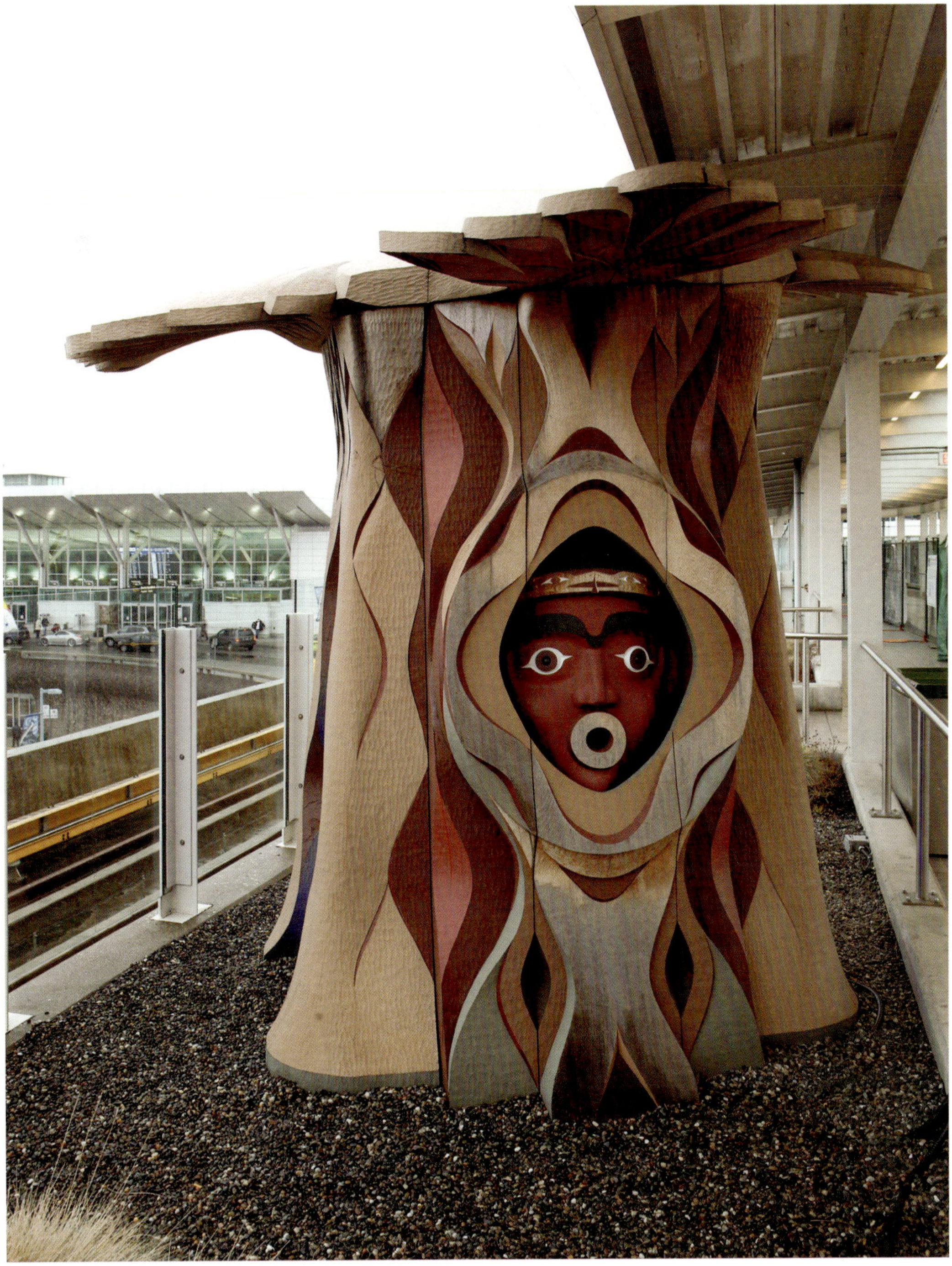

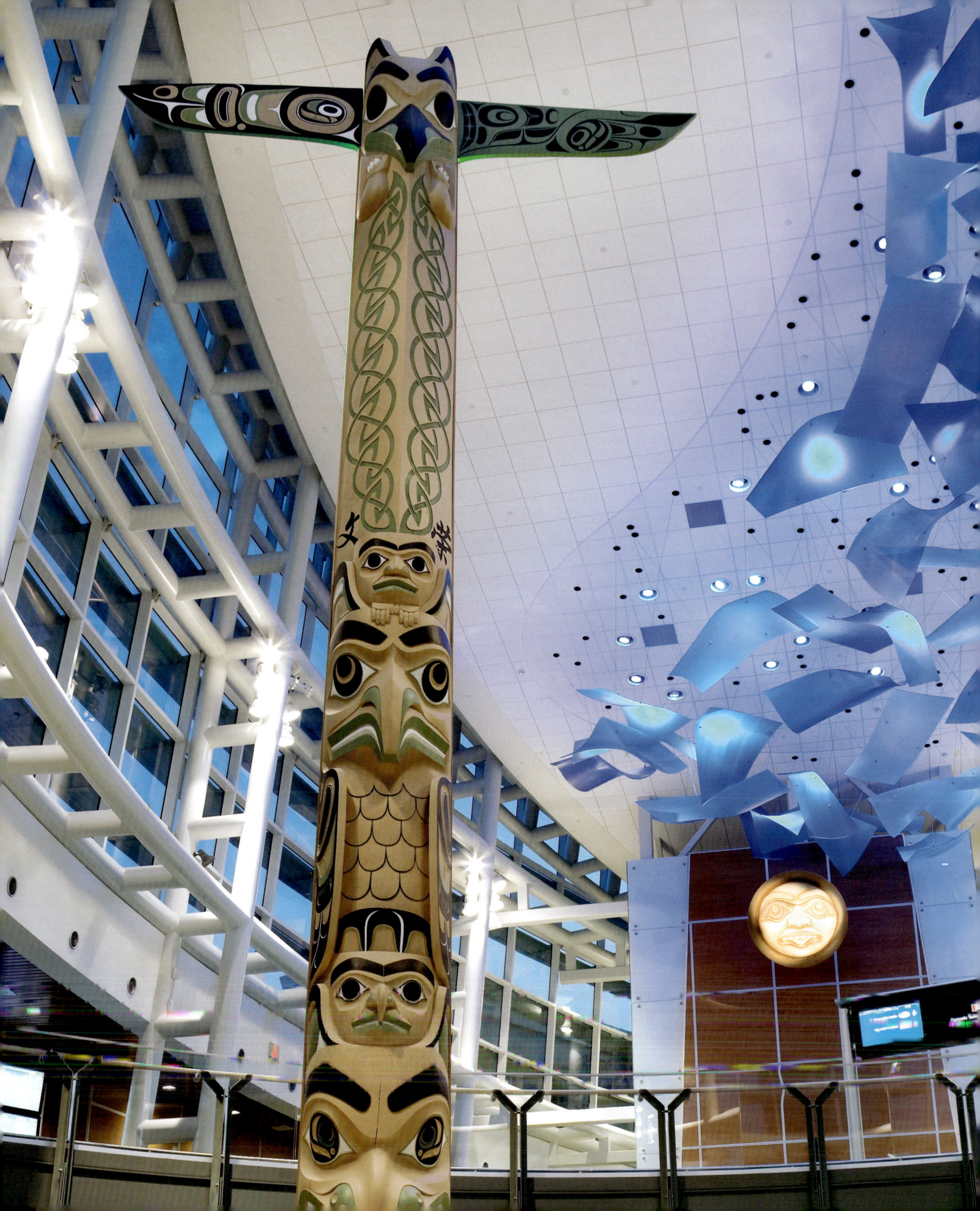

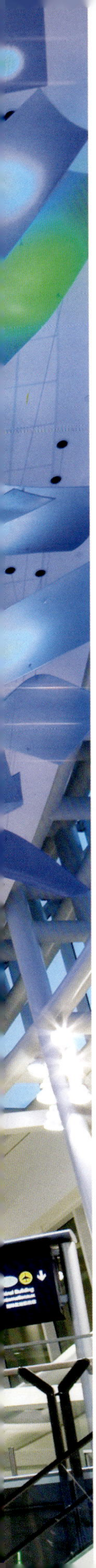

AFTERWORD

In addition to its permanent installations of British Columbian First Nations art, Vancouver Airport Authority's collection also includes over seventy Inuit sculptures and works by prominent Canadian artist Gordon Smith and other non-aboriginal Canadian artists. Sculptures, paintings, photographs, prints, ceramics, glassware and examples of furniture design, industrial design and fashion design are mounted in display cases located at departure gates throughout the airport. The original, handmade works are shown for twelve to eighteen months and are rotated biannually. While affording air travellers many changing examples of the province's lively and diverse visual arts scene, the display case program offers British Columbian artists, designers and craftspeople the opportunity to exhibit (and potentially sell) their work to local, national and international viewers. The airport also showcases works from the YVR Art Foundation's scholarship program for B.C. First Nations youth and mid-career artists. The scholarship program is a function of the YVR Art Foundation's mandate: to support and encourage the creation of First Nations art of the Northwest Coast. One part of the program is for B.C. First Nations youth who wish to become professional artists and further their creative learning. The other is for mid-career B.C. First Nations artists, to help advance their art production and expand their creative practice. All award recipients are selected through a juried process, and all are given the opportunity to exhibit their projects at YVR for a year following their scholarship term.

With ongoing renovation and expansion at YVR, more major First Nations art is being commissioned and created for permanent display. Work by esteemed Haida artist Reg Davidson is scheduled for installation at YVR in 2015. The collection consists of a pole, two standing figures and a large bentwood box. To be located in the post-security area of the Domestic Terminal Building, Davidson's painted red cedar pole and figures recount Haida myths in which Raven is featured as both beneficent culture hero and prank-playing Trickster. Characters portrayed in these works include Beaver, Butterfly, Eagle, Frog, Raven with a Broken Beak and Blind Halibut Fisherman. The bentwood box, standing on legs carved and painted to represent frogs, reproduces classical crest designs from historic Haida storage boxes.

Whether referenced to the past or the present, and whether permanently installed or temporarily displayed, art at YVR continues to engage and delight travellers from all parts of the world. ■

ROBIN LAURENCE

ACKNOWLEDGEMENTS

Vancouver Airport Authority would like to express its sincere gratitude to the visionaries who saw the importance of creating a sense of place at Vancouver International Airport (YVR). These individuals' interests and passions laid the foundation of what YVR is today. To all the artists, including those we were unable to feature in this book, we extend our heartfelt appreciation for sharing your stories at YVR and becoming a part of every passenger's experience. A special thank you to the diverse team that develops and maintains this spectacular award-winning art collection at YVR, including the designers, architects, engineers, program managers, technicians, cleaners, maintenance crews and more.

Without the dedication and hard work of all mentioned here this book would never have been possible.

Robin Laurence would like to thank Rita Beiks, Bill McLennan, Dwight Koss, Frank O'Neill and Clive Grout for generously sharing their time and expertise. She would also like to express appreciation to Terry Chou for overseeing the book project, and to Pam Robertson and Lara Smith for their considerable editing and organizational skills.

ROBIN LAURENCE

Robin Laurence is an independent writer, critic and curator based in Vancouver. She is the visual arts critic for *The Georgia Straight,* and is a contributing editor for both *Canadian Art* and *Border Crossings* magazines, for which she writes regularly. She has published essays about art and artists in more than fifty books and exhibition catalogues, and has produced numerous reviews and feature articles for local, national and international publications.

Laurence holds an MA in art history and a BFA in studio arts, and was educated at the University of Calgary, the University of Victoria, the Banff School of Fine Arts and the Instituto Allende in San Miguel de Allende, Mexico.

15 16 17 18 19 5 4 3 2 1

Cataloguing data available from Library and Archives Canada
ISBN 978-1-927958-26-1 (pbk.)
ISBN 978-1-927958-72-8 (hbk.)
ISBN 978-1-927958-27-8 (epub)
ISBN 978-1-927958-28-5 (epub fxl)

Writing by Robin Laurence
Editing by Pam Robertson
Design by Natalie Olsen
Photography by Kenji Nagai, except image on pages 6–7 by Larry Goldstein
Cover image: Steve Smith, *Sea to Sky*, 2011, mahogany plywood, medium density fibreboard, acrylic paint, 91 cm in diameter.
Printed and bound in Canada by Friesens
Distributed in the U.S. by Publishers Group West

Figure 1 Publishing Inc.
Vancouver BC Canada
www.figure1pub.com

Measurements of artworks are given as height × width × depth.